THE LIONS

WHEN THE GOING GETS TOUGH

Behind the scenes

IAN McGEECHAN

with Steve James

HODDER &
STOUGHTON

First published in Great Britain in 2017 by Hodder & Stoughton
An Hachette UK company

1

Copyright © Ian McGeechan 2017

A CIP catalogue record for this title is available from the British Library

Hardback ISBN: 978 1 473 65658 1
Trade Paperback ISBN: 978 1 473 65657 4
Ebook ISBN: 978 1 473 65656 7

Typeset in Fresco by Hewer Text UK Ltd, Edinburgh
Printed and bound by CPI Group (UK) Ltd, Croydon, CR0 4YY

Hodder & Stoughton policy is to use papers that are natural, renewable and recyclable products and made from wood grown in sustainable forests. The logging and manufacturing processes are expected to conform to the environmental regulations of the country of origin.

Hodder & Stoughton Ltd
Carmelite House
50 Victoria Embankment
London EC4Y 0DZ

www.hodder.co.uk

To my wife Judy, Rob and Heather, and all the Lions with whom I have had the pleasure of touring. The Lions became very special to all of us.

CONTENTS

PROLOGUE

The British and Irish Lions are special; very, very special indeed.

It is a unique concept: four countries coming together in one team every four years (since 1989) to tour New Zealand, South Africa or Australia. For me, therefore, the Lions are the ultimate in team sport. The Ryder Cup in golf is the only thing I can think of that even comes close.

The crucial thing about the Lions is that every tour is different. Every time a tour party is announced, that group of players has no identity, character or meaning until they actually meet up. Some tours might have a rump of players who were on the previous tour, but generally every tour is different because the players are always different.

It becomes distinguished and identified by the year it took place: 'the 1974 Lions' or 'the 1989 Lions', or the like. It is not one team that on the field looks the same or plays the same. It is a team that on its day creates a very unique sort of character and characteristics.

As a coach I always said to the players when they arrived to join the Lions: 'You've all come on different journeys to wear a

Lions jersey, but what you've got to do now is say: "Right, this is what I have learnt on the journey to this point, now what I've got to do is put all that experience out on the table so we can share those journeys and create something even greater."' That is why when the Lions play, they do not generally look like any other team because, if you get it right with the players and their games, their collective game in that jersey is something very different and very special.

And, of course, they are special to me on a personal level. I toured as a player to South Africa in 1974 and to New Zealand in 1977. We lost the series in New Zealand but we won in South Africa, and it remains the greatest memory of my playing career.

I was then head coach on four tours – in 1989 to Australia, in 1993 to New Zealand, in 1997 and 2009 to South Africa – as well as being assistant coach to New Zealand in 2005. And we won two of those series, in 1989 and 1997.

That is a lot of Lions experience, and a lot of my working life taken up being associated with them. So I hope you can understand why I am so hugely, hugely passionate about the Lions and always will be, simply because no one will ever change my mind on the positive impact they have on spectators as well as players. The Lions have a magic of their own.

You only have to listen to Martin Johnson, England's captain in their 2003 Rugby World Cup success and a Lions captain in 1997 and 2001, to know what it means: 'Nobody remembers a Six Nations or Tri-Nations game from 12 years ago, but everyone remembers a Lions series,' he says. 'I played in over 80 matches for England and I can't remember all of them, but I recall every minute of every game I played for the Lions. It is a very special experience. I was walking the dog the other day thinking about that final lineout we lost in 2001. It lives with you.'

The lineout he is referring to was one at the very death of the third and final Test in Sydney, with the score in the series at 1–1 and the score in the match being 29–23 to Australia. The Lions had a lineout 5m from the Australian line and Johnson called the throw to himself at the front of the lineout, but it was stolen by the Australian lock Justin Harrison, and so the game, and indeed the series, was lost.

That feeling about the Lions exists not just in England, Wales, Scotland and Ireland. It is there in the three southern hemisphere countries of New Zealand, South Africa and Australia that the Lions tour. I will tell you a couple or more stories to illustrate where this point hit home to me so quickly and immediately.

I write a weekly column for the *Sunday Telegraph* newspaper and in 2014 I interviewed the New Zealand head coach Steve Hansen for the paper. Hansen was in London for the autumn internationals and, with the Rugby World Cup that New Zealand eventually won about 10 months away, we obviously spoke about that tournament, but what was remarkable was how enthusiastic and animated he was when talking about the Lions tour to New Zealand in 2017.

I didn't bring the subject up – he did. He said that the country was already talking about it. He was certainly talking about it, and he was already planning for it. And this was with a Rugby World Cup fast approaching. It was quite a startling admission, but it emphasised to me how big a deal a Lions tour is, and what it means to people and players in a country like New Zealand where rugby is the number one sport. For the truth is that they see the Lions as the number one opposition.

It is because the Lions, with all their history, have become part and parcel of the countries that they visit. The Lions virtually never play at home, so all their history and all their memories are in New Zealand, South Africa or Australia, and they naturally become woven into the fabric of those countries. For people growing up in New Zealand there is a long history of going to watch the Lions.

In 1977 I took part in a parade in Napier before the game against Hawke's Bay. The whole place just came to a standstill. Everyone in the area had been given the day off and everyone was there for the parade, which finished at the ground before the game. In those days if the Lions were in town, everything stopped. It had been exactly the same in South Africa in 1974, where at one stage we were driven through the middle of Bloemfontein in vintage cars in the build-up to a game.

Take what Sean Fitzpatrick, the great All Black hooker and captain who played against the Lions in 1993, says: 'When I was a kid, the 1971 Lions were our heroes. For the first time, the kids of the entire nation stopped kicking broken-toe style like Don Clarke and started kicking round-the-corner like Barry John [the brilliant Wales fly half who helped the Lions win that series]. We grew up with that kind of knowledge and heritage from the Lions in 1971 and 1977.'

For a lot of Fitzpatrick's 92-Test career, Warren Gatland was his reserve as hooker. Indeed, Gatland played 17 non-international matches for New Zealand but never won a cap. In 2009 in South Africa Gatland was one of my assistant coaches. His attitude to the Lions was remarkable. Initially he said he could not speak to the players as a group because he did not feel comfortable. He said that he had not earned the right at that stage.

He was respecting the Lions jersey as he would an All Black jersey, and indeed he has always said to me that the Lions are the closest thing he has ever seen to the All Blacks. Little wonder then that he went on to coach the Lions in 2013 and will do so again in 2017. He gets the Lions. He understands the concept better than most.

With tours having been shortened now (from, say, 26 matches in 1977 to 10), the greater impact of the Lions is with the supporters. That fabric of the Lions in New Zealand, South Africa and Australia merges with those who visit wearing their Lions jerseys. In the September after the 2009 tour, I met an elderly lady at a charity dinner at my former club, Wasps. It was a convivial evening where we had dinner and then I did a Question and Answer session about the Lions tour.

Afterwards this lady, who must have been in her late seventies, approached me to have a chat. She explained that she was a Saracens supporter (you don't get too many of them at Wasps' events!) but that she wanted to say thank you to me. I looked at her rather quizzically because I did not know what she meant.

'I'll tell you why I want to say thank you,' she said, and she set off on a story that was both moving and revealing. She said that she and her husband had always wanted to go on a Lions tour, so they had saved up for four years to go to South Africa that year. But, tragically, in the February before the tour, her husband had died.

Heartbroken, she had not even thought about making the tour, but her family had persuaded her to go because she and her husband had spent so much time planning and saving for it. They reasoned that her husband would have wanted her to go. So she went and she enjoyed an amazing three weeks watching the three Tests.

'It was brilliant,' she said. 'I'd lost my husband but there wasn't one moment on that tour that I felt I was on my own. I could have been an Irish, Welsh, English or Scottish woman, it didn't matter. As long as I had my Lions jersey on I had a sense of belonging that I never thought I would feel in a rugby environment. God willing, I'm saving up for Australia [in 2013] so if I'm fit and healthy I'll be there as well.'

That is the impact of the Lions – it is simply massive. It extends way beyond the field of play. It brings people and countries together like no other concept.

There are other instances that strengthen the Lions' fabric. At home in my lounge sits a beautiful Waterford Crystal lion, which was sent to me after the 1997 tour of South Africa. A group from that company in Ireland had come over for one of the Test matches, flying over on the Friday, watching the game on the Saturday and then returning home on the Sunday. They had enjoyed it so much that they had had the lion made especially for me and sent it with a lovely accompanying letter.

There was another tale from that 1997 tour of someone who had driven all the way to South Africa, and we had all signed the roof of his car for him, which he had then sold so that he could fly back home!

These are all heart-warming stories of the sort that everyone should consider before questioning the value of the Lions. For since professionalism arrived in 1995 there seems to have been an ever-present question mark against the Lions' place in the calendar. Indeed, even in September 2016, ahead of the 2017 tour of New Zealand, some were again talking about its future in very negative terms. Such people really should first read stories like those just mentioned. They epitomise what the Lions can do, that there is simply nothing else like it.

The Lions can change you both as a player and as a person. I always remember Clive Rowlands, the Welshman nicknamed Top Cat because he captained his country in all 14 of his Tests, addressing the Lions squad in his capacity as manager of the 1989 tour of Australia. He held up the Lions badge on the jersey and said: 'This badge will either get bigger or smaller by whatever you do on the field.' That resonated with everyone, and it still should do so. The badge is either enhanced or diminished by every action, every match on every tour. That is the essence of the Lions.

I have no doubt that the Lions changed me after that first tour in 1974. Being with the best of the best can do that to you. I didn't expect to be on the tour. It was only my second season in international rugby and I had only played 10 Tests for Scotland. I came back and I had a confidence about me that I had never felt before. You even look at your life differently because you appreciate people more.

I certainly did. I appreciated the uniqueness of the Lions and how special it all was. Having been away for the best part of three months, I came home and appreciated my family, the environment I was coming back to, and actually what good people I was coming back to and what good people I had left behind.

After I had become a Lion, playing in the Five Nations was never the same. You just looked at players differently. There was a different rapport. You respected them and they respected you. I particularly remember that 1975 Five Nations and the special feel it had.

Even as a coach it was different. So after the Lions tour of 1997 when I was coaching at Northampton and we were playing our arch East Midlands rivals, Leicester, I would look at the likes of Martin Johnson and Graham Rowntree in the opposition in a very different light. I would never see them in the same way again. There was an inner feeling, something very deep that I struggle to put into words.

We shall come to it later in the book, but it was this that I was referring to when I made an impassioned speech to the squad before the second Test in Durban, South Africa, in 1997.

'You'll meet each other in the street in 30 years' time, and there will just be a look, and you will know just how special some days in your life are,' I said. It might not be immediately obvious to those outside the Lions environment, but it is very true. If a Lions tour has gone as it should, this is one of its impacts on players and also on supporters.

The players must, though, be given the opportunity to create that. They must be given the chance to get to know each other, to bond and to blend. The tours that have missed the mark did not have that. The thinking from the management team must be kept open, especially where selection is concerned. Every player must board the plane convinced that he has a chance of wearing the Test jersey, otherwise you cannot create the environment that makes the Lions so treasured.

I have always thought that every player should be given at least one start in the first three or four matches of a tour, so that the Test players have two starts before the first Test. Psychologically it is massively important that everyone has the chance to wear a starting Lions jersey early on. You need to be able to press your case.

This was not what happened in 2005 with Matt Dawson. The England scrum half was the designated back-up to Wales' Dwayne Peel but there were four scrum halves on that trip – Scotland's Chris Cusiter and Wales' Gareth Cooper – so the others were getting starts early on when Dawson might have had opportunities. He only started once early in the tour, in the fourth match of the tour against the New Zealand Maori side, but thereafter was not risked as a starter because the thought process was that he would always be required as a reserve.

It meant, however, that by the last week of the tour Cusiter had started three games and Cooper two, while Dawson still had had just that one opportunity to prove himself from the start. So it was rightly decided to give Daws a start in the final midweek match, against Auckland, before the final Test. But it was probably too late.

The lesson to be learnt here is that you have to understand how different the Lions are. You need to have an open mind about looking at players, and about managing the itinerary and how it operates. It is about trying to keep the players together as a group as often as possible, so you prevent any divisions forming. And it is also about getting the chemistry right with support staff as well as the players.

So there needs to be a central focus tactically, technically and operationally right from the outset. From the very start all the coaches have to make sure they are clear about how they see the Lions evolving tactically. I think you have got to have a really good picture in your head about the rugby you want to see the team playing, and about how that is going to challenge the opposition in the Test series.

So while you should keep an open mind about selection and try different combinations, you can repeat the same tactical theme in all the practices, even if you are not sticking to any rigid game plan, simply because the players are so good that they will evolve their game naturally.

In 2009 in South Africa that is what we did. All the words we used, all the tactics, they all had the same names – so it didn't matter whether you played on a Wednesday, a Saturday, the following Wednesday, or the following Saturday, all the vocabulary was the same. Under pressure, when a split second call was made, everybody understood what it meant. And when you have got good players, that moment is what makes the difference, because if you give a good player half a second extra or half a yard extra in which to play, then suddenly you have a big advantage.

As coaches on the 2009 tour, we had agreed what we wanted to do and how we wanted to do it against South Africa – running their front five around and playing in the outside channels – even before we got to work, so that in the very first training session we had at Pennyhill Park (England's training base at Bagshot in Surrey), we were beginning to put into practice what we wanted on the field in order to beat South Africa in the Test series.

The problem is that if a different set of coaches are delivering that message, it can cause some problems. That is what happened in 2005 in New Zealand under Sir Clive Woodward. There is no doubt in my mind that Clive deserved to be in charge of that tour. He had led England to a stunning Rugby World Cup triumph in Australia in 2003, which had been building up because of the way his team had dominated everyone else in the world in the run-up to the tournament. And during his time as England head coach he had shown a vision and attention to detail that set him apart from other coaches and managers. In many respects he was ahead of his time. So it was only right and proper that he was granted his wish to try to implement his methods and beliefs upon the Lions.

I truly believed that, so much so that I accepted his offer to be in charge of the midweek side on that tour. I would never have gone if I had thought for even a moment beforehand: 'This is not right.' The challenge excited me. I wanted to be involved and I wanted to see if it could work.

The crux of Clive's thinking was that right from the start of the tour he wanted to have in his own mind the team that would take the field for the first Test. He then wanted to work with that team in preparation for that first Test. All the focus would be on that team. He therefore wanted two separate teams of players and coaches on the tour; there would be a Test operation and a midweek operation. It had been something that had been hinted at by Graham Henry in Australia in 2001 because his Test team appeared to be easily identified from the outset.

Clive had been a Lion himself in 1980 on the tour of South Africa and in 1983 in New Zealand, so he knew how important the midweek games were, despite there being a lot of calls at the time for them to be curtailed. But he also did not want his chosen Test players traipsing around the country for those matches. So there was often one squad in one place with one set of coaches, and another in another place with another set of coaches. It naturally meant that we needed more players, so the tour party began at 45 and ended with 51 players being used.

For the Test team Clive had with him Andy Robinson and Phil Larder, both from the England set-up, as well as Ireland's Eddie O'Sullivan. I was in charge of the midweek team, along with Wales' Gareth Jenkins and Mike Ford, who was then defence coach with Ireland. There were two tactical streams because no two coaches, even when talking about the same things, will deliver their messages in the same way. It was definitely confusing for the players, because they were being taught in a different way by coaches who saw the game plan slightly differently.

Whilst I was very proud that the midweek team remained unbeaten, defeating Taranaki, Wellington, Southland, Manawatu and Auckland, the Test series was lost 3–0. We were up against a brilliant All Black side, with Dan Carter absolutely majestic, especially in the second Test at Wellington where he scored 33 points in the 48–18 victory for the Kiwis.

There were other challenges. For a start, and indeed the very start, there was a match against Argentina at home. The Lions decided to do something different and organise this match in Cardiff to begin their preparations early. Lions games at home are a rarity, for very good reason. The most recent one to this had been when they played the Rest of Europe at Twickenham in 1990. I had actually taken part in one in 1977 when we played the Barbarians at Twickenham – winning 23–14 – as part of the Queen's silver jubilee celebrations, about three weeks after we had returned from our Lions tour of New Zealand.

But this match against Argentina in 2005 created a difficult situation. We only drew it 25–25 thanks to a Jonny Wilkinson penalty deep into injury time, and I felt it was a wasted week in Wales spent trying to prepare a group of players to play a game in isolation rather than getting the tactics and the specifics in place for what we wanted to build on over the next seven weeks.

Then there was the challenge of how we were perceived in New Zealand in 2005. In general Lions tours have been positively received by the host nations and the media, even though in 1977 in New Zealand under coach John Dawes there were some uncomfortable moments in that respect.

Clive decided to take Alastair Campbell, the former Labour spin doctor, as his head of communications. It was always an interesting move and you could see the logic of hiring such a big hitter in that field. But I think he created the wrong impression for us in the eyes of the New Zealand public.

In terms of the actual press dealings, he wanted to be in total control so every media session was exceptionally professional, but it was too sanitised. He actually really impressed me with how he would know exactly what the questions would be in follow-up to your answers. He would give everyone who was doing a media conference a sheet of paper with answers already written on it, detailing what to say and then, if you said what he suggested, what the next question would be, and what your answer should then be to that. And he would always be right – I found that incredible. But the press hated it because they knew they were being manipulated and as the tour wore on they became more and more irritated.

I would like to think that I have always got on well with the media. Even in 1977 when we were supposed to be at loggerheads with them, I can remember myself and my Scotland team-mate Andy Irvine often having a beer with the touring journalists. Sometimes you have to bite your tongue a little bit with some journalists, but overall I was always trying to make it easier for them to do their job well.

There has got to be a trust. You need to know that you can say things confidentially and they will not be written, or you might say to the journalist: 'Can you hold on to that until the weekend or nearer the game or until when it doesn't affect anything?' But if that trust is broken and a line is crossed then that is it, the relationship is over.

I learnt all this very early on from one of the best sports journalists I ever came across, the late Norman Mair of the *Scotsman* newspaper. He had played rugby and cricket for Scotland so he understood the game and sport in general, and we built up a trust that meant we could help each other. Norman was absolutely superb to talk to and he always made me think, whether I was talking tactics or talking about other teams. I could tell him what I was thinking, and then he would put points back to me. 'Why are you doing that?' he would ask and the like. So he was actually helping me in my own role, just by making sure I was clear in what I wanted to get across. He was brilliant in that respect.

Sometimes he would go to a game and say to me afterwards that a certain player was worth having a second look at in terms of selection, whether it was for Scotland or for the Lions. When you can have that sort of conversation and you know that it is respected, I think you build a very different kind of relationship.

Mind you, things have changed an awful lot since my first tour as coach in 1989. Then there were probably only about a dozen journalists on the tour, as opposed to the hundreds now, and I used to do my press conferences at the side of the pitch after training. On that tour we allowed the press to be at those training sessions so that they could see what we were doing. They never knew what time the session was finishing. We didn't give them a time, we just said that the press conference would be at the end of the session, so they had to watch some of the rugby first. We hoped they then might find it harder to be critical! Nowadays the press – except the photographers, obviously, and even they are only given a limited amount of time – are not allowed anywhere near the training field.

In 1989 after we had won the series in Australia, there was still a week left of the tour when we had to play a New South Wales Country team in Newcastle in midweek and then an ANZAC team in Ballymore for the final match. It meant we had some time to relax during that week and one of the many things I did was go out for lunch with some of the journalists. They paid for the meal and a lovely bottle of wine to say thank you to me and my assistant coach Roger Uttley for the way we had cooperated with them on the tour.

That relationship with the press is vital on a Lions tour. To me it is as vital as all the other relationships you need to work on. It is a key part of building the wider environment that is conducive to togetherness and inclusion.

There are obviously other ways of fostering this togetherness. For example, I always think that it is best if players share rooms on a Lions tour. In 2005 they had single rooms. Sharing a room is part of the bonding process. It is about the little things like chatting late at night and making coffee for each other in the morning. You get to know each other and you have to get on.

This is part of the Lions' uniqueness. You have the opportunity to make friends with players you might not ordinarily get to know that well, and that is part of the seven-week challenge. Banter and good communication build a spirit of togetherness. It means you can be more natural with each other and therefore forge a trust, with the result that you want to win for each other because you've got inner respect for what each other does. In conversation you learn what makes each other tick.

If a player wants to go to his room and have some time to himself you have to respect that, and it is perfectly understandable, but what you also need is for that player to know that there is a location in the hotel where everything is happening in one place as regards the operation of the tour and the management of the squad.

In 2005 we were staying in five-star hotels but we did not really have team rooms, centres that we could go to that were just for us. The places available were more like open lobbies, and even when in Auckland where we had an area that had table tennis tables, some seats and some computers, it was in a foyer. Meanwhile the medics were on the fifth floor in another room, so you were dividing the group all the time. I learnt the lesson that you needed one room for everyone.

It is so important to do things together. I think back to that first tour of mine in 1974 and of the 30 players on the bus and all of us singing together. There was one incident when we were going to the second Test in Pretoria. We always had these particular songs that we sang, one of them being 'Flower of Scotland', which was the tour song that the Scotland wing Billy Steele had introduced.

We got to Loftus Versfeld and we hadn't finished singing, so we sat on the bus until we had finished the songs that we always sang. People outside couldn't understand why we were not getting off the bus to go into the stadium for the Test match. But we had to finish our song. It was important to us.

It is little things like that that can be crucial, where you just accept that you do things together and you finish things together – then you are ready for the next challenge. We were not ready for the match until we had finished our singing. It was as simple as that.

What was good about 2005 was the planning. Clive Woodward was always known as a superb planner, and he never spared any expense in making sure those plans were implemented. He had Louise Ramsay as team manager; she had performed the same role with England and was excellent at it. She was extremely organised and efficient.

I was delighted to work with her when I became head coach again on the 2009 tour to South Africa. She was fantastic. She was always able and willing to change things at the last minute with the minimum of fuss. She never panicked, never said: 'Oh no, that's just not possible.' Instead she always just said,

'Leave it with me.' Sometimes as coach you have to change training or travel times, and it can cause huge problems, but with Louise you knew that she would simply sort things. There would be no ripples in the water at all, it just happened.

As I acknowledged in my 2009 post-tour report (which I submitted to the four home unions after every tour on which I was head coach):

> Louise is quite simply outstanding in every respect. It is fair to say she probably took time to work out my idiosyncrasies, but she responded to late changes of decision with the flexibility of approach, which, I think, is vital to create a successful Lions environment.
>
> We were successful because the main programme was planned and agreed months in advance, but the daily/weekly workings were often late calls reflecting the requirements of the situation and environment.

Indeed, despite our travails in the Tests, I took many useful things from the 2005 tour in terms of facilities, travel and attention to detail: for instance, the presence of a chef on tour, a legal expert and the organisation of charter flights in a private jet around New Zealand. The charter flights are especially important because this allows you to travel at the times that suit you best, and to work around training times.

Sometimes you need quiet moments on a tour to appraise where you are and what has been happening, and I was lucky to have such an opportunity late in the tour with Bill Beaumont, the tour manager, who was the ideal man for such a chat. During the last week of the tour, just a few days before the final Test in Auckland, we took the 40-minute ferry from Auckland to Waiheke Island so that we could talk. We had some food and then we went for a walk. We were laughing and joking but there was a very serious side to our talking, too. Both of us knew that this was crunch time for the Lions.

Bill and I have always got on really well. We have always loved talking rugby and that was something I had missed on that trip. There had simply not been enough of it. I have always loved the boot-room chats with other coaches and management staff, whether over a coffee or a bottle of wine at the bar. 'All the management staff did a superb job and we had a relaxed but professional relationship – some meetings did take place in the bar!' I wrote in my 2009 report. I have often found that these informal chats result in the most productive rugby ideas and information. The 2005 tour needed more of them.

I had been worried in 1997 about the Lions, because professionalism had just arrived and had we not won there in South Africa, or at least given a good account of ourselves, then you do wonder what might have happened. And I was worried again now – probably more so. But both Bill and I were adamant that we must be positive and that the Lions must not just survive in the professional era, but that the concept must thrive.

We talked about the good things and the bad things from the tour. But we kept coming back to the overall view that this group of Lions had not really felt what a magnificent experience a Lions tour should be. They had not really got to know each other, they had not experienced the country of New Zealand as they should have done, and in truth they had not got to realise what being a Lion in New Zealand could give them – in other words that, even in the professional era, after all the hard work and the pressure, you can enjoy yourself, have a drink at the appropriate times and savour a unique experience with some special team-mates.

The importance of players getting to know each other is actually heightened in the professional era, because the players from both teams hardly know each other. When I played there would be an official dinner and dance after every Test, and over a few drinks players would mingle and often get to know each other very well. That does not happen so much now. There is a much smaller after-match reception and often teams are keen to leave and prepare for the next match, which sometimes is only a matter of days away. We would quite often have weeks between internationals, so there was no excuse not to have a few beers and let your hair down. Good friendships were made.

All the 2005 tour did in reality was highlight the uniqueness of the Lions and the approach that you have got to have, especially with the tours having become shorter. Yes, what happens with the four home union teams these days is very professional and very well done, but you have to loosen up a little bit if you want to get the environment and atmosphere right for a group of players that really do not know each other at all and have so little time to mix.

Winning for the Lions is so difficult because every series is away from home, and it annoys me that there is this myth that they are a huge failure. Do you know how many Test series South Africa have ever won in New Zealand? One, that's all, and that was in 1937! And while we are at it, do you know how many Test series New Zealand have won in South Africa? The answer to that is one as well. That was in 1996.

Yes, because of the advent of the Tri-Nations competition and its subsequent reincarnations, there are not full-scale tours between these countries any more, but it still does tell a story of the arduousness of the task facing the Lions every time they tour. And interestingly, after the Lions had toured South Africa in 2009, the South Africans then beat the All Blacks in three consecutive Tests in the months that followed. They had not done that since the 1970s. It just showed how tough we had made that series for them, even if we lost 2–1, and the preparation it gave them.

In 2017 the Lions travel to New Zealand to play the world champions, and, as I began writing this in late 2016, before Ireland surprisingly beat the All Blacks in Chicago and then pushed them close in Dublin two weeks later, already some people were saying that it was mission impossible and that the Lions were in danger again because they simply cannot win. But they won their last series, in Australia, in 2013! As Bill and I talked we came to realise that we were very much of the same mind, that certain things were important and had to be a priority for future Lions tours.

Clive Woodward was disappointed with how things panned out. I am pretty sure that if he had had the opportunity to take charge of another Lions tour, he would have done it very differently. It is about learning from your mistakes, moving on quickly and altering things for the right reasons. I am lucky enough to have had the experience of four tours as head coach. I have learnt so much along the way in that time.

One of the key things Bill and I talked about was the relationship between the coach and the manager, and how roles had to be clear and interlink. And over the course of our chat Bill did mention that I should consider being manager of the next tour to South Africa. It was a surprise because at that stage I had never contemplated going on another Lions tour.

So the final Test came and went, with a 38–19 defeat in Auckland. And once the tour was over I was asked to help John Feehan, who is still the British and Irish Lions' chief executive now and had just taken over, in making a tour report, which was unusual because I was only an assistant. But in that report I was able to make all the points I had mulled over with Bill on Waiheke Island, as well as throw my hat in the ring as a possible manager for the 2009 tour.

But as time wore on, it became clear that the Welshman Gerald Davies, who was already on the Lions committee and had toured with the Lions as a superb winger in 1968 and 1971, had also put his name in the ring to be manager. Having given it some thought, I told my old Scotland colleague, full back Andy Irvine, that Gerald was the ideal choice and that I would not put my name forward. In 2007, though, I received a call from Andy, who was by then chairman of the Lions Board. He asked whether I might consider being head coach of the Lions for a fourth time.

It was a shock, to say the least. Thinking about being manager was one thing, being head coach again was quite another. But it was not as if I was out of the coaching loop. I was coaching Wasps at the time and felt that I was coaching as well as I had ever been. I thought long and hard about it, and then asked my wife, Judy, what she thought. 'If you really want to go for it, then go for it,' she said.

I think Bill Beaumont had spoken quite a lot to the Board about the things we had talked about on Waiheke, so I was confident that they were well aware of how I felt and what I would want to do as coach. I knew how hard a task it was to be head coach of the Lions, but I also felt there was a real opportunity here, given the state of the game and the resources available, to drive the tour in exactly the way I wanted.

So I went for it. I said I was interested. I don't actually know who else was in for the job, but I was asked to attend two interviews, one in London and then another in Dublin, because not everyone was available to be in London. Gerald had been appointed as manager but he stayed out of it because he felt that it was not right for him to be involved, which was rather surprising and certainly slightly different from 1989 when the manager Clive Rowlands had got someone to ring me up to see if I fancied being head coach. Clive knew whom he wanted then.

But anyway, in May 2008 I stood before the Lions Board and gave what might be termed my sales pitch. I told them that there were certain principles that I considered vital for a Lions coach to work to. As mentioned, the overriding theme to them was togetherness. Everything had to be as one: the squad, the coaching team, the medical team and the management team.

I said to the Board: 'If you don't agree with those principles, then, for goodness' sake, don't pick me as head coach, because I am not going to change my values. I am not prepared to compromise. These are fundamental principles that I think have to be in place if you are going to have any chance of being competitive in the Test series with a new group of players.' A couple of days later Andy Irvine phoned to offer me the position of head coach.

Those principles will form the basis of this book. My pitch was my blueprint for running a Lions tour, taking in my experiences from all those tours as a coach and player. There have been many good times but I also know that I have made many mistakes and learnt many lessons from them. So this book will consider all points of a Lions tour, from the moment the coach is selected to the moment the players disembark from the aircraft and disperse after their life-changing adventure.

This, through many recollections, anecdotes, memories and indeed quotes from previously unseen official tour reports, will offer the principles I believe are key to making a successful Lions tour.

KEY WORDS

- Making the bond
- Strategic clarity
- Open minds
- Evolving tactics

1974 South Africa, First Test
This is where it all began for me; my first Lions Test as a player.

RAMPAGING LIONS TRAMPLE BOKS INTO MUD

South Africa 3, British Lions 12

from SUNDAY EXPRESS REPORTER:

What a victory this was in the mud of Newlands, Cape Town, yesterday.

It was a triumph which will reverberate from the Cape to the Highveld with the resonance of thunder.

For this was the first time over that a Lions' pack have trampled Springbok forwards into their own Kikuyu turf.

Sure, the margin was only three penalties and a dropped real to a dropped goal. But the scoreline does not reflect the complete, utter superiority of mighty Willie-John McBride's men.

Weary

"We played it exactly as we wanted to play it and controlled the game from start to finish." chortled happy Lions coach Syd Millar as his mud-splattered heroes trotted off while weary Boks trudged behind shoulders hanched, heads down, after losing their first Test to the Lions since 1955.

Millar, who schemed the game with McBride and Gareth Edwards, had summed up perfectly.

Apart from the opening 25 minutes,

with a strong wind at their backs, the Springboks were scarcely in the hunt. Edwards and Phil Bennett, retrentlessly kicking in support of their pounding pack, drove them backwards, backwards and ever backwards.

The Springboks had only one hope against this thunderous driving urgency: they had to run the ball.

But such was the strangle hold of the Lions puck, and so complete their control, that the Boks scarcely got any ball to run. When they did they were cut down like ripe corn by devastating tackling.

Three years ago, when the Lions won the first Test against the All Blacks in New Zealand, I could feel the tension mounting in near-frenzy towards the end of the game.

This time there was no tension. McBride's men exerted such iron control that once they went into the lead just after half-time, the result seemed Inevitable.

Flair

The heroes? Well, out of this bunch of gallants it is difficult to nominate individuals, but "Mighty Mouse" Ian McLaughlan in the front row, McBride and the ubiquitous Mervyn Davies were outstanding up front and Roger Uitley looked perfectly at home on the flank.

Behind, Edwards stole the show and conducted the orchestra with the aplomh, flair and brilliance of an Andre Prevln.

Bennett, too, rose to the big occasion, placing his penalty goals with almost professional detachment as if he had never looked up the word "failure" in his dictionary. J. P. R. Williams, too, was his usual ice-cool self.

But they were all heroes and they played superbly as a team whose watchwords were control and perfection.

They made just one mistake in the game, and this led to the Boks' score. In the 18th minute, Springbok fullback Ian McCallum was wide with a 50-yard penalty. J. P. R. Williams, instead of touching down, decided to run the ball, but left J. J. Williams stranded in goal.

Williams kicked to touch. From the resulting five-yard scrum, the Boks won a quick ball and their fly-half Dawie Snyman dropped a 30-yard goal.

That was their last taste of honey. In the 38th minute their centres were caught offside in front of the posts and Bennett kicked his first penalty for the Lions to turn level at 3—3 with the wind now in their favour.

Five minutes after half-time. Bennett booted them into the lead when Springbok skipper Hannes Marais was offside at a ruck 30 yards out.

Offside

Twenty minutes later Bennett goaled penalty No. 3 for offside at the scrum.

Gareth Edwards applied the coup de grace to the stricken Springboks with a great 35-yard drop goal 10 minutes from the end.

Yes, a great and memorable victory.

- Mike Gibson, the experienced Irish player, will join the Lions as replacement for the injured Alan Old, on June 21, a day before the second Test in Pretoria.
- The New Zealand All Blacks beat Australia 16–8 in the third and final Test at Sydney yesterday. They have won two Tests, with one drawn.

1

THEN AND NOW

I was a professional rugby player in 1974. Yes, professionalism did not officially arrive until 1995, and no, I am not saying that I received any underhand payments, but what I am saying is that I became a professional rugby player on that Lions tour, my first, that year. For me being a professional is not about being paid a salary, it is about your approach and attitude.

In 1974 we were given just 75p a day allowance for the tour. I had to put my mortgage on hold back at home because I could not afford it, and I had to leave my wife, Judy, behind at home and only keep in touch by letter because making a telephone call was so difficult and so expensive.

We would collect our letters from a PO Box and I recently dug out the letters I received from Judy on that tour. Even she admits they are 'hilarious' now. It is because they seem so random and often humdrum in their content, but as she says: 'I was just trying to talk about things that you didn't know about.'

The matches were not even shown live on television at home back then. So family and fans would crowd around radios to listen, while the Test matches would be filmed and sent home so that they could be viewed in midweek. Judy would spend a lot of time with my mother during the tour and they would listen to all the games on the radio.

There was one occasion late in the tour when they travelled up to Inverness to stay with a cousin of mine. They went out for the day to have a picnic but when it came to the time of the game, they realised that they had forgotten the radio. Judy said that it did not matter, but my mother insisted that they had to listen to the game. So Judy had to drive all the way back to get the radio. She got the blame, too!

That was a very different era from now, where satellite television, social media and the internet provide instant blanket coverage, and over 30,000 fans travel in person to watch the tours.

But I still felt like a professional because I was living and breathing rugby for 24 hours a day, training hard at every opportunity (I had done so beforehand too, doing circuits and sprints on my own with Judy holding the stopwatch and shouting instructions!) and watching my diet so that I weighed in at over 12 stone for the first time in my life.

This was a squad out in South Africa to win a Test series and give everything we had on every single day. We had no work to go to. We had hotels to stay in, rugby fields to practise on and train on and games to play. That was all we were concerned with. I understood what taking rugby as a profession meant all right. So much has changed since that first Lions tour of mine in 1974, but at the same time so much has remained the same. *Plus ça change, plus c'est la même chose.*

The 1974 trip to South Africa was a remarkable tour, as we went unbeaten throughout the 22 games and the side became known as 'The Invincibles'. No other Lions side had done, or has done, that. The squad that had toured New Zealand in 1971 had won the Test series 2-1, and remains the only Lions side to have done that in New Zealand, but they had lost games there, not least the very first match of the tour against Queensland, as they played two games in Australia before moving to New Zealand. They also lost one of the Tests and drew another.

Debate still rages today as to which was the better side: 1971 or 1974? Is that for me to judge? Well, why not? I was only on one of those tours so I know that I am not necessarily impartial, but, yes, I do think the 1974 Lions were the better side, the greatest Lions even. We set a record that I do not think can be broken. No Lions tour is going to be as long as 22 games any more, that is for certain.

The much respected Welsh journalist J.B.G. Thomas wrote a chronicle of the 1974 tour and entitled it *The Greatest Lions*, ending the book with the words: 'They must be the "Greatest". If not, please tell me why?' Indeed.

What is certain is that rugby union in the four home countries was in rude health in those times. The Five Nations, as it was then, was a ferociously contested tournament every year, a fact that is no better illustrated than by the result of the 1973 competition when there was a five-way tie for the title. Every side won their two home games and lost their two away games, and there was no other judging criterion used. All five were equal.

Wales – for whom, of course, this was a golden age with outright Five Nations titles in 1969, 1971, 1975, 1976, 1978 and 1979 (with three of them being Grand Slams in 1971, 1976 and 1978) – would have won it had it been decided on points difference.

These days it is, of course, the Six Nations with Italy having joined in 2000 (and in 2017 bonus points were introduced to help determine placings even more), and they are often not alone in struggling in the competition. There always seems to be one or two other countries struggling alongside them. Back in the 1970s nobody ever seemed to be struggling. It was always a monumental scrap.

In South Africa we won 21 games, and we only drew the final Test in Johannesburg 13–13 because the referee Max Baise disallowed a try from Ireland's Fergus Slattery in the final moments. Slattery had been put through by the great Welsh full back J.P.R. Williams and was initially held up over the line by centre Peter Cronje, but then touched the ball down between Cronje's legs.

It was definitely a try – Cronje later told Slattery so – but in fairness there had been a disputed score for us earlier when Roger Uttley had touched down after South Africa had lost control of a scrummage and he and the South African winger Chris Pope had both gone for the ball, with both claiming they had got to it first.

Uttley later admitted that he had not got there first, though. So maybe justice was done in the end, even if it did not feel like it when the referee Baise, under so much pressure to explain the Slattery decision, said something along the lines of it was OK for us as we were going home, but he had to remain and live in South Africa.

But it was not just in terms of the results that the tour was so remarkable. It was in the way the tour was set up and how the key individuals worked and interacted that then had such an impact and influence on me for the rest of my career, both as a player and as a coach. Indeed, the thinking and the principles of that trip still remain relevant today. You have got a group of people who either want to put it out there on a rugby field for each other or they don't. It's as simple as that.

If the attitude is right, the tour will be right. So you do everything to make sure that the right attitude is imbued in the players. You then build a belief because you know that you can trust each other. Out of that comes loyalty because you can trust that someone will deliver when necessary. You have all committed to saying: 'If it is my time to deliver and it is needed, I will deliver.' If you have that collective unity and intent, that is when I think teams grow to a different level. That's the moment when you see Lions rugby as a team sport at its best.

Those principles do not change even though the game has gone professional. Warren Gatland will still need all this when he takes his Lions to New Zealand in 2017. They are things that do not go away. They give a tour its substance and its strength. I can genuinely trace them back to 1974 and that first tour and its impact.

Yes, you have got to be well organised but first and foremost it is about the group of people you have and how they come together and how they then react to one another. This ultimately will have the biggest impact on whether the tour is going to be successful.

That is why sometimes you can actually argue that it is not always Test results that count in the end – some Lions tours have been outstanding even though the team ultimately haven't won the Test series, and without wishing to be too biased I would place the tour of South Africa in 2009 in that bracket.

It shows that when you are managing or coaching a tour – and 1974 proved this – selection is hugely important. This remains the same in 2017. Warren's biggest challenge will have been selection: who might play with whom, how players who might never have played together before might mix and how the chemistry they might produce looks. You are almost looking at a game beyond what the players are producing when you first select them or consider selecting them.

In 1974 there were 30 players for a 22-match tour (two replacements, the Bristol and England wing Alan Morley and the Irish centre Mike Gibson were summoned). We have already seen the size of the squad Clive Woodward took to New Zealand in 2005, but even a more sensible number is still much bigger these days than it once was. For instance, Warren took 37 players to Australia in 2013 for 10 matches, even though he required eight replacements to swell the number used to 45. As I write, it has been said that he will take between 38 and 40 to New Zealand in 2017 for the 10-match tour.

It was in 1997 that we decided to increase the number of players taken on a Lions tour. From 1977 to 1993 it had been 30. But when I took the squad to South Africa on that 1997 trip I insisted on taking 35. I was taking my cue from the New Zealand tour there the previous year – remember that was the first time the All Blacks had won a series in South Africa – when I had actually spent time with them under coach John Hart. I learnt many valuable lessons then, one of them being that you must have extra cover at scrum half and hooker because they are such specialist positions.

If you take at least 35 players it means that a scrum half or hooker does not have to play or do bench duty for every game. Although, as in the case of Matt Dawson in 2005, you do also have to make sure that they have sufficient opportunity as well as sufficient rest.

In 1974 we had just a coach – the Irishman Syd Millar, a former prop who had won 37 caps for Ireland and been on three Lions tours in 1959, 1962 and 1968 as a player, winning nine caps – and a Welshman as manager in Alun Thomas, who had won 13 caps for Wales mostly as a centre and had been on the 1955 Lions tour without winning a cap because of illness and injury. Those two, Millar and Thomas, were the sum of our management staff. They were all we had to help us. There was no other back-up staff, no doctor and no physiotherapist with the tour party.

On each day of the tour one player was assigned as duty boy and it would be his job to go to Alun early in the morning and find out exactly what was happening that day. It was up to him to ensure that, firstly, everyone was out of bed, and then that they were at the appropriate places at the appropriate times. He even had to make sure that all the bags were together and ready to go and that they arrived safely at our destination.

You might think that would not happen today, but even though in 1997 I decided there should be no duty boys in terms of time-keeping, 'Right People, Right Place, Right Time' was something I stressed as soon as we met up, and I did make sure there were two duty boys to help the kit man clear up the dressing room after matches. In 1997 we had a support staff of 12. When I returned to that country in 2009 that number had risen to 26.

All we had in 1974 was a liaison officer who was given to us by the South African Rugby Union. In this case it was Choet Visser, who was from Bloemfontein. Then he had another local liaison officer in each area with whom he worked. It was their job to organise physiotherapy and any other medical requirements we had, as well as keeping us occupied in our down time by arranging things like rounds of golf, game drives, sightseeing and meals at local restaurants. But if you did need physio treatment, or to see a doctor, Choet or one of his helpers could only ring a local practice to help. You still had to go there and take your place in the queue with everyone else. There were no favours in that respect.

Although I do remember there being favours in many other respects. For instance, Syd knew that most of us did not have much money and that we had made big sacrifices to go on the tour, so, when we went to the De Beers diamond factory, he said to me, 'Don't worry about paying anything for that' when I chose a diamond that I wanted set into a ring for Judy.

The local hospitality was outstanding. Whichever golf course we wanted to play would be made available at the drop of a hat. The Scotland lock Gordon Brown even got to play a round with Gary Player, the great South African golfer, who actually gave the South African team (rugby, that is) their pre-match talk before the decisive third Test in Port Elizabeth.

On most Sundays we would be entertained at huge family homes with a *braai* and a few drinks around a swimming pool before being driven back to our hotel. This was because everything on the tour was organised for us by the South Africans. Whereas these days it is completely the other way around: all the organisation is in the Lions' hands and all the information will be gathered beforehand by a Lions person. It is an intricate and detailed operation that is years in the planning.

The advance logistics people are crucial on tour in setting everything up 24 hours ahead. That is why I used Guy Richardson, an ex-military man, as my director of operations in South Africa in 2009. He continued the role in Australia in 2013. For the 2017 tour of New Zealand, the Lions have appointed Gerard Carmody, the former Ireland team manager, who was the logistics officer in Australia in 2013.

The training kit in 1974 was mainly our club kit, although we did get one training jersey, I think. My club, Headingley, had given me a club jersey to train in and two pairs of socks, as well as six club ties so that I could use them to thank people who helped me on the tour. We got a Lions duffle bag to put our kit in and we had to bring our own suitcase.

If you were a Test Lion you kept your Test jersey. But for all the other games you had to hand your jersey back in so that it could be washed and sometimes patched up. I think there were only about half a dozen sets.

For the fourth Test, however, we had run out of jerseys. So Syd and Alun had to get a set made in South Africa. If you look at the numbers on the jerseys for the fourth Test they were completely different from those in the other three Tests. They are actually rugby jerseys made in South Africa. I cannot see that happening today, somehow!

Also, we were provided with two blazers, a tour one with a large Lions badge and a formal one with a smaller badge. We were given two pairs of trousers and a tie. Now the players have got kit coming out of their ears, with every playing jersey beautifully embroidered with the game for which it is worn, complete with their initials.

In 1974 the travelling press corps was only about half a dozen strong. And we knew them all – the likes of the afore-mentioned J.B.G. Thomas of the *Western Mail*, another Welshman Vivian Jenkins, a Lion himself in 1938, who was writing for the *Sunday Times*, the *Daily Telegraph*'s John Reason, Terry O'Connor from the *Daily Mail* and Chris Lander from the *Daily Mirror* – and we all travelled together.

These were very different days, as Thomas indeed detailed in his book, *The Greatest Lions*. 'My creed is that the players' private lives should remain their own,' he said. 'If, occasionally, an odd glass or chair is broken and the damage made good by immediate payment, then I do not think it requires headlines.'

That has changed a little, as has the number of journalists seeking such stories. But, as I have already mentioned, there are ways of dealing with the press and of cultivating a good working relationship with them. We certainly had that relationship in 1974.

As a squad we were an eclectic bunch. I was a secondary school teacher then, and we had other teachers in the squad, doctors (J.P.R. Williams and Ken Kennedy), an RAF PE instructor in Billy Steele (he was probably the only one fitter than me after my intensive personal training sessions before the tour), farmers, a carpenter, a solicitor, a banker, an accountant, a steelworker and so on. All amateurs, but, as I said, essentially professionals from the moment we met up at a London hotel to leave for the tour.

It was a controversial tour, though. Protests against apartheid in South Africa had been increasing and there was a lot of pressure for the tour to be cancelled. The Labour Party wrote to us asking us not to go. Some players like the Welshmen John Taylor and Gerald Davies did just that, refusing to join the tour.

Call me naïve but I believed then, as I do now, that sport and politics should not mix, but I was worried that I might not get permission to go. Leeds (where I was teaching) was a Labour council, so their position was clear. But I was lucky that my headmaster knew the chief education officer and he was able to get a quorum for a meeting of the committee. One afternoon I was told to take the afternoon off school and go to the council offices for a meeting, where I asked for permission to go to South Africa. That small committee gave me that permission.

The matter was raised at a later meeting of the full committee but I had already been granted permission, and, anyway, there were a number of people who were very supportive of me, and to them I have always been very thankful.

But even as we gathered in London there were still concerns about the tour. It was here that Willie John McBride first showed me his truly great leadership qualities. It was Willie John's fifth successive Lions tour but his first as captain. He began as he was to continue. He gave a brilliant speech.

'I know there are pressures on you,' he said. 'But, gentlemen, if you have any doubts about going on this tour, I want you to be big enough to stand up now and leave this room, because you are no use to me, and you're no use to this team. There will be no stain on your character, no accusations if you do so, but you must be honest and committed. I've been in South Africa before and there's going to be a lot of physical intimidation, a lot of cheating. So if you're not up for a fight, there's the door.'

Nobody left. And nobody was left wondering what sort of captain Willie John was going to be. He had a real understanding of the players, what they wanted and what they needed. And this is what Willie John himself wrote about this incident: 'I believe that was the moment when the 1974 British Lions united and we became a special team. When we went off to

South Africa the next day, there was a special bond already among us, quite unlike any I had ever known before on a Lions tour.'

Before the first Test in Cape Town we were in our hotel for the final team meeting and he was sitting there puffing on his pipe. We were waiting for him to say something, but he said nothing. We sat there for about 20 minutes and still he said nothing. Eventually he just said: 'Are you ready? Let's go.' He later said that he thought we were ready, so he did not feel the need to speak – a brilliant lesson for any captain, or indeed coach.

Willie John was clever in how he got different players to speak up at different moments in the tour. Whether it was during one of our visits to the local schools or after training, or even after matches, he would call upon different players to say a few words.

'I'd say that, without exception, every man in that 1974 Lions squad could stand up in any company by the end of the tour, give his view on things and talk with people he had never met,' he said. 'It was always important to say thank you. The 1974 Lions never forgot that lesson.' It was so true. The Lions had indeed become part of South Africa.

There were many remarkable aspects to that tour, and so many great players involved, but, when I look back, it is the relationship between Willie John as captain and Syd as coach that stands out most. It is always a critical relationship and I saw there how powerful and good that combination was in terms of its impact on the group. It stayed with me throughout my coaching career, as did some of the initiatives the two of them implemented.

For instance, they had a senior players' committee that we called the 'Mafia' and they all got black hats and black ties and would turn up in them at team dinners. But joking aside, it was a very clever idea because, with one player from each country, it unified the group and gave it a rounded decision-making process. That committee drove the discipline internally but also allowed us to have a lot of fun outside of training and matches.

Syd and Willie John are from Northern Ireland so they had a Dubliner in Fergus Slattery on that committee. From Scotland there was Ian McLauchlan. From England there was Fran Cotton, and from Wales Gareth Edwards. It built up a great sense of belonging. Whatever you were doing, people had responsibilities, but they were responsibilities that could make the tour work for everyone. That was where Willie John was so good. I was quiet on that tour but he would often come across and have a word with me, just so that I knew he was thinking about others.

So as Lions coach I always had a senior players' group and in both 1989 and 1997 I took that a little further because I had the captains – Finlay Calder, the tough-as-teak Scottish flanker, and Martin Johnson, the great English lock – as part of the selection panel too.

The players knew that Finlay and Johnno were there as well. It was not necessarily that they were going to make selections or have a vote, but what we wanted them to do was express an opinion while we were discussing selection. It was all about finding the right combinations. It was a rugby challenge. We just talked it through until we felt we had the strongest mixture of players.

Finlay and Johnno had to take the field with the players. They knew whom they wanted to rub shoulders with. They knew better than Roger Uttley and Jim Telfer (my assistants on those trips) and me what the feeling was like in training and who was delivering what. When we were talking tactically about which players we wanted to introduce, it was good to have those conversations with them.

It is all about giving crucial feedback. Willie John was doing that with Syd in 1974. In 2009 in South Africa captain Paul O'Connell was not in on the selection meetings but I always spoke to him beforehand. I always did that with Scotland with Finlay too. We would always have telephone conversations before selection. And it was the same when Finlay was Lions captain in 1989. I could trust him and he was straight down the line in his opinions, so you knew where you stood.

I have to say that O'Connell was an outstanding captain. I always felt I could go and talk to him. I spent a day at his house out in Ireland before the tour because I wanted to go through in detail my thoughts, aspirations and intended way of working on tour; most especially the tactics we would have to use to beat South Africa. I spent five hours with him just talking this through.

It meant we only had to have 15- or 20-minute conversations on tour because we were on the same wavelength. We only had to pick up on certain things. He knew that I wanted his feedback.

The doctor, James Robson, was important in this respect, too. He has been on six Lions tours, and I have always said that I would trust him to the ends of the earth. That is a true measure of the respect and affection I have for him. For that reason I have always believed he is as great a Lion as any player.

He would always give me a good impression of what the environment was like and how people were feeling. Players talk on the physio's table! For instance, he might say that the players were tired and needed a break or that they were feeling great and were up for a big session. He was always brilliant at assessing the mood and the atmosphere.

His first tour was to New Zealand in 1993 and this was what I wrote about him in my tour report to the four home unions:

James, I feel, was an inspired choice as doctor, simply because he is sports-minded, and is a physiotherapist as well. He and Kevin Murphy [the tour physiotherapist] worked wonders in the medical room and did it so professionally that the players had total confidence in their ability to make them right. James is very aware of the sports needs in the players, and his medical knowledge in that field helped, with the use of the correct drugs and treatment, to dramatically shorten the injury period of a number of players.

In fact, only one player, Richard Webster [the Wales flanker], was injured for longer than a week, and potentially a number of injuries could have taken two to three weeks for recovery. I would also suggest that, if the four home unions consider the development of a medical group in sports injuries, James Robson should be part of it, as he is the best doctor I have ever worked with in the sports injury field.

There must always be humour and enjoyment on a Lions tour as well. In 1974 Willie John and Syd knew there had to be a valve to release after all the tensions and pressures around the games and training. But they always made sure you had to earn those fun times first. 'I believe there is a great secret in life,' said Willie John. 'It is realising when to work, and when to play.'

So on that tour there were trips to the stunning Victoria Falls in what was then called Rhodesia and to the huge game reserve, Kruger National Park, where there was some drinking and some fun and games. Apparently on the previous tour to South Africa in 1968 there had been some quite unruly behaviour (and Willie John and Syd had been on that tour!) but there was nothing particularly untoward on this one, just the realisation that some down time was required at the right times.

What impressed me most about Syd as a coach, and it stayed with me, was the clarity of his messages. Believe it or not, despite it being such a hugely successful tour, we actually copped some flak for our style of rugby on that trip. In particular John Reason wrote a book demeaning our achievement, saying that we had kicked too much and that the South Africans were no good anyway! It did not go down well.

We had an excellent set of forwards, so we did take the South Africans on up front, but that in itself was a brave approach because every South African pack, in any era, is strong. They pride themselves on their physicality and on being able to impose themselves up front. We surprised them by taking them on and indeed beating them at their own game.

Syd was insistent that you cannot ruck on hard grounds like those in South Africa, because you cannot control the ball, as it will bounce when you are putting it down. So Syd said to all the forwards that they must try to keep the ball off the ground. That meant mauls. Lots of them. The forwards therefore spent hours and hours mauling in training sessions.

This was something I took and used when head coach in Australia in 1989, in fact taking it another step forward. On that trip Finlay Calder was captain at flanker and Scotland were renowned for their rucking game, but there were also a lot of English forwards present, and an English forwards coach in Roger Uttley. And England were very good at mauling.

Initially we wanted to use the rucking game but Finlay and I had to change things because it was obvious that the English forwards were very strong and we had to use that strength. It was about finding a balance between rucking and mauling.

In the end I called it 'hand-rucking'. What I wanted was mauling, but at the height that the Scottish forwards played. We wanted the English game but with the bodies positioned lower like the Scottish forwards: very compact and dynamic.

Did we ruck? No. Did we maul? Yes, but it was not an upright, slow thing. It was quite dynamic. People like the

English back-rowers Mike Teague and Dean Richards were clever players. They could handle the ball in tight situations and they would hit and spin in contact.

In the tour report afterwards I wrote about the early aims of the coaching part of the tour and I said:

CONTACT

We must be able to make contact on our terms and control contact and the distribution of the ball. In London (we trained at London Irish before the tour) tackle bags were introduced very early and some players were obviously not used to hitting them or even holding them – by the second week of the tour this aspect of our practices had improved no end, out of all recognition.

First Conclusions

Not ruck or maul but:

Body position on contact.

Ball in hand to control – on the ground to keep momentum, the aim was to develop hard rucking and mini-rucks at hip height but looking forward, tight, dynamic, aggressive on feet, burst through any weak tackles of spaces.

Backs to move ball and attack spaces at outside centre and link quickly.

But that is not to say that the backs were ignored in 1974. We played some brilliant rugby at times, and scored some breathtaking tries. Syd might have been a forward himself but he could coach backs and he did that by making things very simple.

I still remember to this day that he kept on to us about being able to move the ball from Gareth Edwards at scrum half to J.J. Williams, Billy Steele or Andy Irvine on the wing – not missing anybody out, putting it along the line and not making one bad pass. So we practised that time and time again. We used to apologise to each other if we put a pass on somebody's hip rather than out in front of them. We got extremely good at it, it was unbelievably slick.

We scored tries in the Test matches just by putting the ball through our hands and getting J.J., Billy or Andy free on the outside. It was all because Syd was clear about what he wanted and because we were so accurate. We were going to take them on up front, but, as soon as we got on the front foot, we had to release the wingers on the outside. That was where we were playing next. It was that simple.

You still have to do that with players these days. The game going professional hasn't changed that. The basics are still the basics. If you can do the basics to a world-class level, then you will be world-class.

This idea of keeping things simple helped me enormously before the first Test in Cape Town. I was so nervous the night before that match. I was worried that I would let all these superstars down. I had watched the likes of Gareth Edwards and others win the series in New Zealand in 1971. I had watched it on TV and I wasn't even playing international rugby then.

Now here I was about to take the field with them in that Lions jersey. I remember going for a walk to the waterfront and staying there for about 15 minutes thinking about what I had to do. I just cleared my head, and thought about my specific role the next day. It had been raining for days in Cape Town so conditions were bound to be soggy. There would be a lot of kicking and chasing, and therefore a lot of tackling. I steeled myself for the tackling in particular. It goes back to giving that clarity. Millar had given it to us as coach, now I was giving it to myself.

It worked. We won the Test 12–3, with three penalties from Phil Bennett and a drop goal from Gareth Edwards. I tackled myself to a standstill. I remember looking up at the clock and seeing that we had only played about 20 minutes. I did wonder if I could carry on as I was. But I could. And I did. It was a superb victory and a wonderful moment for me personally.

Syd brought clarity to other areas too. These were the days when there were no neutral referees. We had to have South African referees whether we liked it or not. The only choice was that they gave us a list of four, whom they regarded as the best, from which we had to select one.

Syd had come across the aforementioned Max Baise before. When the list came out Baise was on it and Syd chose him. And in the first Test he was fair. Suddenly for the second Test his name was not on the list. On the list instead was Cas de Bruyn, who had refereed us against Eastern Province earlier in the tour. It had been a running battle and he had completely lost control.

Syd got us all together and said: 'I've got the list of four. I don't trust any of them, but there is one name on the list who will never ever believe he is going to referee a Test match because he was so bad. I'm going to pick him. He might be so grateful to get a Test match that he will be honest.'

And he was. De Bruyn refereed the third Test too, but he was off the list for the fourth Test and Baise was back on it. By then it seemed Baise was looking after himself and he was the one who disallowed Fergus Slattery's try at the end of the Test, which would have won us the match.

That was what Syd had to deal with. And you look at his decision to choose De Bruyn under that pressure and you have to take your hat off to him. I learnt so much from him.

The 1974 tour was also remarkable because only 17 players were used in the four-Test series. It is easy to reel the side off: J.P.R. Williams; Billy Steele, myself, Dick Milliken, J.J. Williams; Phil Bennett, Gareth Edwards; Ian McLauchlan, Bobby Windsor, Fran Cotton, Gordon Brown, Willie John McBride, Roger Uttley, Fergus Slattery and Mervyn Davies. And then Andy Irvine came in for Steele for the last two Tests and Chris Ralston in for Brown for the last Test.

So 13 players out of the 30 (plus the two summoned replacements) never got involved in the Test matches. But it was those 13 who made the tour. That is always the case on a successful Lions tour. The competition in training was such that you could never coast.

You could never turn up and think to yourself '50 per cent will do' because whoever was opposite you was going to be taking you on and was going to try to show you up in search of your Test place. As Gareth Edwards has said: 'The strength of the tour was the unity of the whole squad. I'm sure most of the lads would tell you that some of the hardest moments on that tour were training against, dare I say it, the B-side, which was a shadow side more accurately. They were as tough as any team we played.'

It was why when we won the third Test in Port Elizabeth, and with it the series, the first thing Willie John did – having just finished a Test match and won it with all the elation that that brought – was to walk over to the stand to applaud the non-playing members of the squad. They stood up and applauded back.

It was a magnificent moment, and it would not be untrue to say that there were tears in the eyes of both sets of players. In the changing rooms afterwards we were sharing beers together. It showed that it was one squad in it together. It showed the uniqueness of the Lions and it showed how a Lions tour can and should work.

But I remember the forwards having fights on that tour because nobody would take a backward step. What it meant was that you went into the Tests very well prepared because you had been battling all week in every training session to make sure you delivered.

That intensity in training was a huge eye-opener for me. It changed my whole approach to rugby. I had never been challenged in that way before, but I knew I had to do it because I wasn't first-choice centre in anybody's eyes before the tour began. So I had to do things on the training field that showed I was there for real and that I was going to put everything I could out there and, if it wasn't good enough for a Test place, then so be it.

The way the other two centres who did not win Test selection ahead of myself and Ireland's Dick Milliken – England's Geoff Evans and Wales' Roy Bergiers – handled the situation was unbelievable. They were extremely competitive, yet so gracious and helpful. What it meant was that as the tour went on nobody wanted to be wearing the first Lions jersey that lost. That sort of competitive environment had a massive effect on me, which continued in my playing career, and it was also one of the in-built principles that I looked for as a coach.

The 1974 tour was instant evidence for me that the chemistry between players can really surprise everyone. Who would have thought beforehand that I would partner Milliken at centre in all four Tests? I did not know Dick at all before the tour, but we became very good friends off the field and it led to an inner understanding on the field where we each knew what the other was going to do.

I have already mentioned the pre-match speech about the 'look' in 1997 that has become quite well-known because of the tour video. I was referring to shared experiences but you would also have the 'look' because of the understanding you had built on a Lions tour. I definitely had that with Dick and that was when I first began to understand it. It was the inspiration for that comment many years later.

The moment on that tour when we gave each other the look that mattered most was before the third Test in Port Elizabeth. This was the match that could decide the series for us, and to say that the South Africans, who had made all sorts of changes to their side to avoid what they considered the humiliation of a series defeat, were fired up would be the greatest of understatements.

They came hurtling down the ramp onto the pitch and sprinted out so fast that you wondered whether they would ever stop. As they did so, Dick and I looked at each other. 'Here we go,' we were both thinking. But I knew he would look after me, and he knew I would look after him.

It was brutal. South Africa picked nine forwards for that game. They picked a No. 8 – Gerrie Sonnekus, who was one of six debutants – at scrum half. They were only going to play one way. I can safely say that the first 40 minutes of that Test was the toughest rugby I ever played in my whole career. And most of it was played out 20m from our own line. We broke away and scored (through Gordon Brown) just before half time, but we had taken a lot of punishment.

We went in 7–3 up. We ran them off the park in the second half, with two tries from J.J. Williams, to win 26–9. It was because we had a collective belief and understanding, when there is absolute trust that the line will not be broken. When you have got that feeling it is unbelievable. And indeed that match was unbelievable. It will forever be known as the Battle of Boet Erasmus Stadium.

Another of the debutants was a lock called Moaner van Heerden, who was going to sort us out apparently. He was soon up to his stuff, but Willie John just said to him: 'If you want to leave this field in one piece I suggest you leave it in the next 20 minutes. If not, you will be carried off.' The game went on and in the next 20 minutes van Heerden did indeed go off injured. They tried to rough us up but there was no backward step. The forwards were so good and so powerful. As I've said, their training sessions were ferocious and it meant they were never going to face anything in a game that was harder than what they had encountered in training.

It was in this Test that the famous 99 call (a shortened version of the 999 emergency call) was used. It had come about after the aforementioned horribly violent match against Eastern Province in the fourth match of the tour. Willie John and Syd had called a meeting at which it was decided that we could not let the South Africans get away with such behaviour.

You have to remember that these were the days before citing officers. A long time before then. Rugby had to police itself at times, and this was an example of that. We had to stand up to them, and if that meant quite literally fighting back, then so be it. But it also meant that everyone had to be involved because, if that were the case, the referee would never send all 15 players off.

I only remember the call being used once, in that third Test when there was a stand-up fight. Did I get involved? Well, in truth, the likes of myself, Dick Milliken and Phil Bennett were never the keenest to be involved in such stuff.

So I watched it. It was good viewing. J.P.R. Williams came from 50 yards behind me to get involved. It was basically two sets of forwards plus J.P.R. And, yes, I think it was J.P.R. who caused van Heerden to leave the field early. With a punch.

There is another famous story from that match. Gordon Brown hit his opposite number, Johan de Bruyn, so hard that the South African's glass eye flew out and landed somewhere on the pitch. Nobody knew where, though, so we had the bizarre sight of all these forwards on the ground in a Test match looking for a glass eye. It was found and de Bruyn put it back in, but at the next lineout Brown looked over and burst out laughing. The eye was back in but all around it was grass! He really had just plonked it in without even thinking about cleaning it.

Gordon sadly passed away in 2001 and in a lovely touching gesture de Bruyn presented his widow with the glass eye in a specially made trophy.

For me the only Lions Test that compares with that match in 1974 for its brutality is the second Test in Pretoria on the 2009 tour, when we agonisingly lost another ferocious match 28-25 because of a long penalty from Morne Steyn in the dying seconds.

We had been leading 19-8 as we went into the last quarter but then calamity after calamity struck us. Both props, Gethin Jenkins and Adam Jones, were injured, as were both centres, Jamie Roberts and Brian O'Driscoll. The latter was clearly not right when the winger Bryan Habana ran past him for a try. The South African replacement Jaque Fourie then scored a try even though it looked like he might have had a foot in touch. None of the television angles available could provide a conclusive answer.

It was 25–22 when the Welsh fly half Stephen Jones kicked a brave penalty from long distance to level the scores, but then in the dying seconds replacement Ronan O'Gara kicked ahead and chased. He too had suffered an injury and was covered in blood. He was probably not quite thinking straight because he might have been better off slamming the ball right downfield. Instead he challenged Fourie du Preez in the air and it looked horrible. The penalty was duly given, and Steyn did the rest. The whistle went. That was it. As I have said before: 'Without question, it was the lowest I have ever felt.'

The dressing room afterwards was a scene of utter desolation. I have never seen such sadness and emptiness after a match. I told the players I was proud of them, and I was. Hugely so.

It is not just in a Lions context that this match should be remembered. It remains one of the fiercest and most physical Test matches ever played. As Paul Ackford wrote in the *Sunday Telegraph*:

Has there ever been a game like it? This was one of the great matches of all time, a drama which defined how good Test rugby can be.

South Africa won it with the last kick of the match to take the series 2–0 but, frankly, victory seemed an irrelevance after such a pulsating occasion.

It was also a match that brought the brutal nature of international rugby into horrible relief. Both teams suffered a

Willie John McBride in reflective mood in South Africa in 1974.
He was a truly great captain.

Willie John McBride celebrates with Gordon Brown and the rest of us after
we won the third Test in South Africa in 1974.

J.P.R. Williams. The Wales full back was a hard man, a true Test-match animal.

Gareth Edwards. I never played with or against a greater rugby player.

It showed how good the 1974 Test side was that Andy Ripley could not get into it.

The first half of this third Test in 1974 was the toughest rugby I ever played.

J.J. Williams runs away to score one of his two tries in that third Test.

Gordon Brown and Bill Beaumont in action in New Zealand in 1977.

Phil Bennett introduces Prince Charles to John Dawes in 1977.

The front row for three of the four Tests in New Zealand in 1977, from left to right: Graham Price, Peter Wheeler and Fran Cotton.

The 1977 tour party. Too many Welshmen? Probably.

Jeff Squire, Derek Quinnell and Gordon Brown provide the
protection for Dougie Morgan in 1977.

Finlay Calder proved himself to be a fine leader in 1989.

The English contingent of the 1989 tour in front of the Sydney Harbour Bridge.

catalogue of nasty injuries. Andries Bekker, a Bok replacement, suffered a sickening accidental blow to the head, while the Lions finished with a makeshift front row and a makeshift midfield as the men in the starting positions were forced off with broken bodies.

At times the commitment of both sides bordered on the insane and five Lions were last night en route to hospital. How they will get a side out for the third Test is beyond me.

Indeed none of those five – Roberts, O'Driscoll, Jones, Jenkins and O'Gara – would play in the final Test in Johannesburg, but we did get a side out and, remarkably, we won 28–9.

And all this happened in Pretoria after Schalk Burger was very lucky not to be red-carded in the first few seconds of the match when he gouged the Irish wing Luke Fitzgerald. He received a yellow card but it should have been red, and I was amazed afterwards when the South Africa coach Peter de Villiers said that it did not even merit a yellow card, and that it was part of the game. What?

In a subsequent press conference de Villiers bizarrely also said:

I am against anything that is against the spirit of the game. If we want to eye gouge lions, we'll go down to the bushveld and eye gouge them there, then see if they can haul us in.

Rugby is a contact sport and so is dancing. If you guys [the media] were clued up you'd know that there were so many incidents that we could have complained about, like the incident where a Lions player maliciously jumped into one of ours with their shoulder.

But we didn't do it because this is a contact sport. If you are going to complain about every incident we might as well go to a ballet shop and all get tutus.

I felt I had to respond and said: 'I'm very disappointed he said that. I can't see that ever being part of the game. It certainly wouldn't be part of a game that I want to be associated with. I could never condone actions like that. I would hate to see that sort of thing happen again. It should automatically be a red card.'

That said, it was one of the best collective performances I have ever seen from the Lions. In the first half in particular, after which we led 16–8, we played the sort of rugby that I had always been looking to implement. We simply took the South Africans apart. And this in their beloved Loftus Versfeld and against a side that was then the best in the world.

We won four halves of the six halves of Test rugby on this tour, as Warren Gatland's side did in winning the series 2–1 in Australia in 2013, and as we did in winning 2–1 in South Africa in 1997.

The margins are so small. Some of the rugby we played in 1997 was as close to what I would term perfection. It was brilliant. I said to the players that we had to surprise the southern hemisphere because they didn't think we could play that sort of rugby. It was similar here in 2009.

Yes, the official rankings showed that New Zealand were marginally ahead of South Africa in late June and early July of that year, but, after the Lions tour South Africa then beat New Zealand three times in succession in the following months and took the No. 1 spot. They kept it until November, when the All Blacks regained it. The Lions always facing an impossible task? Come on. We were superb on that tour.

The England lock Simon Shaw showed that day what a world-class player he was. He won 71 caps for England, but he should have won many more. They kept saying that he couldn't play alongside Martin Johnson because they were both front jumpers at the lineout. Why not? I would have played him and Johnson every time.

They said he was too heavy and could not be lifted in the lineout. Well, he could run, handle, hit rucks, maul, tackle and, what's more, he was a highly intelligent player. That's a lot of positives against maybe one negative.

I tried to get him into the Test side in 2005 in New Zealand without success, but in fairness we had made a mistake in South Africa on the 2009 tour because we didn't pick him for the first Test. We got that wrong. Unsurprisingly Shaw was Man of the Match in Pretoria and he was so emotional in defeat that he welled up during the post-match interview.

The bank of red that day was incredible. They reckon there were 30,000 Lions fans there that afternoon. In 1974 there were no travelling fans. The only support we had was from the non-whites, who always supported the visiting teams because they saw the Springbok team as the embodiment of apartheid.

We used to go to their end at the grounds, where they were standing with the sun in their eyes, and they would cheer us back. It made for a fantastic atmosphere, even if on this tour I found the reality of apartheid both disturbing and distressing, especially in places like Bloemfontein.

It is often not until later that you recognise the impact this had on some people. So when we toured South Africa in 1997, we had just arrived in the country and were ready for the very first press conference of the tour when Fran Cotton, the manager, and I were ushered into a side room at the airport. There we met the sports minister, Steve Tshwete.

I was simply amazed by what he said. I had no idea about his life. He had been imprisoned on Robben Island for 15 years for his stance against apartheid. He had been there with Nelson Mandela.

He looked at Fran and said: 'Lions tighthead prop, you played in all four Test matches in 1974.' He turned to me and said: 'Ian McGeechan, Lions centre, you played in all four matches too, and you dropped a goal in the second Test.' It was amazing. He went on to explain that he had listened to the Test matches on a radio on Robben Island, cheering on the Lions and being so excited that we had won the series.

I looked at Fran and we were both overwhelmed. It was impossible to understand the suffering that someone like Tshwete had undergone and yet he was talking to us and explaining the joy we had brought him and his friends, including Mandela.

I received what was possibly my greatest ever compliment on that 1974 tour. It came from J.P.R. Williams, who probably does not recall ever saying it, but it meant so much to me at the time.

Dick and I were not a big centre partnership by any stretch of the imagination. In fact every opposition pairing were considerably heavier than us. That meant that we had to be very clever to make up for it if we were not going to let anyone past us in midfield.

And as far as I can remember, we did not let anyone past us in any of the Test matches and J.P.R. never had to make a tackle on an opposing player who came through us. At some stage during the tour, J.P.R. said to us both: 'It's great playing behind you two.'

Wow, J.P.R. had said that! Both Dick and I reckoned that we could die happy after that comment. Dick and I are still good friends today and we still catch up. It is the sort of chemistry that a Lions tour engenders and part of the uniqueness of Lions rugby.

For example, during the 1989 tour of Australia the England hooker Brian Moore and Finlay Calder became very good friends. If I am honest, it was an unlikely alliance, but they had a mutual respect and understanding. In short they both knew that they were hated by rugby folk in the other country. But they both knew that in Lions rugby they could totally and utterly rely on each other to deliver.

'I'm so glad that people now see in Brian the man I have known all this time,' said Finlay in the excellent history book,

Behind the Lions. 'He's an extraordinary human being. I've never seen a man as driven about anything and everything in my life. He's just a compulsive winner. Scotland is a funny nation because if he was one of us we would have been so proud of him, but because he wore an English jersey he became this figure of hate.'

Wales' Jamie Roberts and Ireland's Brian O'Driscoll as a centre pairing in South Africa in 2009 were another example of a pairing at centre that clicked instantly. I could just see that it was right. I would see them together off the field all the time, chatting to each other in airport lounges, going out for coffee, comparing notes, looking at training sessions on their laptops. Sometimes you see that players have really hit it off together and this was a classic example, even though they had never played together before. Their games and their personalities fitted together very well.

McGeechan and Milliken in 1974 and Roberts and O'Driscoll in 2009. It is a neat link between very different eras, and it shows that a Lions tour is still all about the players, how they interact with each other, with their surroundings and with the Lions ethos.

The success of any tour will come down to how close it gets to these principles. The game may have gone professional and the numbers involved in the tours may have risen dramatically, but actually what you are trying to do is the same. It is just that organisationally you have to be far more astute and detailed because you are doing it with almost twice as many people.

But you cannot get away from the fundamental truth that a Lions tour is about one single group of people. When it mattered everybody showed up together to do the right things together. That has stayed with me ever since 1974. It wasn't about two or three groups then and it isn't about two or three groups now.

KEY WORDS

- Flexible approach
- Chemistry and partnerships
- Right person, right place, right time
- Knowing your opponents
- Knowing yourself even better
- Good training = good performance
- Players' committee
- Coach/Captain partnership
- World-class basics
- One group

1974 South Africa, Third Test
This was brutal. The first half was the toughest rugby I ever experiecned as a player.

LIONS, TEAM OF THE CENTURY

South Africa 9 pts, British Lions 26

by our Correspondent
PORT ELIZABETH, 13 July

AFTER a start that pointed to a thorough taming by the Springboks, the Lions shook off their lethargy, built up a commanding lead and ran away with the Test series.

Two brilliant tries by J. J. Williams late in the game underlined the Lions authority and left the bewildered South Africans mourning the demise of a domination of touring sides that has stood for decades.

The Lions thus become the first international side to beat the Springboks in a Test series this century and, incidentally, the first side to beat South Africa in Port Elizabeth for 64 years.

In the early minutes the hopes of the 55,000 crowd, including Prime Minister John Vorster, soared as the Springboks made most of the running and took the lead with a penalty.

Even a 15-minute equaliser, which Andy Irvine sent plumb between the posts, failed to dent their enthusiasm. For the green-and-gold Springboks were a far sharper outfit: first to the ball and stronger in the mauls.

The game erupted into its first free fight near the Lions goal-line after the Springboks had come desperately close to scoring. Roux had kicked a high ball which Kritzinger picked up and was brought crashing down a yard from the Lions line. In the resultant pile up of bodies, players from both sides began trading punches, with the referee trying to cool the situation.

With 37 minutes gone the Lions launched one of their rare attacking moves. J. J. Williams went charging down the line but Schlebusch came rushing over to bundle him out of play.

Then Gordon Brown, against all the run of play, brought the non-white spectators to their feet in their enclosure. He picked up a loose ball from a line out and made five yards to dive over for the simplest of tries.

Irvine, from a position five yards in from the 25, failed with the conversion and at half-time the Lions were 7-3 in the lead.

When play resumed, Irvine had another chance to increase the score after a penalty award 40 yards out for off-side. But, with his third penalty attempt of the afternoon, he screwed the ball just wide of the post.

But Irvine made amends minutes later by kicking a prodigious penalty goal from two yards inside his own half to make the score 10–3.

The Lions were now going from strength to strength, launching their best attacks of the match, J. P. R. Williams just failing with a drop kick.

Then, after eight minutes, the second punching incident flared up, the exchanges erupting after a clash between Brown and Polla Fourie. Slattery joined in the sparring and players from both sides were locked in a brawl until Cas de Bruyn again restored order.

Then 15 minutes into the second half, Bennett, showing no worries from a knee injury, put Lions 13–3 ahead with a snap drop goal. His performance was almost casual, having picked up the ball from a set scrum 15 yards from the Springbok's line.

The Lions were now rampant, the Springboks looking far slower than in the early stages, and their pack running out of steam. And with 24 minutes gone the Lions went 17–3

ahead with a brilliant Inter-passing move between J. J. Williams and J. P. R. Williams.

It was a spectacular try. Winger J. J. made 15 yards, passed to J. P. R., who made another 20 before giving the return to his namesake, who sped over the line like a train. Irvine converted.

But soon after, with 12 minutes left, the Springboks narrowed the score to 19–6 with a penalty by Snyman.

The spirit and inspiration seemed to have gone out of the Springboks and despite the set-back the Lions were still in full command.

But with 34 minutes gone the Springboks gained three more points after a penalty award against Windsor for foot up. Snyman, 15 yards in from the line near the 25, made no mistake with the kick to make the score 19–9.

But the Lions came back dramatically with a try which put the match beyond doubt. J. J. Williams sprinted 35 yards, kicked ahead, picked up the bounce and then slid over the line to make the score 23–9.

Bennett failed with the conversion, but on time he dropped a goal to make the score 26–9 and clinch the series 3–0.

2
SELECTION

It begins a year, sometimes even further back, out from a Lions tour and everyone – every fan, every player, every coach and every pundit – seems to join in. It is all marvellous fun, filling reams of column inches and hours of time in bar rooms. I am, of course, talking about picking your own Lions squad, or at least the Test team.

And everyone thinks it is easy. Well, as someone who has actually had to do this for real rather than scribbling the names on the back of a beer mat, I'll let you into a little secret.

It is pretty easy – but only for the first 25 names. Selecting those is usually fairly straightforward, and that is the case whether the tour party comprises 30 players, 35 or even more. It is picking the last 10 or so that is so difficult. And they are often the most important selections because they can make a crucial difference.

Just because the first 25 names might be easy, it does not mean that you should embark on a tour with a fixed Test team in your head. As the tours of 2001 and 2005 have proved, you must never do that.

You must approach every Lions tour with an open mind. You cannot pre-determine or pre-set anything. Picking your Test side before you have started and then ignoring the evidence of the play on tour can be very dangerous. You only have to look at the Test-match selections of the likes of Scotland's Tom Smith and Ireland's Jeremy Davidson and Paul Wallace in South Africa 1997 to show that.

We knew we wanted to play a certain way on that tour and in the end when it came to Test selection we had to say that those three thoroughly deserved their chances, simply because of the way they had played and in particular the way they had slotted into the style we wanted to adopt. I did not think at the start of the tour that they would be the Test-starting Lions. They weren't in line at all, but we wanted to give them the chance, and that is what we did. So Smith at loosehead prop, Wallace at tighthead and Davidson in the second row actually started all three Tests. It was an important lesson.

Wallace had not even been in the original party and had only been called up when his Irish colleague Peter Clohessy pulled up with an injured back during the pre-tour get-together in Surrey. Wallace had been in Limerick preparing to go on an Ireland Development tour of New Zealand.

The converse of this method of selection is obviously the 2005 tour, where too many English players were inked in beforehand and then did not show the requisite form on the tour. That caused obvious problems, not least because Wales had won a Grand Slam that year and had a number of players pushing very hard for Test selection.

How long should you give the players until deciding upon your Test team? That is a question that is often posed. Well, there is the argument that the Test team should play together the week before the first Test but that does not necessarily have to be the case in my view, because I have always genuinely believed that as long as the message is the same it doesn't matter what the combination on the field is. You are doing the same things. It is just that a different selection goes out and delivers it the next week.

Those last 10 selections in the original party are critical. They are not in everyone's minds, sometimes they may not even be playing international rugby at all, but these are the players who are really good at doing the bits and pieces all the time, fitting in and making the tour work. They are really strong characters in a different way. You feel they can add value, perhaps in unexpected ways, the type who won't go off tour, won't get too down and won't upset things. They determine the chemistry and environment of the tour, how quickly it builds and how strong it becomes. So that is why you spend the most time on them during selection. They can make or break a tour.

The only time I can remember not spending a lot of time on players like that was the 1993 tour to New Zealand, where the squad was selected by a committee consisting of manager Geoff Cooke (England), myself, assistant coach Dick Best (England), Derek Morgan (England), Bob Munro (Scotland), Ken Reid (Ireland) and David Richards (Wales).

I was persuaded to take players about whom I was not entirely sure. I probably ended up with four or five players that

I would never have taken had I had the final say. I look back at that now with a great deal of regret. It was wrong. But I was still learning.

For example, our selection around the front five needed better discussion and we probably should have taken England's Jeff Probyn and Ireland's Peter Clohessy. Yes, I went into that meeting lasting six hours at the Edwardian Hotel at Heathrow with a list of 25 key players (the easy selections, remember), and, yes, all those 25 were selected, but it was the other five in the 30-man party that troubled me later. There was never actually any vote at the time, more an amicable consensus, but I should have been stronger and more forceful in my views.

The fact that we so nearly won that three-Test series, fashioning a magnificent victory in the second Test in Wellington, shows just how close we were to getting that selection correct.

I wrote a diary of the tour with captain Gavin Hastings entitled *So Close to Glory* and that was indeed the case. It is the first Test defeat in Christchurch, by just 20–18, that still rankles because of a couple of crucial refereeing decisions. I have talked already about the difficulties faced by the Lions in years gone by with referees, but here we had an Australian official in Brian Kinsey. We spoke to him before the game and we thought we knew how he was going to referee the game, but, as it turned out, we were speaking a different language. He wouldn't then speak to us after the game. It was so frustrating.

First, there was an early disputed try for the New Zealand centre Frank Bunce. The Welsh winger Ieuan Evans also had his hands on the ball as the pair went over the line, having caught Grant Fox's high kick. Evans never let go of the ball.

'If I live to be a hundred, I will never understand how Mr Kinsey could award that,' said Evans in his autobiography. 'How he could have given it from his position some distance away was beyond my comprehension. Seeing it again on video, he looked for guidance towards the touch judge who gave the nod for the try. There was no way he could have known because I was going backwards with my back to him. It was to prove the crucial score.'

Too right it was. I spoke to a number of international referees afterwards and they all agreed on two things: firstly the fact that Evans had first touch of the ball and never let go surely meant that there must have been considerable doubt as to whether Bunce had scored, and secondly that, if there was any doubt, then a scrum should have been awarded. Oh, for the benefit of a Television Match Official in those days!

With nine minutes remaining of that match we went 18–17 ahead thanks to a superb penalty kick from Hastings, who slotted it despite the long range, the angle and a horrible wind. Apart from that dubious try New Zealand had not looked like scoring, and were relying on the boot of Fox for points.

There was just one minute left and a famous victory was beckoning when referee Kinsey made another huge call. Bunce was tackled on our 10m line by No. 8 Dean Richards, who quite legitimately turned him towards our side while he was still holding onto the ball. The ball was eventually released and retrieved by the England scrum half Dewi Morris, but, inexplicably, Kinsey awarded a penalty to New Zealand that Fox duly kicked to win the game.

I watched that incident many, many times afterwards on video and I came no closer to explaining why Kinsey had penalised us. It was heartbreaking, but when I look back now there were many other reasons why we lost that series and I do think getting that small remainder of the party right in selection might have helped us get over the line.

The problem was that each position was looked at and selected in a mostly technical sense without thinking too much about the wider picture: the all-important environment. And selection took place too soon after the conclusion of the Five Nations, so that form in the last couple of rounds was too fresh in the memory and therefore too influential in the thinking behind the selection.

I tried to ensure this did not happen again, writing in my tour report: 'The final selection meeting should not take place immediately after the last international weekend. It would be more beneficial for seven to 10 days to elapse before this final meeting.'

There were 16 Englishmen in that original 30-man party in 1993, as well as eight Scots, five Welshmen but just two Irishmen, in forwards Mick Galwey and Nick Popplewell. Considering Ireland had beaten England 17–3 in that season's Five Nations, we had got the balance wrong. I do not think that I am being unduly harsh either if I say that there were some Scottish players on that trip who should not have been there. Funnily enough, it was the selectors from other countries who pushed hard for some of those players, but they did not cope well with the pressures of a Lions tour. Too many players went off tour on that trip to New Zealand.

This was a crucial lesson I took with me into selection for future tours: that you need strong characters, especially those who might be in the midweek side. And that included a captain for that side. As I wrote in my report: 'The major weakness in our squad was the absence of a strong character who would captain the midweek side and give it purpose and focus. I would recommend future selection actually selects a player with this responsibility.'

In 1989 in Australia we had had the Irishman Donal Lenihan in that role. He would be exactly the type of player I was talking about at the start of this chapter, one of those who had different qualities from the other second rows on that trip, Wales' Bob Norster and the two Englishmen Wade Dooley and Paul Ackford, but one who could play a huge role on that tour and in the 2-1 Test series victory, even if he did not physically take part in any of the Test matches.

His midweek team became known as 'Donal's Doughnuts', a name which I think began one day when Roger Uttley called him a 'doughnut' for messing something up in training. It stuck and every player who appeared in the midweek side had a T-shirt emblazoned with the nickname and it became something of a badge of honour to wear it.

I know that Donal has since tried to downplay the significance of this team – 'it's a complete and utter pain in the arse to be honest,' he has said – and expressed his view that captaining them to an unbeaten tour was no consolation whatsoever for missing out on the Test side. 'It was the first time in my career I did not make a side I had my sights set on,' he wrote in his auto-biography. But that team played a vital part on that tour, especially after we had suffered defeat in the first Test in Sydney.

Of course, Donal was disappointed not to make the Test team. Everyone should be. But there are ways of dealing with that and of reacting to it. Donal did it in the right way. Others, including quite a few on the 1993 tour, have not done so.

'Donal's Doughnuts' turned that 1989 tour around. They played Australian Capital Territory in Canberra after the first Test, and got off to an awful start, going 21-11 down at one stage but, with Donal urging his men on, opting for a scrum-mage instead of a penalty at one critical moment and the England centre Jeremy Guscott playing so well that it won him a start in the second Test, the team came back to win 41-25. It was a seminal moment.

As Mike Hall, the Welsh centre/winger said: 'When we came back to the dressing room after the match, the players who were not playing – the Test team – lined the narrow corri-dor and clapped us in. We sat in the changing room for a long while and said that we were not going to lose another game. There had been a momentum shift. Every tour has its decisive point where it can go one way or the other. How we responded when we were 21-11 down was ours in 1989.'

It certainly was. And Donal played his part in that – a huge part. In fact I firmly believe the Test series would not have been won without him.

I made some strong points on the selection policy in my 1993 tour report: 'The manager, but more particularly the coach, must have significant, even final, decision on the composition of the tour party. It would be beneficial for the manager and coach to have no national involvement during the season prior to the tour.' I also made some general points about the difference in interpretations made by referees in the northern and southern hemispheres. I am not sure much has changed to this day.

There were significant differences in law interpretations, but we did expect this [I wrote]. The only point I would make is that, in New Zealand, the referees are told the type of game they have to referee towards, and this allows players to develop continuity.

They view very harshly the following: the player on the ground should be penalised at all times if he either does not release the ball or move away and that he is rucked dynamically if he is directly in the way of the ball. This undoubtedly helps continuity.

The lineout throwing is geared to give the side throwing in possession. Scrums hit and continue driving so again the ball is put in quickly and favours the side in possession; squint put-in was almost never penalised.

I know we have a meeting between coaches and referees; the significant difference between the two hemispheres is that referees are dictated to more in the southern hemisphere to produce a certain type of game and, under the new laws, contact, continuity and the availability of the ball are seen as a priority.

This is allowing Australia and New Zealand to develop faster, more continuous rugby, and our own players did benefit from this approach. If a home unions team is ever to win the World Cup, then we have to look carefully at the way we want our game to develop, and we must interpret the laws positively towards that end. It might not be the purest approach, but it is the practical approach, and it is the only way in which we will be able to compete in the world environment and competitions.

Whilst in New Zealand, both Geoff [Cooke, the team manager] and I heavily criticised their interpretation of the third man 'who can be off his feet and scooping back'. This, more than anything else, took us time to adapt to, particularly as we had emphasised that we wanted our players on their feet.

It was such a shame that the selection process in 1993 was so different from 1989.

I was very fortunate that Clive Rowlands was tour manager in 1989. He had wanted me as coach, even though I hadn't even taken over as head coach of Scotland by then; I had just been the assistant coach taking the backs. But Clive had enjoyed the Scottish back play.

In 1993 I was interviewed for the job and indeed so was Dick Best, who was then appointed as an assistant when he was told I had got the head coach's job. I got on well with Dick, so well that he is now actually my agent, and his work with the forwards was excellent.

But in 1989 there were no interviews, just a phone call to ask if I would be interested in taking the job. It was on a Sunday evening in August 1988 from Ken Smith, the Scottish representative on the Lions committee. 'Clive Rowlands would like you to coach the Lions in Australia next year, would you be able to do it?' he said. I remember being in the lounge at home after taking that call. I was in a state of shock. Part of me might even have been thinking it was a hoax call. I said to my wife Judy that I'd had a phone call and they had asked if I wanted to coach the Lions. It was completely out of the blue really. 'He must see something special that he wants,' she said.

I was thinking: 'I have been assistant coach to Scotland for three years, and have only just been appointed as head coach, and now Clive Rowlands wants me to coach the Lions! Somebody with that standing in the game wants me as coach of that team!' It did wonders for my confidence, even if my mind was spinning.

Judy and I had a chat about it as she was doing a degree in music and PE full time and we had two small children, Robert and Heather, at school. But it was just too big an opportunity to turn down. It's only when you look back you think: 'Crikey, Judy took a lot of the responsibility to allow me to do it.'

It was the same in 1974 when I was first selected. She had never been left on her own before. She had been living with her parents before we got married and we had been married for five years then. But she just got on with it. There is no doubt that it is the womenfolk that make it all workable.

Judy did not even fully understand then who the Lions were and what they meant. 'I didn't know they existed,' she says with a giggle. In fairness rugby union did not exactly embrace women in those days and Judy had never even been to a match before she met me.

Women have not necessarily been that well looked after on Lions tours. It was actually stipulated in a letter written to us in 1974 that no wives were to be permitted on the trip. In 1997 Judy helped organise trips out to South Africa for a number of wives and girlfriends but even in 2009, when things looked better organised, there was an uncomfortable incident after the second Test in Pretoria when the wives were left stranded without knowing where their bus back to the hotel was. Pretoria is not the sort of place you want to be in that kind of situation. Judy got a message to me about it and I was not best pleased to say the least. 'It was awful,' says Judy.

We went out to Australia for the 2013 tour and that was actually much better. 'It was the first time I was treated like I was accepted,' says Judy. And about time too.

I got on with Clive Rowlands immediately in 1989. As I have written before: 'Emotional, excitable, cheeky, passionate, fair, supportive, intuitive and caring – all these facets I would experience rubbing shoulders with him.' I got on with him even more so when he assured me from the start that I would get the squad I wanted, even though there were other selectors in England's Mike Weston, Scotland's Robin Charters, Ireland's Noel Murphy and Wales' Derek Quinnell.

Because there was not much video footage of players at that time, the selectors had to watch players around the four countries, but Clive said that my view would count most and he even gave me two wild cards so that I could disagree with up to two of the final choices and change them for players I wanted.

That privilege was not given to me for the 1993 tour and it was a mistake. By the time I went to South Africa in 1997 it had been returned and the tour was the better for it. You have simply got to be comfortable with the group you are coaching.

The other thing I learnt about selection before that 1989 tour was that you should never select and announce a squad on the same day. You should always sleep on it. That is something I always tried to do in later selections. I would have to wake up happy about what had happened at the meeting the night before. Sometimes, even in the professional era, you just have a gut feeling for a player and you have to go with that.

So when we gathered in Cardiff to select the squad in 1989 Clive asked us to come armed with at least three players per position whom we thought were in contention. We managed to whittle it down to a squad of 30, but we had to sleep on it.

And that was where I played a wild card. I was uncomfortable with one of the selections, so I played it and changed the selection. I can't say who the player was, because I do not think that would be fair. But it turned out to be quite important because the selection was not about technical prowess or basic rugby ability, rather it was about the environment. It was somebody I wanted in who probably wouldn't make the Test team but whom I felt would be instrumental in helping create the right environment. I knew how important that was.

I remember doing the same in 2009. I asked everyone to sleep on it at the end of the meeting. I said I wasn't signing it off. The next day there was at least one change. And I had a conversation with captain Paul O'Connell before we finalised it.

In 1989 I think we got the five extra players in the 30 right. In 1993 we obviously didn't. It was crucial. It was why in 1997 I insisted on reverting to what had happened in 1989.

I said to the manager Fran Cotton and to Jim Telfer, my assistant coach, that I just wanted the three of us to pick the players. I did not want anyone else involved. I said to them: 'If I'm going to fail, I want to fail with the players I've chosen and not somebody else's choices.'

Picking the Lions is not like picking any other squad or side. You have to use different criteria. So I based a lot of my selectorial judgement on my experiences as a player on those two Lions tours in 1974 and 1977. And they were very different experiences.

I can sum it up in two short sentences. In 1974 you felt you were part of the best group of players in Britain and Ireland. In 1977 you had the feeling you were a guest on a Wales tour.

One tour worked, as we have seen, the other one did not. That 1977 tour of New Zealand promised so much, but it ended up being a huge disappointment, not helped by New Zealand having one of its worst and wettest winters ever. 'A grim, doomed, endless slog. It was interminable, not enjoyable in the slightest.' That was how I described it.

It was longer than the 1974 tour and I know it was even harder for Judy back at home because we had just moved house (we also moved house in 1993 and 2005 when I was on or about to be on Lions tours!). 'I was living in a new house on a building site basically,' she says now in recollection. 'There were no street lights. I didn't have a phone. It was just the dog and me. It was a bit desperate.'

We lost the Test series 3–1 despite our forwards dominating the New Zealand pack throughout the tour. In fact 'dominating' might be too mild a word because by the time of the fourth Test the home pack was so beaten and bewildered that they resorted to three-man scrummages. What an embarrassment that was for New Zealand rugby and its great traditions.

But we still could not capitalise on that to take the series. Why? Well, there was the tremendous expectation after the tours of 1971 and 1974 and there were some great players missing. Gareth Edwards, J.P.R. Williams and Gerald Davies were all still playing but did not tour. Neither did Fergus Slattery. Roger Uttley had to withdraw through injury. But I don't see them as excuses. We still could and should have won the series.

John Dawes, the Welsh centre who had been captain of the 1971 Lions, was coach and the Wales fly half Phil Bennett was the captain. Scotland's George Burrell was team manager, but he was not the sort of character who would challenge Dawes or anyone else for that matter. We realised that when there was a senior players' committee consisting of myself, Bennett, Fran Cotton and Mike Gibson, upon which Burrell sat.

It was Dawes' tour party and initially he selected 16 Welshmen, and then two more, Charlie Faulkner and Alun Lewis, came out as replacements. Scrum half Lewis, of Cambridge University and London Welsh, never played for Wales. Elgan Rees and Brynmor Williams were also uncapped at the time of the tour.

There were some very good Welsh players on that tour, but that is where the balance is so important, because there were also some fairly ordinary Welsh players out there. They were the ones who made it quite difficult in the midweek games to keep everything in really good focus. We are back to the matter of those tricky players to select outside of the obvious 25. That was wrong again on this trip.

In principle there was nothing wrong with having a Welsh coach and a Welsh captain, because I had that Scottish connection with Finlay Calder in 1989 and with Gavin Hastings in 1993. I did have an Englishman in Martin Johnson as captain in 1997, though, and an Irishman, Paul O'Connell, in 2009.

It just did not click in 1977. Bennett admitted afterwards that he should not have been captain and indeed Dawes admitted that the No. 8 Mervyn Davies would have been captain had his career not been brought to an abrupt and sad ending the year before when he suffered a brain haemorrhage playing for Swansea in a Welsh Cup semi-final against Pontypool at Cardiff.

Dawes became distracted as coach, not least because of a difficult relationship with the press. There were a lot of stories that were very negative towards us, thus it became known as the 'Bad News' tour, but our attitude towards the press did not help the tour one bit.

Tactically we were poor. We had to be if we could not win with all that possession and superiority. But just as importantly, the problems had begun before we even left. It was a poorly selected squad, and too many of those Welsh players lost their way quite quickly on the tour.

Some might raise their eyebrows at this and cite the example of the number of Welshmen in the 2013 tour party to Australia under Warren Gatland, with Wales flanker Sam Warburton as captain.

But that was very different. Yes, there were 15 Welshmen in the original 37-man party but Gatland managed it well. For a start most of those Welshmen were Test starters (10 were picked for the final Test), but he also used people like Paul O'Connell and Brian O'Driscoll as key leaders.

O'Connell helped Warburton a great deal. They shared a room together when the squad had one of their two pre-tour get-togethers in Cardiff and was always on hand to advise at the right moments. 'Paul's help with the captaincy was invaluable,' wrote Warburton is his tour diary, *Lions Triumphant*. 'I actually think that was one of the primary reasons why I enjoyed doing the job so much. He took so much weight off my shoulders.'

So, early on in the tour, because Warburton was injured, O'Connell and O'Driscoll were instrumental in how the tour was laid out. Between them they captained three of the first four games. They were effectively taking the reins from a player's perspective.

That was where O'Connell was always so good. He was excellent for Ireland when O'Driscoll was captain – an outstanding number two even though he was a natural leader. That helped Warren and the environment on that trip.

By the time we came to select a squad for the 1997 tour, much had changed, not least the game had gone professional. It meant, for example, that we had so much more video tape footage to aid selection. The principles of what we were looking for did not necessarily change, but the detail that could go into the identification of those players to suit what was intended certainly did.

Again I was not interviewed for the job, I was simply asked by manager Fran Cotton. He telephoned me early in 1996 and I went up to Manchester to his office and we chatted about our thoughts and, because we seemed to see most things in exactly the same way, it was pretty much decided there and then that I would be head coach.

Fran asked me whom I wanted as my assistant and I had no hesitation in suggesting Jim Telfer, even though he was not on the home unions' list of nominations and he had not coached for nearly four years, having given up coaching at Melrose in 1994 when he became director of rugby at the Scottish Rugby Union. He had not coached internationally since the 1991 Rugby World Cup, but we went back a long way. He had been on three Lions tours, two as a player to New Zealand in 1966 and to South Africa in 1968, and once as a coach to New Zealand in 1983.

I wanted someone I knew well and someone whom I knew I could trust implicitly. As I have said, we wanted to play a fast game but I knew that we had to get the set piece right first. Jim could do that.

'I regard Jim Telfer simply as the best forwards coach in Britain and it was again a privilege to be coaching alongside him,' I wrote in my tour report. And, despite being very different – 'a long-haired skinny lad from Leeds and a gruff back-row forward from the Border hills,' as I once wrote – we also made a neat combination, a good cop/bad cop-type scenario.

Jim was renowned for his hard edge as a coach, a short temper even, with those who he felt were not pulling their weight, thus his famous scrummaging session in Pretoria in 1997 when he vowed to sort out our poor efforts in that area with a session on the hydraulic machine that has become legendary for its intensity and ferocity. Some say it consisted of 42 scrums in 46 minutes, which may or may not be true but it was certainly brutal, as well as hugely beneficial.

He has become famous for his speech to the forwards before the first Test on that tour and I hope in repeating it in full here that it does not upset him, because I know that he was surprised by the reaction to it in some quarters when it came out on the hugely popular *Living with Lions* video. There is some industrial language in it and I know his mother was shocked by it, but all I will say is that none of us was sure how detailed the video was going to be. It was all new to us.

This was the first time that anything like this had been done and there were quite a few dissenting voices about it, mainly people claiming that it would destroy the mystique and the magic of the Lions by allowing the general public inside the camp. I have to admit that I did have some similar reservations at first. And when I first saw the finished version, I said there wasn't enough rugby in it. I wanted more rugby, I wanted more of the training shown.

But what did amaze me was that the producers had picked up the very essence of what we were trying to do tactically on that trip. They said it wasn't difficult because the message throughout the tour was so clear, especially as the rugby we wanted to play hadn't been played by anyone else in the northern hemisphere. That was a great thing to hear.

As it turned out, that video was one of the best things that has ever happened to the Lions. It raised the profile enormously. It was a massive point in Lions' history, actually. The video captured the public's imagination because it was so inspirational (and I suppose it helped that we won the series!) and passionate. There was indeed a good deal of swearing in it but I cannot believe that anyone would think there would be anything different in a rugby changing room. They are places of high emotion and tension.

So this is what Jim said to the group of forwards seated around him in the team room that day in Cape Town:

The easy bit has passed. Selection for the Test team is the easy bit. You have an awesome responsibility on the eight individual forwards' shoulders, awesome responsibility. This is your f***ing Everest, boys. Very few ever get a chance in rugby terms to get to the top of Everest. You have the chance today.

Being picked is the easy bit. To win for the Lions in a Test match is the ultimate, but you'll not do it unless you put your bodies on the line. Every one jack of you for eighty minutes.

Defeat doesn't worry me. I've had it often and so have you. It's performance that matters. If you put in the performance, you'll get what you deserve. No luck attached to it. If you don't put it in, if you're not honest, then we're second-raters.

They don't rate us. They don't respect us. They don't respect you. They don't rate you. The only way to be rated is to stick one on them, to get right up in their faces and turn them back, knock them back. Outdo what they can do. Out-jump them, out-scrum them, out-ruck them, out-drive them, out-tackle them, until they're f***ing sick of you.

Remember the pledges you made. Remember how you depend on each other at every phase, teams within teams, scrums, lineouts, ruck ball, tackles.

They are better than you've played against so far. They are better individually or they wouldn't be there. So it's an awesome task you have and it will only be done, as I say, if everybody commits themselves now.

You are privileged. You are the chosen few. Many are considered but few are chosen. They don't think f*** all of us. Nothing. We're here just to make up the f***ing numbers. Nobody's one's going to do it for you. You have to find your own solace – your own drive, your own ambition, your own inner strength, because the moment's arrived for the greatest game of your f***ing lives.

It was seriously inspirational. But what people probably didn't appreciate about Jim was that he was also a very good listener. It was not just about his way, he would also listen to others' views and opinions.

When we coached Scotland together we would disagree, but it was never a case of us falling out. We just had an open relationship where we were both trying to drive things forward. We thought the same way and we each had absolute confidence in what the other was doing. We were from very different backgrounds but we became very close as friends, our wives became very good friends, and we discussed, very personally, things that I would never have discussed with others. That is how close we were.

Andy Keast was a revelation to us as a technical analyst on that tour in 1997. It was Martin Bayfield, the former England lock whom I knew from Northampton and from the 1993 Lions tour, who first mentioned his name to me. Andy was an assistant coach at Harlequins at the time but he had coached at Natal before that, so he had useful knowledge of the South African players. Harlequins were clearly trying to move ahead very quickly at this time and were already using a computer program to help with their video analysis.

Dick Best was director of rugby at Quins then, so I spoke to him about Andy and he was very complimentary. I went for it and never regretted it for a moment because Andy was quite superb on that tour.

He worked so hard. The rest of us came back home with sun tans but he was as white as a sheet because of all the hours he spent inside poring over videos. Each player had a video prepared individually for him, detailing his own game as well as his immediate opponent's. It was cutting edge stuff at the time, and it gave us a huge advantage as a squad.

We also had a kicking coach in Dave Alred. Fran Cotton had pleaded with the Lions' committee to allow him to be taken on the tour, and again it proved an inspired decision because the kicking was vital on that trip and he did work that none of us others could do.

'It ultimately gave us the edge over South Africa,' I wrote in my report. 'Our kicking both from hand and at goal in the Test matches was of the highest quality and showed how invaluable it was to have Dave Alred specifically practising and monitoring all the kicking involvement from each game. Our kicking strategy progressively improved.'

I also had no hesitation in nominating James Robson to head the medical set-up, and I just asked him to pick whomever he wanted to assist him. He originally chose England's Kevin Murphy, who had been on the three previous Lions tours, as the physiotherapist, but he pulled out at the last minute after a dispute with the home unions over payment to cover his practice at home while he was away. He was replaced by Wales' Mark Davies, who won three caps for his country in the 1980s and proved a popular choice on that tour and subsequent Lions tours.

We had a bigger support staff than before, up from just five in 1989 (myself, Roger Uttley, Clive Rowlands, Dr Ben Gilfeather and Murphy), which, ridiculously, was seen as something of an extravagance at the time, to 12 now. We had Richard Wegrzyk as the masseur, Stan Bagshaw as the kit man (rarely can someone have had such an appropriate name!) and Samantha Peters ('our very own Lioness,' I called her) as the administrative assistant. They were all invaluable in their different ways, simply because everyone had their roles, which were complementary and clear, thanks to Fran.

I was coaching Northampton then and I will always be grateful to chairman Keith Barwell, who gave me the flexibility and time to go elsewhere and look at other things that year. It did impact on the club, even though we did end up with five Northampton players on the tour (Nick Beal, Paul Grayson, Matt Dawson, Tim Rodber and Gregor Townsend), but it was important because not only could I spend time watching videos but I also could go to see players live.

Because we wanted to be more thorough and organised, we selected an initial group of 62 players. Myself, Fran and Jim were the official selectors but we were helped by four selection advisers in Donal Lenihan (Ireland), Derek Quinnell (Wales), Ian Lawrie (Scotland) and Peter Rossborough (England). We would meet every six weeks.

That initial 62-man group met in Birmingham's Metropole Hotel in March, where Fran and I outlined our plans, and draft contracts were signed and fittings for blazers and other kit were taken. This was the first time this had been done, and it caused some comment, not least because the England captain, centre Phil de Glanville, was not amongst the 62 names announced.

Nor was Jonathan Davies, who was 34 by then having returned to union and was not first choice for Wales, with Arwel Thomas being preferred. Davies would have been the Test fly half in 1989 had he not gone to rugby league, and I considered it a huge blow at the time when we could not call upon him. He was clearly not happy about being left out of the squad in 1997.

'Selections for Lions tours invariably cause controversy but no one really appreciates how it affects the players concerned,' he wrote at the time. 'Disappointment is hardly the word to describe it. Despair would be a little nearer the mark. And that's when you miss out on the tour itself – when you don't even get into an original 62, you are under serious threat of total demoralisation.'

It is good that players are disappointed, but I think Davies has since admitted that he was maybe not quite as quick by then, that his legs had slowed up a little. He was certainly a fantastic player in his pomp.

In fact for a long, long time on the wall of my office at home I had a photograph of Davies on a calendar. It might not be one he was particularly fond of, but for me it was a brilliant example of how to play the game, and especially of how to attack. It was taken when Wales were playing the All Blacks in 1988. Davies was actually the outstanding player on that tour in a Wales side that got badly beaten. The picture is taken from right behind Davies, who was at fly half, and it shows the All Black prop Steve McDowall running at him. Half a metre either side of McDowall you can see the whole All Black pack, and they are not flat, either – they go back about 20m.

Sometimes principles in the game do not change, and that one of support certainly has not. I liked the picture because it reinforced what I was thinking at the time and it was a principle I used throughout my coaching career, about the importance of the ball carrier being at the head of a group.

Anyway, back to 1997. Some 24 of the 62 were not necessarily first-choice players with their countries. As Fran said in his tour report: 'As the selection policy was not consistent with the individual unions, the initial reaction to the first public announcement was one of furore. However, in my view in staying consistently to the selection policies it ensured that on tour we had two teams of similar capabilities and enormous flexibility. This resulted in no "dirt-trackers", only one squad.'

There were three uncapped English players in Leicester centre Will Greenwood, Sale full back Jim Mallinder and the Bristol back-rower Martin Corry. Greenwood would go on to make the eventual squad of 35.

Sometimes you just see a player and you know immediately that he is what you want and that he will be a perfect Lion. It was like that with Jeremy Guscott. I went to watch Bath play in the season before the 1989 Lions tour and I remember saying to the manager Clive Rowlands afterwards: 'I would love to take him on tour.'

We did, even if it took the withdrawal of Will Carling with shin splints to get him in. And it was the start of a wonderful relationship, firstly between Guscott and the Lions, with the centre going on three tours in all (in 1993 and 1997 as well), and secondly, I like to think, between Guscott and me.

He had not been capped by England when we selected him for Australia (although he did play against Romania before the party left). He was obviously raw when he first came on tour. But I talked to him a lot and we gained a real understanding of each other. A lot of people have said that he was difficult to deal with, but for me he wasn't.

Yes, he would tell you if he thought something was not right, but I had a real rapport with him and enjoyed coaching him. I certainly always knew his thoughts, which is so important for clarity. Seeing him mature and play on three Lions tours was very satisfying for me. I even picked him for the 1997 tour when his former club coach at Bath, Jack Rowell, was not selecting him for England.

But he was just another example of how we laid out in the plainest terms what sort of player we were looking for and what sort of game we were looking to play in South Africa. I still have my hand-written notes describing exactly what I wanted in every position for that tour. I wrote them on Monday 9 September 1996, so basically at the beginning of the season that preceded the Lions tour.

They read:

MERITS BY POSITION

Forwards

Props – physical presence, good scrummagers. Technique.
Loosehead – steady, rock-solid – mobility.
Tighthead – key scrummager. TOP PRIORITY.

Hooker – physical presence, scrummager, good lineout thrower, mobile, good rugby player, able to play out on wing.

2nd Row – part of back five, essential link to back row, good scrummager, not necessarily a 'giraffe', adaptable.

Back Row – specialist seven – must be quick with vision.

'Brave' seven must be excellent rugby player, key tactical player.

Six – physical presence, mobile, OFFENSIVE DEFENCE, line-out support skills. Good one-on-one lineout player.

Eight – physical presence, explosive pace (back of scrum), high work rate, good hands/ball skills, lineout jumper (if needed six or eight), excellent defender, BIG HITS one-on-one.

Vision as a unit.

Backs

Nine – one of key players, quick service, strong running/breaking player, link with back row and backs, good tactical brain, good tackler.

Ten – good hands, change point of attack, longer passes, good in contact, good runner.

Centre – take ball up quickly, kick well, good hands, strong defender, quick, reactive runner.

Outside Centre – good passer under pressure, playmaker/vision, good defender and defensive awareness, pace.

Wings – pace, ability to beat first man, full-back skills, good awareness in defence and strong one-to-one tackler.

Full Back – attack-minded, pace, ability to beat first man, good catcher – brave, good kicking awareness and kicking skills.

Goal kicker is essential – two top-flight.

Captain – Test player. Same playing vision, strong personality.
Midweek Captain.
Personality/Character. Intensity. World champions three times
 in two weeks on their own patch. Need a good profile.

Size was important, because you always have to match the
South Africans physically, but the game we wanted had to be
quick and at times off the cuff. The best way to beat South
Africa was to de-structure the game, to get the ball in and out
of contact swiftly so that it was always on the move.

We knew we had to scrummage well and be accurate at the
set piece, but that we were going to play the game somewhere
else. Ultimately the set piece went so well that in the second
Test in Durban a driving maul led to the position where Guscott
dropped the goal to win the Test and the series. It meant we
were playing the game we wanted rather than being dictated
to.

So amongst the forwards we needed ball-handlers. That,
along with the increased video clips available, meant that we
selected Neath's Barry Williams because he was so mobile
and athletic and we reckoned he was amongst the best three
hookers, with Keith Wood and Mark Regan. Williams had only
won one cap for Wales at the time, and was nowhere near the
national side, but we had been impressed with his performances for Wales A that year.

And that was why we ended up with such a large rugby
league contingent on the tour, players who had turned professional when union was still amateur and who had by now

returned to union. We picked six in the end: four Welshmen in Scott Gibbs (Swansea), Scott Quinnell, Allan Bateman (both Richmond) and Dai Young (Cardiff), along with the England winger John Bentley and his Newcastle team-mate, the Scotland centre/wing Alan Tait.

They definitely helped the environment, simply because union had only just gone professional, while these players had experienced professionalism for much longer. Their attitude rubbed off on the others. They also helped a lot in terms of the defensive work, which was becoming more and more impor-tant, especially the line speed. We actually spent one whole day doing defence every week on tour at a time when many clubs did not do defensive sessions at all.

It made me chuckle when some people questioned the inclusion of Bentley. What was there not to like? Fran Cotton knew him well from old. Bentley had so many of the qualities we were looking for. He was strong, powerful and a good runner, and he was an excellent on-field communicator. He was also a tremendous character off the field. He became the life and soul of the tour party.

And then there was the choice of captain: Martin Johnson. Again it surprised many, mainly because he was not captain of England at the time and had not captained Leicester that often. But it was not a difficult decision for me. The selection of the captain is a very personal decision for the coach. He has to be able to trust him and have a strong relationship with him. I thought I could do that with Johnno, and so it proved.

Yes, I did have to do some work to persuade Fran and Jim Telfer that he was the right man, because initially they favoured a more experienced international captain. So the likes of Wales' Ieuan Evans, Scotland's Rob Wainwright and Ireland's Keith Wood, as well as the England prop Jason Leonard, were all in the frame. Will Carling had already made himself unavailable for the tour, mainly because Fran had told him he would not be picked.

But I was thinking: 'Who would I want to be following out onto a Test-match rugby field?' I wanted a physical presence. When the two captains lined up in the corridor to toss the coin for the first Test, I wanted the Springbok captain to have to look up to the Lions captain. And as it was, Johnson was a bigger man than Gary Teichmann, the Springbok No. 8.

I also have it on very good authority that when they met in the corridor to toss the coin for that first Test, Teichmann would not look Johnno in the eye. As I wrote in my tour report afterwards: 'The point I wanted making had been made.' It was the first time I had come around to that way of thinking, but I wanted a big man to make an immediate statement to the opposition. I also wanted someone who was hard-nosed and ruthless, and Johnson fitted the bill perfectly.

I was thinking of Willie John McBride in 1974 and that speech he made to us before we left. That tour worked because we were a group of players led by a captain who was not going to take a backward step. I thought Johnson could do the same. That was when I started using the phrase 'Test-match animal'. You just looked at Johnno and thought immediately that that was what he was.

It helped that I was coach of Northampton at the time because Leicester were our biggest rivals and I could see the effect he had on his side as well as the opposition. I remember one game at Northampton when he got yellow-carded, but would he sit in the chair where he was supposed to or stay out of the way? Would he heck. He stomped up and down the touchline. The crowd were at him, and there was a lot of emotion and passion around, but it just did not bother him. All that concerned him was winning the match.

He had come over to New Zealand as a replacement for Wade Dooley on the 1993 Lions tour when he only had one cap for England and he had played in two Tests out there. I was impressed with him then and just became more and more so when I was at Northampton.

His Leicester team-mate Dean Richards was one person whose view and feedback I trusted and treasured. I had used him a lot on the Lions tours in 1989 and 1993 for feedback on training and general matters, so I said to him that I was thinking of making Johnno captain. Dean never said much, a bit like Johnno, but the gist of his reply was: 'He won't let you down.' And he didn't.

The more you talked to Johnson the more you realised what a feel he had for the game. And I do quite like captains to be in the back five of the pack because I think they have a good feel for the way the game is going, and they are at the heart of everything.

I had the same relationship with Finlay Calder, even if he could be a little short of confidence sometimes. He actually offered his name forward to be dropped after we lost the first Test in Australia in 1989. I just said: 'No chance.'

Johnno was instrumental in getting the right attitude amongst the players. Once the tour began, he was part of the selection process and I always felt he would say something if he felt it was not right. He was the reference point we wanted.

He did have some disciplinary problems, but I always thought he got yellow-carded every January so he could have a few weeks off before the internationals! I thought that was very clever. I'm only joking, especially as just as I am writing, the England captain Dylan Hartley has been banned for six weeks, a punishment that sees him available only just in time for the 2017 Six Nations.

The truth is that sometimes you just want that edge as captain. It was what sprang to mind when I wrote a column for the *Sunday Telegraph* after England's Rugby World Cup disappointment at home in 2015 and their subsequent search under new head coach Eddie Jones for a captain to replace Chris Robshaw. To me it was obvious that captain had to be Hartley, and without wishing to indulge in too much braggadocio, I said as much long before his name was mentioned as a possible captain:

This situation needs a strong personality and character to lead England [I wrote]. And Hartley is that man. He has been captain of Northampton. It is not as if it is a new role for him.

Yes, there is an element of the gamble about it because of Hartley's disciplinary record, but that is where you back yourself as a coach. You have to give Hartley a very clear under-standing of what you expect from him. Yellow cards simply cannot be a part of it.

Whenever I have spoken to Hartley, I have found that you can have a very good rugby conversation with him. It seems to me that he has a good rugby brain, and I think he could form a really good rapport with [Eddie] Jones because it is so impor-tant that the coach and captain have a close and special relationship.

The captain has to have the respect of his team-mates not just for the way he plays but also for the presence he brings. He also needs the respect of the opposition too. Actually it is through your captain that a team makes its statement of what it is and what it wants to be collectively. Hartley can make that statement alongside Jones.

Some have said that Wasps' Joe Launchbury could be a pick rather like Martin Johnson once was as captain. But I disagree. Johnson had a presence that Launchbury, for all his qualities as a typical modern-day lock, does not have at the moment.

I went for Johnson as captain of the 1997 British and Irish Lions just because I liked what I saw, even though he was not a captain then. When Northampton, where I was then, played Leicester, Johnson had as much influence on our players as he did on those in his own team. We had players like Matt Dawson, Tim Rodber and Gregor Townsend, but Johnson was always the most dominant figure on the pitch.

That was what impressed me. It soon became clear that he was also highly intelligent. He could read games tactically, and for a coach he was good because he would challenge you too. He was that important to England eventually that I am not sure they would have won the 2003 Rugby World Cup without him as captain.

England had a lot of leaders in that group but they needed a huge presence to draw them together and Johnson was that man. He could get hold of a game when things were getting loose.

And then there is a name like Maro Itoje, who has been mentioned even though he is only 21 years old and still uncapped. We need to see him at international level first. He has shone at European level but it is still a big step up and we need to see that he can make that first. I am sure he will (probably as a blindside flanker), but let's not get ahead of ourselves.

If you appoint a young captain like England once did with Will Carling at the age of 22, your team needs quite a bit of maturity. It needs leaders, which England had in 1988 in the likes of Dean Richards, Brian Moore, Peter Winterbottom, Jeff Probyn, Wade Dooley and Rob Andrew. And it needs power in the right areas so that you can control the game when you want to, which England had with that formidable pack. So in that instance you could put a young captain in and let him grow in the environment.

England promptly won all 13 Tests in 2016 with Hartley as captain. QED. And when he was sent off to trigger that six-week ban, it was for Northampton in a European Champions Cup match against Leinster, not for England.

Picking Finlay Calder as captain in 1989 was fairly straight-forward, as it was in handing Gavin Hastings the reins in 1993. Yes, there was obviously talk about England's Will Carling in 1993 and it was a choice between those two, but there were some significant reasons why I went for Gavin.

Firstly, he had been on a previous Lions tour in 1989, which Carling had not. Secondly, he had a lot of experience of playing in New Zealand and was highly rated and respected there. In my eyes that counted for an awful lot. New Zealanders do not dish out their rugby respect easily.

He had played there for three weeks in 1987 as part of Scotland's RWC campaign and had actually stayed on to play some club rugby in the Auckland area afterwards. He had been outstanding for Scotland on their 1990 tour of the country, where we really troubled the All Blacks, especially in the second Test at Auckland, where we only lost 21–18 and outscored them by two tries to one but were let down by the referee, who awarded five penalties to New Zealand, kicked by Grant Fox. That match remains high on my list of greatest rugby disappointments.

Gavin had also impressed the All Blacks in the 1991 RWC third-place play-off match against them in Cardiff, where Scotland had only lost 13–6. Carling was, of course, a highly successful captain of England, having won Grand Slams in 1991 and 1992, but I thought Gavin was the better choice because of that respect he already had from the New Zealanders.

In 2009 I faced a choice between the two Irishmen, Brian O'Driscoll and Paul O'Connell. But there was a third contender for the captaincy on that tour of South Africa in the England prop Phil Vickery, for whom I have always had the utmost respect as a player and as a person. I certainly considered him, but in the end it did come down to a choice between O'Driscoll and O'Connell. Brian had, of course, been captain of the Lions in New Zealand in 2005 before his tour was ended early in the first Test by a horrible double tackle from Tana Umaga and Keven Mealamu, and he was captain of Ireland's Grand Slam side in 2009, their first such success since 1948.

And he had played very well in that season too, but in contemplating the Lions captain I was thinking back to 1997. I was thinking about a big man, a big physical presence to toss up beforehand and to lead the Lions out. I wanted Brian to relax and play his own game. And I knew that Paul was an outstanding leader. I knew that I could have the same sort of relationship with him as I had had with Martin Johnson.

Often you just have to go with what feels right for you because the coach/captain relationship is always so important. It was the same with Warren Gatland and his captain Sam Warburton in Australia in 2013. Warren felt comfortable with Warburton because he had brought him through as captain in the 2011 RWC in New Zealand, but what people can easily forget is that Warburton was not actually captain of Wales when they beat England 30–3 in Cardiff to win the 2013 Six Nations. Warburton had been having a few issues with his fitness and form during that championship, so it was not an indictment of him that he was held back from the captaincy.

Rob Howley, who was standing in for Warren as Wales head coach, did exactly the right thing in making Gethin Jenkins captain for that England match. What gets you on the plane for the Lions is playing well. But leadership qualities never go away. Your form or fitness can. At the end of that championship Warburton proved his fitness and form, and so Warren felt very comfortable in making him captain of the Lions.

But in 2009 I made sure that I rang Brian before Paul was announced as captain, because I thought he deserved that phone call. I just wanted him to go out there and enjoy playing for the Lions. He said: 'Can I ring Paul and give him my congratulations?' I said: 'No, you had better not just yet because Paul doesn't know he is captain yet!' Then I rang Paul.

He was being harassed by an insurance person from England so he wouldn't answer his phone. I was trying to get hold of him to tell him he was Lions captain! And it was after that that I spent that day with him out in Ireland at his home, where I went through my template of how we should play.

But in essence the 1997 tour became the template for all subsequent tours, apart from 2005. Even the 2001 tour pretty much followed that template. They actually tried to persuade me to be coach on that tour too. Syd Millar, as Lions committee chairman, and Donal Lenihan, who was to be manager on that trip, were very keen for me to do it, but I had just taken the Scotland job again and I didn't think it was fair to go into that and try to do the Lions as well. I felt I would be compromising Scotland.

When Graham Henry was selected he came up to Edinburgh twice and we had dinner and we talked through what had happened in 1997 and what I thought was important. They were good chats.

So it is fair to say that selection has changed quite a bit over the years. I have mentioned some instances where untrustworthy characters were omitted. Well, that is less likely to happen nowadays. Professionalism has altered that. You cannot drink at the wrong times and behave badly and still be a professional rugby player these days.

In 2009 I had thought about releasing a big squad of some 60-65 names again, as we had in 1997, but decided against it. We didn't feel the need and anyway, as the England flanker Neil Back showed in 1997, players could make a strong enough case to be selected even if they were not originally named. We just felt that it would be better to work with the national coaches when looking for the type of players we wanted – strong characters who could also play the expansive, handling game I desired.

Warren Gatland was, of course, with Wales then, Martin Johnson with England, Declan Kidney with Ireland and Frank Hadden was at Scotland.

Instead of selecting and announcing a preliminary squad this month, we have decided that we should instead work closely with each of the four home union coaches in the lead-up and during the Six Nations to determine which players are showing the form and application that will make them suitable tourists [I said at the time]. Becoming a Lion is the pinnacle of a player's career – it is a unique experience and nothing compares to it.

We want to ensure that all players continue to see they have a chance of playing themselves into contention for the final squad that we will be announcing in April, as planned.

Selection of the tour party is the most important element of the tour, as far as I am concerned. I want to ensure that we have every opportunity to make the best selection decisions and that we utilise expertise from outside the group, such as the national coaches of the home nations, to select the final group of players that will represent the British Isles in South Africa.

Here is word for word what I wrote in my tour report about selection:

PRINCIPLES

PICK ON FORM NOT REPUTATION (Shane Williams?)
Select final group late (22nd April 2009)
Allowed follow-up with final 10/12 selections
Initial group of 60/70 decided not feasible
Speak to all national coaches
Aim for 35 players so all get game time

November Tests and Heineken Cup:
Identified 120 players

RBS 6 Nations:
Enlisted the help of Jim Telfer
3 Selection Meetings

Pre-selection in January cancelled, good decision:

1. After first 2 games of RBS 6 Nations

2. End of RBS 6 Nations

3. April 20th (and pre-meeting in Reading week before)

Selection by position

No voting – out of discussion

Pre-measuring during RBS 6 Nations valuable

130 players covered

Paul O'Connell as captain:

Forward, good and got on with playing, spoke very well

Spent day with him in early April

Brian O'Driscoll phone call – deserved that, was excellent on
    tour.

The Shane Williams case was interesting because we would have liked the Wales winger to have been in better form during the season, but I always considered him a match-winner and therefore worth taking. On the tour he proved that decision to be absolutely correct, scoring two tries in our third-Test victory in Johannesburg.

I have to say that all the coaches were a tremendous help, as you would expect from such people in a Lions year. It needs everyone pulling in the right direction, and they were very honest and considered in their views, especially when I asked about the character of players, about how they would react under the most extreme pressure that only a Lions tour can bring.

I thought long and hard about whom I would take as support staff to South Africa in 2009. Gerald Davies was manager, but,

crucially, he recognised that he had not been part of the professional game and so vowed to stand apart from the rugby intri-
cacies and the internal workings of the group. That would ultimately work well throughout the tour. Gerald was very good at
picking up chats with individual players, and this helps to hold
everything together.

In fact, this is what the role of Lions manager has become.
He is more of a PR social representative, whereas the rugby
responsibility sits with the head coach and the support staff,
which is in a way what you want. So you've got a diplomat, a
front-person whom everyone respects, and behind him you
have got an interconnecting group that is trying to make sure
everything is right by the time you get to the pitch.

There was a strong Wasps connection in 2009. Warren
Gatland (forwards), Rob Howley (backs), Shaun Edwards
(defence), Craig White and Paul Stridgeon (fitness), Prav
Mathema (physiotherapy) and Rhys Long (analysis) all had
spent time at Wasps, where I was director of rugby at the time,
even if I took something of a sabbatical in the year before the
tour.

Was that Wasps connection wrong? I was asked that at the
time. 'I've been extremely careful in choosing this coaching
team, because in the uniquely pressurised Lions environment,
where the challenge is to achieve something extremely difficult in a very short space of time, trust is so important,' I said.
'I work closely with Shaun, I've worked with Rob and after
talking matters through with Warren, it's clear to me that we
think along similar lines.

'People might say there is a Club Wasps feel to this. Is that a bad thing? What we need is uniformity of thought and complete understanding. We won't always agree as a coaching team, but I know this much: we'll be honest with each other. If someone has a problem – and this goes for the players as well as the coaches – there must be no innuendos, no whispering, no hiding in corners. I want it out in the open like a shot. Only by being prepared to talk things through will we reach the answers we need.'

This approach undoubtedly accelerates progress and understanding.

Graham Rowntree was also used as a scrummaging coach and he was someone I knew well from two Lions tours in 1997 and 2005. His coaching career had taken off quickly and he had joined the Rugby Football Union from Leicester as a national academy coach in 2007 before being asked by head coach Brian Ashton to be England's scrummaging coach at the RWC that year. I always rated him. I just liked his whole approach.

These were all people I knew well and whom I trusted. Often our discussions were very informal – as I have mentioned they were often over a drink at the bar – and they might last a couple of hours, but we all knew that we could have a pretty honest and open discussion, not just about players but about the way we were playing too. We knew we all had a similar approach that we could keep evolving, which I felt was important. There are only five or six weeks to the first Test after you arrive. You need people who you know are of a similar mind so you can move things along quickly.

I used other people with whom I was familiar as backroom staff, of which there were now 23 for this tour. James Robson was obviously there but so was the masseur Richard Wegrzyk. And as I have mentioned, we had Louise Ramsay as operations manager. She was absolutely brilliant, undoubtedly the best administrator I have ever come across.

I'm back to the importance of chemistry in a squad, and the chemistry among the support staff and their subsequent interaction with the playing squad and coaching management were quite magnificent. Nowadays tours are so short that you have to hit the ground running. Selection of the support staff comes into that too. Things have got to be as right and as powerful off the field as they are on the field.

In 2009 we assembled all the support staff together in London for a weekend a few months before the tour. I asked everyone from each area to talk about how they saw their responsibility and then I spoke about how we would all operate together.

We all then gave feedback. It was such a valuable exercise. Wives were invited as well so we all went out to the theatre in the evening after the meeting. But crucially, we left the weekend with a clear understanding of what we were going to deliver as a group and how best we were going to deliver it. That really got us up and running. We were on the front foot. 'In many ways this felt like a reunion but importantly, it was a meeting of minds,' I wrote in my tour report.

On the media front we had Greg Thomas, Christine Connolly and Louisa Cheetham. Gary O'Driscoll was another doctor, with Phil Pask and Bob Stewart as other physiotherapists. Guy Richardson was the excellent logistics officer and Rhodri Bown helped Long with the analysis. And we had our own chef, Dave Campbell, a Scotsman who had been on the 2005 tour.

Patrick O'Reilly, the kit man from Ireland, the man they all call Rala, was a brilliant personality. He was just the kind of person you needed to put the players in the right frame of mind at the right time and to relieve the pressure on them. On that tour it was certainly the first time I had ever walked off a training field and had a coffee waiting for me on the touchline. Whatever you wanted, Rala just produced it at the right time. Selection, you see, is not just about the players who go onto the field, especially on a Lions tour.

But what about when you are selected as a player. What is that like? Utterly magical, I would say.

I think I will let Gareth Edwards take up the story at this point, because I still rate him as the greatest player I have ever seen, and I was fortunate enough to be in the same Lions Test side as him in 1974.

'It's hard to put in so many words what is special about the Lions,' he has said. 'Suffice to say every player aspires to play for his country. Then you realise there is a further step to take. You read about it and, OK in later years, you're able to see these tours on TV. But we grew up reading about them, Cliff Morgan, Jeff Butterfield, Tony O'Reilly and all those guys on these long, long trips to the far side of the world. It's a gathering of the clans, isn't it? And there's the uncanny factor, too, that you battle and try to tear each other apart only weeks before and, all of a sudden, you are standing shoulder to shoulder against a common enemy a long way from home.'

Gareth is so right. When you get picked for your country it is obviously very special, but when you get picked for the Lions you take another step. You are going from being the best in one country to being part of a group where you might end up being third best in your position.

The challenge then is to compete for that Test place. So you have to be mightily competitive. You have to be ruthless in saying to yourself that you will deliver no matter what. But you also have to have the ability to manage the disappointments. That is the beauty of Lions tours. Every player is asked: how do you manage your own behaviour and performances if you don't get picked?

These days the players discover their fate via television when the names are read out live. Only the captain, who is present at the announcement, knows beforehand (although I did, of course, tell Brian O'Driscoll as well in 2009). All the others will wait expectantly, and watch. It is unique, because no other rugby team does this. Some might say that it is rather old-fashioned, but the suspense adds to the magic, in my opinion.

The announcement of the squad is very special. It was something I was keen on making a big thing of in 1997, so we got Sky Sports television all booked up and arranged it so that the unveiling at their headquarters in West London was beamed out live, and that year we tried to ensure that the letters to the players confirming their selection arrived that day.

I know most of the players learnt by letter that year, the first professional Lions tour. I remember reading that Neil Back had received his letter and promptly burst into tears. He had been in the international wilderness, having only won five caps at that stage. He had not played for England for two years and had not been in that original 62-man party we had named. There was still a debate about his size but in fairness Jim Telfer had pushed hard for his inclusion, and it worked out rather well.

He appeared in two of the Tests and from there his England career took off. He reminded me a bit of Simon Shaw in that they both showed what they could do in a Lions shirt, taking their game to a different level and still looking very comfortable.

Now the players do genuinely discover their fate on the day. There is drama. There is real theatre, and that is good in my view. You can never have such a build-up with any other team, with those months spent with everyone picking their Lions team, with the Lions hovering over everything and everybody looking at who is playing well and who is not, and who is going to be in their team. That builds its own narrative and creates the very powerful message that the Lions are different and that this is a completely different journey that is about to be embarked upon, whether you are selected as a player or a coach.

In 2005 the squad had been read out in alphabetical order. In 2009 Gerald Davies read it out by position so that it made more sense to everyone. He began with the full backs, then the wingers and so on. I remember the Bath and England hooker Lee Mears saying how tense his wait had been. He thought the props would be read out last, but it was actually the hookers, so his name was not announced until last but one, with only Wales' Matthew Rees after him.

'It was like waiting on *The X Factor*,' joked Wales' Tom Shanklin, who unfortunately missed the tour through injury, having been originally selected.

For 20-year-old Wales' full back/winger Leigh Halfpenny it was very emotional. 'I'm absolutely speechless,' he said. 'I would never have expected any of this at the start of the season. I leaped in the air when I saw my name on the television, I nearly hit my head on the light. Then I broke into tears with my friends and family, it was just a massive occasion.'

I can relate to that. I had no thoughts whatsoever of making the Lions tour during the 1974 Five Nations. It was only when I was flying back from our game in Ireland that season and I picked up a newspaper that I received the shock of my life.

There in the *Sunday Times* Vivian Jenkins was selecting his Lions squad and my name, complete with a picture, was there. I was completely taken aback. I looked at some of the other names, the likes of Willie John McBride, Gareth Edwards, J.P.R. Williams, Phil Bennett, Ian McLauchlan and Fergus Slattery, and could scarcely believe that I was being talked of in such company.

But it was only speculation. I had to wait for the letter like everyone else. When it dropped through the door, it was the most wonderful experience, though. On the outside was the acronym B.I.R.U.T., denoting the British Isles Rugby Union

Team. That was what we were called then and it was emblazoned on our tour bags. Indeed, in his 1989 tour report Clive Rowlands was still referring to captain Finlay Calder as 'a very successful captain of a B.I.R.U.T. team'.

The letter in 1974 was from the manager, Alun Thomas. 'Dear Ian,' it began. 'A quick note of much congratulations on your selection. It is a great honour, and I know you will take full advantage of it. You will soon be hearing from my assistant manager, Syd Millar, and from our captain, Willie John, on what we require from you between now and the day of departure . . .'

Notice how the coach was termed the assistant manager because coaches were not really recognised as such back then. It went on to emphasise a couple of points in a separate letter from the secretary of the tour committee, Albert Agar, namely that we should keep the assembly hotel and departure details secret (due to the apartheid demonstrations) and that we should make sure we only played once a week until the end of the season and then not at all after April 20 (the first match in South Africa was on May 15).

We were asked to provide some personal details, including our shoe size. 'I am hoping to "scrounge" a pair of Dunlop Green Flash shoes. No half sizes available and also a pair of Norvic Chukka "Scallywags" (leisure wear), half sizes available,' wrote Thomas. I wonder what modern-day players think reading that. It makes me chuckle for certain. It was a different world.

We were asked to do some reading too. 'Could I recommend you read *The Lions Speak* (by John Reason), which describes brilliantly the attitudes behind the success of the '71 Lions. If you were on that tour, read it again and any general book on South Africa, e.g. Alan Paton's *South Africa and Her People*.'

And we also had to do some writing. 'Would you write to the South Africa Tourist Corporation, Piccadilly, London W1 telling them who you are and they will send you a marvellous map and tourist guide. It is important you do this.'

For all this, though, it was the Lions badge at the top of the letter that kept attracting my attention. I kept looking at it. The four quarters with the four symbols of the home unions with a Lion above it. That brought reality. I was a Lion.

But then you actually have to meet up. That can be as daunting as it is exciting. As I mentioned about 1974, I was rather in awe of some of those legendary names. I was not even sure what I should call Gareth Edwards. Sir, maybe? To think that I was eventually given that title before him.

Yes, I have mentioned that players of that era knew each other better than those today, but still it was hugely exciting seeing players that you have probably never played with before in the same room and on the same training field.

These days the players meet up on what I first called 'Messy Monday', where all the kit is handed out and all the administrative chores are seen to. I can see why so many of them liken it to the first day at school.

'Meeting up is like your first day at secondary school,' says the Wales flanker Martyn Williams, who was a Lion in 2001, 2005 and 2009. 'You've got your group of mates from primary school – or in this case, the guys you play with for your country – so you tend to stick together.

'You have to break down all the barriers as quickly as possible. If you are going to be a successful team, you have to get to know each other off the field.

'It is up to the senior boys who have been on a Lions tour before to set the tone. On my first tour in 2001 it was the likes of Keith Wood, Lawrence Dallaglio and Martin Johnson who reinforced the point straight away – "Forget your nationality, you're all Lions now".'

Indeed. That is the moment when you realise you are a Lion. I never anticipated losing on that 1974 trip (and we didn't), merely because of the presence of such great players. But that initial dynamic is important. There will always be more reticent players amid those eager to take a lead and how they gel is vital.

KEY WORDS

- Selection and strategy
- Support staff make the environment
- Select on merit not reputation
- Wildcards
- Sleep on selection
- Captain must have presence
- Confidence breeds success
- Media support
- Trust and respect go together
- Head – listen – support

1993 New Zealand, Second Test
We will come to this game in detail later but it was, I think, a good
example of getting selection right and the influence of a captain, with
Gavin Hastings not really fit but still managing to lead superbly.

TENACIOUS TOURISTS OVERCOME CAPTAIN HASTINGS' EARLY ERROR
TO SHOW NEW ZEALANDERS THEIR COMPETITIVE EDGE

ALL BLACKS GET A MAULING AS LIONS ROAR BACK IN STYLE

New Zealand 7 British Isles 20

by Norman Mair

New Zealand, 1993

HAVING **chosen to play into the wind and sun, the Lions at once took the game to the All Blacks. Their most voracious start, by popular consent, since those home matches with the Christians.**

An eminently kickable penalty to the tourists was rendered stillborn by a touch-judge's flag. It had been prompted by an altercation, featuring Peter Winterbottom, Ben Clarke and Mark Cooksley, born of alleged Lions' stampng.

The Lions were unblinkingly putting that reversed penalty behind them when they suffered a second hammer blow. Fed from a ruck emanating from a Lions' drop-out, Grant Fox hoisted what Bill McLaren would call a Garryowen but Kiwis term "The Bomb".

Gavin Hastings has been a wonderfully reassuring sight under the high ball on this tour but now, as he half turned to make the classic cradle, the ball spilled from his clutches. Eroni Clarke, off the mark so quickly that there were vain, if highly optimistic, cries of "Offside!" from among the 2,000 Lions' supporters, swooped to score.

Because of his damaged hamstring, the Lions' captain had missed out on fielding practice all week and, besides, so early in the match, the injury may still have been in his mind, breeding uncertainty. He himself, though, would have no excuses. "No," he told a Sassenach scribe, "the sun did not come into it. I simply made a mistake. It happens."

Fox kicked the goal and, agonisingly, the right-footed goal-kicker that is the Lions' captain, from the starboard flank and across the face of the wind, missed with two penalty goal attempts, hitting a post with the first of them.

The Lions, though, were not to be denied, Hastings kicking a good penalty goal. Sean Fitzpatrick had fallen foul of Monsieur Robin's firm conviction that the new law requiring a player at a maul to retreat behind the hindmost foot offside line, before joining or rejoining behind the line of the ball, is one of the best things the legislators have done for the game in many a day.

The All Blacks looked rattled. As they once again infringed within range of the posts — this time for illegally handling on the floor — Hastings's boot bit further into the deficit.

Against what was not a heavy wind but still strong enough to be decidedly influential, the Lions, in one of the greatest halves in their history, had laid claim to a sixty per cent territorial advantage. And, before half-time, Ian McGeechan's parting gesture at the Lions' final pre-Test session on the Friday morning had paid off ...

Tossing the ball to Rob Andrew, he had called to him to drop a goal with his left foot. Now, as Martin Bayfeld turned the ball down from a lineout and Dewi Morris found him with an exemplary pass, Andrew did just that.

Lionised: captain Gavin Hastings savours victory

Nine-seven ahead with the wind to come was great going but there was scarcely a New Zealander in the stadium who was not comforting his neighbour, not to mention himself, with a reminder that, on all past form, the Lions; were only a forty-minute side. Nor could the second half have begun more inauspiciously, Andrew, as if in a time warp, restarting the game with a kick which crossed the enemy goal-line.

A scrum back — but he had not forgotten the change of law. Just over-hit downwind a deliberately raking kick-off.

Chatting to Fox in the morning, one had asked him if he found the so often wind-swept Athletic Park a difficult pitch on which to kick goals. Not really, he had answered, because the wind did not swirl but blew straight down the field.

Now, however, across the slant of the wind, he hooked a penalty attempt badly; perhaps the worst kick one has seen him perpetrate.

Whereupon Patrick Robin, as one had watched him do when he had charge of a match between the colts of Hawke's Bay and Waikato, vouchsafed the young men and women in the crowd a sight of something of which their grandparents may have told them: a referee in New Zealand blowing for in squint at a scrum!

It was an anachronism which was to be worth three points to the Lions. Andrew, obliquely, pumped the free kick high to the posts. Hastings, hamstring by now forgotten, secured a rebound and was tackled, a large section of the indigenous population being adjudged to be on the wrong side of the ball.

Fox, like Hastings before him, had struck a post with a penalty kick before the Lions produced a try which, simultaneously, destroyed any chance of an All Blacks revival and McGeechan's image as a phlegmatic Yorkshireman.

Inside the Lions' half, Fitzpatrick, a tremendous player over the years but, on the day, a symbolically attired Accident Black Spot, lost the ball in a tackle. Morris gathered to counter-attack on the break.

The scrum half linked with Jeremy Guscott who gave a lovely pass, having done just enough, in the words of McGeechan, "to give Rory Underwood the yard he needed to beat John Kirwan and leave him for dead".

A thrilling score which had McGeechan rubbing his hands in glee where Scotland's 1990 Grand Slam and the 1989 Lions' victory over the Wallabies had been hard pressed to induce much more than a wan smile.

Hastings missed the angled conversion but, before no-side, he had garnered his fourth penalty goal when the All Blacks, who had lost not a little of their discipline, were penalised under their own posts for stamping.

3

THE ENVIRONMENT

It might have been Scott Gibbs who suggested it, but it was definitely the captain Martin Johnson who came striding down the team bus to speak to me and the others at the front.

What am I talking about? An incident after the first Test in South Africa in 1997, that's what.

We had won 25–16 in Cape Town after a never-to-be-forgotten try from England scrum half Matt Dawson – only playing because the Welshman Rob Howley had had to return home for shoulder surgery – as he fooled the South African defence with his outrageous one-handed, high-over-the-head dummy to score and put us ahead after we had been 16–15 down.

The Scottish winger Alan Tait also scored a try and the Welshman Neil Jenkins, a fly half who was playing at full back in that series so that we could play the better attacker, the Scotsman Gregor Townsend, at 10, kicked five penalties.

It was a stunning victory. South Africa were world champions and had just won seven Tests on the trot. Later that year they would begin a run of 17 consecutive wins. It was a time for some celebration, but it was also a time that needed to be managed carefully. We could not get ahead of ourselves. We

Gavin Hastings was another inspirational Lions leader in 1993.
He was hugely respected in New Zealand.

Ireland prop Nick Popplewell in New Zealand in 1993.

Not many backs ever have the total respect of the forwards. Scott Gibbs did!

had only won one Test, and there was still a series to be won. We also had to play a midweek match against the Free State Cheetahs on the following Tuesday. The side for that match would be training in Cape Town on the Sunday morning after the Test match.

We had booked everyone into a Mexican restaurant, Cantina Tequila in Cape Town, on that Saturday evening. It would have been easy for everyone not to give the next day the slightest thought. But on the bus the call was made by Johnson: 'We are all going training with the midweek side in the morning. We are all going to be there at 9 a.m. to hold the tackle bags.'

I was very happy with that. We had a good night but everybody was back in the hotel before 1 a.m. I actually ended up in the team room watching the video of the match with some of the players. Tim Rodber, Keith Wood, Rob Wainwright and Barry Williams were all there with me.

Crucially, not one player was late to get on the bus the next morning. The weather was poor but everyone was there. Interestingly you will not find that bus ride the next morning or the training session that followed on the famous *Living with Lions* video. The cameramen did not make it, but the players did. The point is, though, that at that moment I knew that we had the right environment on the tour, and that the players understood what it was to be a Lion.

This is what you strive for on every Lions tour. The captain giving that rallying call would have been superb, another player saying it made it even better. Everyone was on the same page. 'I thought it was a brilliant call and I wish I had thought of it,' wrote Johnson of Gibbs' call to arms. 'It was fantastic for team spirit.'

It was. Gibbs had a magnificent tour as a hugely physical presence in the centre – and I always felt that the subtleties of his game, especially his deft hands, were often disregarded. He was a hugely popular member of the tour party and will always be remembered for smashing the huge South African prop Os du Randt out of the way in the second Test in Durban. He would often be the player rousing the team in the huddle before a game.

That was Johnno's way of captaining. He only spoke when he felt that there was something worth saying – and how the players then listened! – but he was always very comfortable in letting other players have their say, relying heavily on senior players like Gibbs in that respect.

Gibbs certainly embraced the Lions concept. He got it all right. As he said afterwards: 'When that squad was announced in '97, I think there was an element that this squad was different, this management was different, and all those elements came together to create one playing entity.

'There was never anyone who felt alienated in any way. That's a true strength of a squad, that inward support from everybody. That was there in abundance in '97 and that was why it was so successful on the field and off the field. We made a lot of friendships.'

The great thing about that incident in Cape Town is how well the midweek team then did in Bloemfontein. It was actually the only occasion on that tour when the party was split, something I never intended but sometimes it was unavoidable, mainly because of the rigours of an itinerary designed to suit the home side and test us to the limit.

The first two Tests were in Cape Town and Durban at sea level, but the South Africans wanted a midweek game at altitude. It did not make sense, so that was why we did what we did. We all flew to Durban from Cape Town on the Sunday afternoon, but then on the Tuesday morning the midweek team flew up to Bloemfontein for the match and then straight back to Durban that night. It was not ideal, even if it was only a 45-minute flight, but it had been agreed before we left simply because it was deemed the best use of time and resources.

I was due to make the trip but was told to remain in Durban by James Robson because I had a flu bug. He was concerned that in the tight confines of a charter flight the bug would spread easily. I was not even allowed to watch the game on television with the Test squad. I had to sit in my room all alone and watch it.

We beat the Cheetahs 52–30. Fran Cotton described it as one of the 'greatest performances in Lions history'. I certainly thought it was our most complete performance of the tour. The quality of the rugby we produced against good opposition was sensational, especially the continuity of our play as we scored seven tries, with John Bentley scoring a hat-trick.

Back in Durban all the Test squad stayed up late that night, awaiting the return of the side from Bloemfontein, clapping them into the hotel as they arrived, and staying with them to have a late supper. We were as one again.

The match was marred only by a horrific injury suffered by Will Greenwood. Just before half time he was tackled and thrown to the ground, hitting his head on the hard surface. He was obviously concussed. It looked bad but none of us knew quite how bad it really was at that moment.

Put simply, James Robson saved his life. Will had swallowed his tongue. His pupils were not reacting to light and James was ready to make an emergency opening of the airway. As it was, James thinks Will's gumshield saved him, preventing his teeth from completely clamping together and allowing some air through. I was obviously not there but it was clearly a terrible situation that was handled magnificently by James. How lucky we were to have him.

We made Nigel Redman captain for that match. The Bath and England second row had been a replacement for Doddie Weir, who had been injured in a despicable incident in the midweek match against Mpumalanga. Indeed, I do not think I have ever seen such a horrible act on a rugby field.

Weir, the Scottish lock, was standing at the side of a ruck when the home side's lock, Marius Bosman, for no reason whatsoever, kicked him on the knee with his studs up. Doddie's ligaments were severed and his tour was over, and, unbelievably, Bosman was not sent off. He received just a fine. It was a joke.

I was angry and so was everyone else, but it did give Redman, whom everyone calls Ollie, an unexpected opportunity. He was on tour with England in Argentina, from where we also summoned Mike Catt to replace the injured Paul Grayson.

There was a bit of a fuss about that, too. Jack Rowell, the England coach, did not want to release Catt until after the second Test, which was ridiculous. We wanted him in South Africa immediately, and, while there was some wrangling behind the scenes, Catt was actually forced to make a trip from Buenos Aires up to Mendoza and then back again.

It might be unbelievable to think now that the Lions did not take instant precedence – what would the player prefer?– but those were the days when things were still run by out-of-date committees and there was always red tape to be encountered. Take, for example, the case of the England lock Wade Dooley in New Zealand in 1993. Wade had to fly home because of the sudden death of his father, to be replaced by Martin Johnson, but once he had taken care of everything back at home Wade indicated that he would like to return to the tour for the final two weeks.

The committee of the four home unions would not permit it, even though the New Zealand Rugby Union said they would allow it and would pay for the extra player to be on tour. But there was no relenting. Rules were rules, apparently. You maybe could understand that in the case of injury, but in the case of a family bereavement? It was insensitive and just plain wrong.

New Zealand saw the rugby element of it; our committee did not. The tour manager Geoff Cooke and I were very disappointed with the decision. This was what you were dealing with, just two years before professionalism; it was still very much a group of blazers. Some of them were well-intentioned.

For example, Bob Weighill as chairman was really good. He was a really nice man, but some other alickadoos just did not appreciate what we were asking of players, and how intense the international game had become by the 1990s.

Another example was in 1989 when the Lions came back from the Australia tour and were asked to play France as part of the bicentenary celebrations of the French Revolution. The Lions wouldn't pay for the wives to go to Paris for two or three days and that was why a group of players, including captain Finlay Calder, would not make themselves available.

It was a pity because we had such a good rugby rapport. And it showed when we played France because we beat them 29–27 with a lot of players who had not even come on tour. But the players who had been on the tour ran proceedings. It was absolutely brilliant, and the two training sessions we had there were outstanding. It shows that an understanding can get embedded into a group if you approach it just right.

So, back to 1997 and the hassle of securing Catt's release from the Argentina tour. Fran Cotton had to make an awful lot of phone calls and it was only at the very last minute that Derek Morgan, who was chairman of the Rugby Football Union's playing committee, gave the green light for Catt to join us. I am still shaking my head at the ridiculousness of it now.

When one player arrives, there is always the disappointment of the player leaving to consider. And so I thought it was another wonderful example of the togetherness of the squad in 1997 that a couple of players, Jeremy Guscott and Jason Leonard, took time to take Grayson out for a few beers to console him. It was typical of the squad that they should spare a thought for him when he most needed it.

Catt came to South Africa and made a real impression, playing at fly half in the final Test. I remember saying afterwards that it would have been very interesting had he been on the tour from the beginning. Yes, Gregor Townsend did exceptionally well in that position, but you could see how much Mike enjoyed playing in the style we adopted.

And Redman made an impression too. His press conference just after arriving had everyone chuckling. He was asked how he had found out about being called up. 'I got a call from Jack Rowell in the hotel to go to his room,' he said. 'I assumed that I was going to be dropped. When he said that I was going to South Africa I said: "I don't believe it." "Neither do I," said Jack.' That was typical Jack Rowell, but it made us all laugh.

At the conclusion of my tour diary of that trip I had a bit of a Steve Redgrave moment – 'Anybody who sees me in a boat has my permission to shoot me,' said the rower after gold in the 1996 Olympics before winning another gold in 2000 – vowing not to do another Lions tour. But I also think I encapsulated the allure and enchantment of the Lions by mentioning Ollie's story.

'Someone asked me about the next Lions tour in 2001,' I wrote. 'There is no way I could beat what I have just been through. It is an enormous privilege to have had three shots as it is. I have toured all three southern hemisphere countries so that is it. It has been a fantastic adventure. The magic of this particular experience was best summed up by Nigel Redman.

Who could have imagined Ollie leading the Lions out at Bloemfontein? We all have different dreams and they do sometimes come true. They did for Ollie. And they did for me too.'

Ollie was a special character but he was also entering a special environment when he arrived. We had worked very hard at nurturing that environment on the 1997 tour, and it had borne fruit. This has always been one of my guiding principles with the Lions. If the environment and chemistry are right, it has a huge impact on the group and gives you the best lead-in to a Test-match performance.

The Lions should always be able to put a good Test team out. There are always going to be egos because the squad is full of big players in their own international jerseys, but what you have got to get right is the environment that creates the way they play. There is the mental environment and the physical environment: one leads into the other. When you start to feel they are going right, you are onto something good. We had that.

I knew in 1997 that we had to be careful with our initial preparation. Leicester had played in the Pilkington Cup final against Sale on the Saturday before we met on the Monday. And there were six Leicester players in the squad – Martin Johnson, Neil Back, Graham Rowntree, Eric Miller, Will Greenwood and Austin Healey.

Johnson had injured his shoulder and he had an ongoing groin problem, but we did not tell anyone that he was injured. We just did not pick him until we played Western Province in the third match of the tour. We simply said that we were not going to overplay our captain. It actually helped him, I think, to have that break.

However, it underlined that our preparation when we met at the Oatlands Park Hotel in Weybridge, Surrey, had to be carefully planned. We had to make sure that we did not play too much rugby and we also had to make sure we blended the group together. As ever with the Lions, these players had been knocking lumps out of each other only a couple of months before. Some knew each other, some did not. Some would be confident, some less so.

But most importantly for me, they would all be quite stale after a long season. Of course, they would be able to rouse themselves for a Lions tour. But for endless training sessions? No, I didn't think so. That became a problem in Australia in 2001, apparently.

So I said to Fran Cotton: 'This could be a real problem if we do too much rugby too early and mentally we will tire them out,' I said. We needed to bond them through activities that did not involve rugby. Fran was put in touch with a number of companies who specialised in this sort of thing: bringing employees together and helping them work as a more cohesive and co-operative unit.

I had been involved in something similar with the Scottish Life Assurance Company, for whom I worked for four years in the early 1990s whilst also coaching, but I was insistent here that any activities had to be done outside and to be practical and not be done inside and in a conference room.

Fran and I interviewed four of these companies. I had written down what I wanted to do and reckoned we could get the principles of how we wanted to play into other activities. It was all about nobody being on their own – how you couldn't succeed on your own.

To implement this in our playing style we were looking at the idea of a 'plus one' player in attacks, never leaving a player on his own, as well as using a second line of attacks. I had spoken to some of the rugby league players and they reckoned this would work, especially against South Africa.

By the 'plus one' tactic I mean that there was a player behind another all the time. The player who was going to hit the line would move very late and take the ball off the player standing closer to the line. We had two runners who were always on the shoulder.

So if the ball carrier was going for one shoulder of the defender, then the support runner was going for the other. Without looking, the ball carrier could pop the pass up knowing that someone else would be there. We wanted to coax the South Africans into making big hits but actually look to play one pass wider out from that hit. We did the same drills and practised them during the whole tour.

We immediately got a real rapport with a company called Impact, who were based in the Lake District. They were really good. They saw it straight away and knew exactly what we wanted.

The key was that none of the activities were achievable by a single person. They all had to be done in twos, threes or even more. It fitted in perfectly with what I wanted and what I had stressed to the squad when I had first spoken to them. Looking back on my notes I had written at the top:

'Personal Responsibility – "Be at the right place at the right time, all the time." E.g. no duty boys, information under door each evening about what is happening and when. Although early sessions together, as tour develops different groups will be involved in different activities, depending on involvement in a game.'

And at the bottom I had written: 'TEAMS WITHIN TEAMS, GAMES WITHIN THE GAME.'

That was what we were doing here. All the management staff were involved and a lot of fun was had. There was one exercise – it may even have been the very first one – where we were split up into groups of nine and had to stand with our arms out and our fingers pointing straight out at about shoulder height.

The aim was to balance a piece of cane on our fingers and then to get it to the ground without it leaving anyone's fingers. It sounds absurdly easy, but it was most certainly not. There needed to be excellent communication and leadership, and it took some time to establish that.

There was another exercise where your group had to build a tower of beer crates with one person standing on top of them. Tom Smith was a really quiet and subdued character, and new to the international scene, but his group got about 30 beer crates up with him perched on top. He was about 35ft in the air.

You got respect for things you did which were nothing to do with rugby. The others suddenly saw Tom and saw the concentration and bravery he had used to make it work. It made a big impression.

There were other height challenges, for instance climbing trees with rope ladders, and a number of people – both players and coaches – were quite uncomfortable doing the tasks and needed help to complete them. Then we went on the River Thames and canoed in groups of three, where there was much hilarity as some of the bigger lads tried to get across a weir.

I think we only actually did three rugby sessions – at London Irish – during the five days we were based at Oatlands.

I felt comfortable as a coach at this stage of my career. Often coaches feel the need to do something to justify their position. Here in no way did I feel that I needed to prove myself. It meant that I could easily make decisions to cancel training sessions. I was more concerned with the players' welfare than having to prove myself. So on the very first day we cancelled a session when Martin Johnson mentioned that the players were feeling jaded, and again we did the same a few days later. I made sure we did what was right at the right time, not what we had decided to do some time earlier. There was nothing that was totally prescriptive.

There was a big breakthrough, though, on the Friday afternoon before we left. It was here that we got the players to talk about and decide upon a set of guiding principles and core values for the tour. These became known as the 'Lions Laws'. Once they had been decided upon, their headings were printed on yellow cards and laminated in plastic so that every player had one to carry around with him. He could read it himself as a reminder of what had been determined or he could even brandish it to a team-mate if he thought he was stepping out of line.

We said to the players: 'If one of your team-mates starts to produce that card in front of you, you know that you are doing something wrong.' The words on the card were: 'Winners, Highest Standards, Discipline (Self and Team), Identity, Cohesive, Supportive, Openness, Honesty, Desire, Dedication, Belief (Self and Others), Positive, Constructive, Trust, United, Committed, Enjoyment, Flexible, Respect, Personal Space, Punctual, No Cliques.'

We were split into groups to discuss certain aspects in more detail. One group discussed discipline and decided that there would be a disciplinary committee comprising myself, Fran, Johnno and Rob Wainwright. 'Any decisions must be unanimous,' it concluded.

Another group looked at 'selection and polarisation'. It agreed on these points:

1. Non-selected players should congratulate the players selected in their positions.
2. Selected players to publicly recognise the role of non-players.
3. Any selection queries are taken to the coach, not discussed with other players.
4. Before Tests, on a strictly confidential basis, non-selected players should be forewarned by the management. For other games selection is announced at meetings only.
5. Focus must be maintained by all 35 players and coaches before every game, especially the final two midweek games.
6. Make a concerted effort to get to know all members of the party, e.g. training, seating at dinner, etc.

7. Make the team room the focus of the party – not the bedrooms.
8. Once a week to go off site from the hotel to go out together.
9. Have one daily meal together as a squad, e.g. lunch.
10. Entertainment for people through non-rugby-related events.

Another group looked at internal and external communication, agreeing that there should be bi-weekly team meetings, with the management leaving for the last 10 minutes of them, and that there should be opportunities for players to voice concerns to the management through a senior players' group (the 1997 version of the 1974 'Mafia').

Team spirit was another element that was examined. 'It is the backbone of the side, it keeps us together whatever,' the message from that group read. 'How will we know if we are getting it right? Mood in camp, the atmosphere, positive, smiling, enthusiasm. Team spirit will motivate each other, drive standards and stop complacency. We should continue our non-rugby team-building in South Africa.'

And lastly there was the code of conduct. It read:

1. No one to go out on pre-match nights.
2. Alcohol. Individual responsibility, nothing that is detrimental to you or team performance.
3. Punctuality. Player input into itinerary. No excuses for lateness unless it has been communicated beforehand. Roommates take responsibility. Court to decide fines.

4. Dress code. Training as instructed by coaching staff. Functions as requested. Travel is casual. Hotel is casual, but we have a duty to our sponsors. In free time, players' responsibility, but still have duty to sponsors.

I think the crucial part of this was talking to the players about what they wanted to do if they weren't selected for the Tests. 'How are you going to handle it individually and how do you want us as a management to handle it?' we asked them.

We agreed that letters would be slipped under doors at 8 a.m. the morning after the previous night's Test selection and then that evening we would all go out for a meal together. Test players and non-Test players would sit next to each other. We were trying to convey that the Test side was only a group representing all of us in the next game.

And going to a nice restaurant in a busy part of town also showed the players the support that was arriving for the Test, the thousands of fans who were out and about. You then had no doubt about the impact the Test was going to have. The letters were important because it was felt that it was better for players to deal with their emotions in relative privacy first before meeting up with the group.

At the end of it we all knew what we were aiming to do around all the key decisions and moments of the tour. We had a plan for those trigger points where we were going to feel challenged.

It was interesting to read Warren Gatland's comments in 2016, not long after he had been appointed as head coach for the 2017 tour:

The challenge for us is getting things right off the field. If we can do that and get some harmony into the squad, we can go a long way towards getting things right on the field. We weren't perfect in 2013, but we were pretty good.

The big thing for me is there wasn't a huge amount of negativity coming off the squad after the tour. There are always guys that are going to be disgruntled because they didn't get selected and I understand that. That is one area we have got to continue to work on in terms of how do you handle the players' disappointment in terms of missing out on selection? They are often players that are used to being number one in their club side and the national team and they might come on a Lions tour and be number two or number three. It's pretty tough emotionally for some of them.

It's how they prepare and cope with that disappointment and are supportive of the team. I have still got to make sure we are better at that on this tour.

Sound familiar? These are always the problems, but Gats knows as well as anyone how to cope with them, using guiding principles that stand the test of time.

Going back to 1997, to keep the balance we had a good night in a pub on the last night in Weybridge. We didn't go mad but had a few pints and just relaxed. We were getting on the plane the next day. We had had a good week, we had worked hard and got a lot from it, so we went for a drink at the end of the week. That was what we did on tour, too.

But things were a little different then, as Will Greenwood quite neatly summed up some time afterwards. 'Rugby had only just turned professional then,' he said. 'You watch the *Living with Lions* video of that tour and you see Keith Wood downing tequilas. These days it would be viewed as an Andrew Flintoff "pedalo"-type incident and be on the back page of the newspapers. But that was the way it was. It was a last hurrah of innocence and youth, the Corinthian spirit.'

The players' vow to continue the bonding in South Africa was duly carried out in the form of a players' court. Keith Wood was at the heart of much of the fun on tour – as well as much of the passion on the field, too – and he even became my personal barber when shaving my head after we had gone 2-0 up in the series. While some of the players were having short haircuts before the tour, I had said that I would have my hair cropped too if we won the series. So as soon as we did, the likes of Austin Healey and Matt Dawson were reminding me of my pledge. I could not back down!

Wood was the obvious choice as judge of the court. His clerk was Ieuan Evans. Rob Wainwright was the prosecution lawyer, while Mark Regan was in charge of the defence and Tim Stimpson was the fines master.

Dai Young, Simon Shaw and Tom Smith were chosen as the henchmen. It produced some fantastic moments.

The cameramen for the *Living with Lions* video were with us in Weybridge, following our every movement. Sales of the video were incredible and it attracted non-rugby folk as well as avid rugby watchers. As its blurb says: 'This film is unique, it is more than just a sports documentary. It is a deeply moving, often romantic and passionate study of men. It is an insight into a world rarely observed, "a world where legends begin".'

It captured the mood of the tour magnificently, from the rousing speeches to the agonies and dramas of injured players like Doddie Weir, Rob Howley and Will Greenwood, to a very different type of agony for John Bentley when he had waited up all night for his letter and then found that he had not been selected for the first Test, to the singing of our adopted tour anthem, Oasis' 'Wonderwall' (even I knew the words to it by the end), and to those hilarious court sessions conducted by judge Wood.

What the video did best, though, was portray the importance of the Lions. Nothing beats it. And the presence of the cameramen did not affect the environment; they knew their boundaries and limits. They would switch off the cameras when asked to and were accepted as part of the wider set-up.

There was none of that in 1989, but we did have an exceptional environment, with much of that down to Clive Rowlands as manager. You can only create the correct environment if you have a clear direction from all concerned at the top. That comes from the coaches, the manager and the captain. Clive certainly showed the way in that respect.

You learn a lot as you go along because everyone is open, which can trigger a different line of thinking. That used to excite me more than anything else, because on a Lions tour you have the best players and the best minds, so you can delve into a real depth of what I call 'collective intelligence'.

However, you have to make sure all that intelligence is brought out and utilised. There were certainly tours in 1977 and 1993 when that did not happen. The chemistry and environment were never quite right on those trips. You need open minds but total support.

Clive was not only a brilliant manager, he was a brilliant man manager too. He knew when to raise the bar. He knew when to pull players up; he knew when to let it go a bit. Most of all, he knew when my assistant Roger Uttley and I were under pressure and when we needed to relax a bit. Often before dinner he would say 'I need a meeting in my room' and the beer would be out ready and we would sit down, relax and just talk rugby.

That was how Clive was all tour. He could recognise when players might need picking up, and when they might need the pressure taken off a little bit. He could be tough too, even on Robert Jones, who was his son-in-law at the time, to make sure he delivered.

He just had a great feel for it. Fran Cotton was the same in 1997, as indeed were Geoff Cooke in 1993 and Gerald Davies in 2009. They were clever at recognising whether players needed support or needed to be challenged.

At the very first meeting in Oatlands, Fran had given an excellent speech about how everyone should behave, paving the way for those 'Lions Laws' in fact, but above all stressing that there should be no cliques because there had been cliques in New Zealand in 1993 and that had obviously proved to be very problematic.

Notice the similarities with Clive, who wrote this after the 1989 tour: 'It soon became obvious that team spirit had been fostered at an early stage and that each and every member of the party was willing, indeed was anxious, for this to be retained. Rory Underwood was appointed accommodation officer with a brief that the same two players were not to share a room throughout the tour with the exception of the pre-Test evening. This rule can prove vitally important on tour when the formation of cliques can prove a hindrance to community spirit.'

Like Clive, Fran knew his role and knew how to perform it. As Martin Johnson said of Fran: 'He was very good at understanding the sensitivities of the players. Often you didn't even really notice him lurking in the background, but he was very sharp at picking up on the little things that matter. He was in a good position as well. As a former player himself, no current player could turn around and say: "What do you know? You haven't been through this. You don't know what it is like." Fran had done all this and more.'

Clive was really good at giving me space and just talking. Even before we went, Clive had made his mark and showed why he was such a good manager.

I was still teaching at the time at Fir Tree Middle School in Leeds. They had been very good to me over the years there, allowing me time off to play for Scotland and later to coach. But a new headmaster had come in and brought with him a different attitude. I could do my coaching but it would have to be without pay. It meant we were struggling because I did have to take a lot of time off, and I do have to say that the Lions' daily allowance of £1.25 a day did not exactly solve the financial riddle at the time.

So Judy decided to take a full-time honours degree, and just before the 1989 tour she had to complete a particularly difficult teaching practice. There was a lot of pressure, with our two young children, and at school too. I remember one Lions meeting that had been scheduled in Cardiff but I couldn't leave home until we had sorted Judy's preparation for the teaching practice the next day. She had so much to do and it was getting on top of her. So we sat there and went through it, and then I got in the car in the early hours to drive to Cardiff.

Clive knew something was up, and some time afterwards he called a Lions meeting over Easter. My first reaction was to think: 'Oh no, how do I tell Judy that I am going to be away again?' And then he said that the meeting was in Tenby. He said it would take a while to get there but added: 'By the way, the Lions know it is a Lions meeting but what they don't know is that I have booked a room for you, Judy and the kids, and I have booked it for four days.'

It was indeed a long, long journey in my old Ford Capri, especially with the Easter traffic. But it was worth it. I think we actually had five days in Tenby. On the first night Clive came with his wife Margaret. We had dinner, a few drinks and a really good chat about the Lions and where we were and what we needed to do. And then he said: 'That's it for the Lions chat, that's the official bit over, now just enjoy yourselves.' He said to the manager of the hotel: 'Look after them.' The bill went to the Lions because we had had a Lions meeting.

That is the beauty of someone who can read a situation and make the necessary changes. When someone goes out of his way to smooth over any problems, even if they seem incidental to others, you know that you will have the correct environment in place. People underestimate that sometimes.

It was the same when we got to Australia. Clive had arranged for us to stay in five-star hotels rather than the ones allocated to us, as we knew they were not brilliant from a recent England tour there. Roger Uttley had been coach of that England tour in 1988, so, as our first game of the tour was in Perth, Clive asked Roger about the hotel we had been allocated, and when Roger gave it the thumbs down he asked what the best hotel in the area was. 'The Burswood Casino and Country Club,' said Roger.

'Leave it with me,' said Clive. That became one of his favourite sayings on tour (as well as 'the badge is getting bigger'), and, crucially, if he said it, he did get the matter sorted.

Here he personally changed all the reservations so that everyone stayed at the Burswood. The Australians hated the fact that we were being treated to such luxury. But we walked in and it was the first time I could remember on a Lions tour everyone thinking and indeed saying: 'This is the best.' The players could not believe it.

You have to remember that we still had to fly by economy class in those days. Even though it was the second recommendation on Clive Rowlands' tour report afterwards that 'the standard of air travel should be improved from economy class to club class', it was not until 1997 that we flew business class. There was a lovely touch from Virgin Airlines on the way home from that tour when they changed the V of their logo on the tail of the plane into a victory salute.

But this was a five-star place. Suddenly the impact on the players and everything we were doing was really positive. We were thinking: 'This is going to be right.' It was no coincidence that we then won the game against Western Australia 44–0.

Clive was excellent at taking the pressure off and making sure the environment was right, and I learnt a big lesson there. If the players know that you have gone out of your way to get things right, you already have everyone thinking differently in the first week. When you are on a seven-week tour or the like, that is vital.

We even had Clive doing some on-field stuff with the players before the tour. He had been a scrum half, of course, and it seemed natural that he should help his son-in-law Robert Jones and Scotland's Gary Armstrong as they did some passing and box kicking work in one of our training sessions at London Irish.

I couldn't resist a joke, though. Clive is well remembered for the Wales versus Scotland match at Murrayfield in 1963 when there were a remarkable 111 lineouts in the match. You could kick straight to touch outside your 22 in those days and Clive did that quite often it seems, as Wales won 6–0, with a penalty from full back Grahame Hodgson and a drop goal from Clive himself.

'I was never at any time tempted to open the game up and let my backs make the running,' said Clive afterwards. 'That's what Scotland were praying we'd do.' His name will always be synonymous with that game and that number of lineouts, so I could not help shouting across at Jones and Armstrong:

'Don't let him get too involved, otherwise you will have 111 lineouts!'

It was good, though, to get Clive on the field. In 1989 the schedule was a lot less crowded so we had a bit more time before the tour. I asked if I could see the squad on two week-ends before we got together and that was what I was granted. So we met at London Irish and trained there. It gave Clive, Roger and me the chance to talk to the players about what we wanted to do.

The game was still amateur then, though, so I wanted the squad to work hard on their fitness levels. I seconded Rex Hazeldine to help. Rex, who is famous for his rugby fitness work and has written books on the subject, was at Loughborough University and beginning to help with the England team at the time. I wanted to do it scientifically, not just simply say that the players had to run further or faster , so Rex put some tests and programmes together.

On our first weekend of tests, some of the players did very poorly and I have to say that it was mainly the Welsh players (there were seven of them in the original 30-man party). They looked very unfit, and I think it frightened them. Ieuan Evans said to me afterwards that the best wake-up call they got was that weekend.

I go back to Willie John McBride in 1974 and that pre-tour speech. In a way I was trying to convey something similar, saying to the players: 'If you commit to wearing that jersey you have got to be in the best shape you have ever been in in your life.' I mentioned this in my tour report and said that I had reminded the players that 'fitness had to be taken for granted in our team development'.

I had taken aside some of the Scottish boys (there were nine of them in the party) and we had done some extra training beforehand. I knew they were fit and they actually showed the Welsh boys up. At that time we had a very confident group of Scottish players. I had told them I wanted them to take the lead in the fitness stakes. That was the way we were trying to play anyway, with a very fast and high-tempo game.

Mind you, it probably tells you a lot about what the game was like in those days if I tell you what happened to Wade Dooley. He had to miss one of the testing days because he was at his grandfather's funeral. So when he arrived, the rest of the squad were already at the pub. They made him down two pints of beer and then do the bleep test. He actually got a very good score!

But in general I wanted to give the players some answers to their fitness concerns. So Rex gave them detailed individual programmes, saying that if they followed these in the next month they would be in the right shape once the tour arrived. Two weeks later we did the same tests and you could already see the improvements.

In 1993 we did not have as much time to prepare. 'As in 1989 I felt it was imperative to have a separate training weekend together,' I wrote in my report. 'But this proved very difficult to organise and ultimately we had to release players to play in league games on the Saturday of our get-together.'

We were at Weybridge again and again we did some testing with Rex Hazeldine involved, especially speed and reaction work. The theme of the training was pace and continuity, because those were two things that I did not think New Zealand would expect from us. As I wrote in my report:

A number of reports which I gleaned from New Zealand suggested that we were capable only of playing set-piece rugby, and would not be quick enough to adapt to the physical intensity. Consequently I felt that from the word go we had to look at tactically the shape of the game we wanted to develop as a group and the avenues we wanted to pursue, which would break the perception of 'British rugby'.

In training we devised a pattern for carrying ball into contact, what roles the support players had and the specific jobs the first, second, third or more players arriving had. We also differentiated between reaction to ball in hand and ball on the ground, but made no allowances for any upright positions. Everything we did had to be aggressive, powerful and driving forward. The more we practised the better we had to be at it so that, although it might not be second nature in these early practices, it would become second nature by the time it mattered in a Test match.

We also had those 'teams within teams'. 'I also divided the squad into six teams, with each team having a captain,' I wrote. 'These captains were experienced players and I felt that we could then have separate captains' meetings, if there were any particular discussions to have as the tour progressed.'

Sadly, now most of what I can recall really about the preparation for that tour is the wrangling and subsequent reaction over selection. The environment created on that trip was not good. You only have to read the comments of England flanker Peter Winterbottom to know that.

'It was very unfortunate that the tour party split in two,' he said in *Behind the Lions*. 'You felt for some of the boys in the midweek side, because quite a few of their team-mates didn't do the shirt justice. Some of them had given up. The key to a successful Lions tour is you have to have quality players, but you also have to have team spirit running right through it. Whether you are in the Test side or not, everyone has to pull in the same direction. In 1997 Geech and Fran Cotton had clearly identified that non-Test players had to pull their weight, and before the tour they got the guys to say before they left how they would contribute if they didn't make the Test side. In 1983 and 1993 we didn't do that, and the Waikato and Hawke's Bay matches in 1993 [losing 38–10 and 29–17] were embarrassing.'

By 2009 the scheduling had become ridiculous, and it has not improved since. The last game played in the domestic season was at the end of the week after we had to come together. That was how it was for Warren Gatland going to Australia in 2013 too and how it will be going to New Zealand in 2017.

Nowadays you simply do not get the chance to have every player with you before you depart – not for training anyway. Just for 'Messy Monday' maybe. That was what I had asked for in 2009 and ended up getting (or nearly did) – that the whole squad should come together on the Monday before we flew out on the following Sunday.

Leinster and Leicester were playing in the Heineken Cup final in Edinburgh on 23 May 2009. There were five Leinster players in the squad – Gordon D'Arcy, Rob Kearney, Luke Fitzgerald, Brian O'Driscoll and Jamie Heaslip – and two from Leicester – Harry Ellis and Tom Croft. And Northampton were in the Challenge Cup final against Bourgoin at the Twickenham Stoop that weekend. They had one player selected in the Scotland prop Euan Murray.

Because two of the three Test matches in South Africa were to be played at high altitude, I had planned to take the squad for some high-altitude training to Granada in Spain, at the foot of the Sierra Nevada mountains and almost 750 metres above sea level, but it proved impossible because of the unavailability of so many players and I cancelled it.

But at least I got that agreement from the committee to get them all there at our camp at England's training base at Pennyhill Park in Bagshot, Surrey, on the Monday before we left. I called it 'Messy Monday' because it meant we could get all the messy stuff out of the way: we could get the paperwork done, all the organisation, the photos and all the kit distributed, even if the players didn't have to take it all with them afterwards.

Still, one player did not make it and that one player not given permission to come was Northampton's Murray. That was disappointing, for us and for him, because he missed the tour photograph.

After lunch I spoke to the players about what we were about and what we planned to do during the week, so that even those who weren't going to stay and wouldn't be there knew what we would be doing. I had already told those players playing in the finals that they would not be involved in the first game against a Royal XV in Phokeng; they could use that first week in South Africa to get up to speed. I wanted every player to understand what the first two weeks of the tour were going to look like and what we were going to concentrate on.

What I had agreed with the other coaches was that we were not going to target individual provinces. We were going to aim towards getting a game in shape that we knew could challenge South Africa in the Test matches. And we did that from day one. In the very first session I went out and did some pattern work that we wanted to implement, just to give players the idea. I had gone through these plans with captain Paul O'Connell when I had seen him at his home in Ireland the month before.

This is what, verbatim, I reported in my post-tour analysis:

RUGBY – TACTICAL APPROACH

Wanted to play with WIDTH and sustain it through multi-phases

Move South Africa front 5 around the pitch

Work the ball from touchline to touchline

Work and recycle the players so that we had tight and wide attacking options, particularly after 3 phases

Every 4th phase would be able to attack with a full back-line plus two back-row forwards

Work a blitz defence

Be accurate through contact (on our feet) to allow the continuity into phases

We wanted to implement these developments through the first six games. The aim was to put together a game that would be effective against, and beat, South Africa.

RUGBY SPECIFIC

Preparing to beat South Africa from day one

Not separate tactics

Provinces unimportant

LIONS SHAPE AND APPROACH

Basis attack pattern and starter plays

Full lineout – 5 man lineout

Back → 4 set-ups → options

Introduced 1st session

All sessions filmed and TACTICS BOOK built up practically on the computer

Players can then download plays

LESS PAPER MEANT FEWER OPPORTUNITIES for information to be left around

Tactics introduced over 4 weeks so not overloaded by game one

Risk: some things not covered

Double sessions in 1st two weeks and:

Conditioning, but 35min to 70min max

3 phases to show stages in Tour

Build-up

2 weeks before Tests

Test weeks

Saturday morning sessions: Rustenburg, Bloemfontein, Johannesburg (Wednesday).

That final point was something we had done on the Saturday morning of the Tests in 1997, where Jim Telfer and I had taken the non-Test players for training sessions. We had some of the best and most enjoyable sessions then. The players were brilliant.

In 2009 a couple of things were key, firstly the fourth defender principle and secondly the use of one word to signify not just one move but a series of them. This meant that there wasn't a huge amount of communication required. One word might mean three moves and everybody could understand it. We would get to a touchline and then we would target where their fourth defender was, because South Africa tended to tighten up a bit in defence. If we could get to their fourth defender we knew that we would playing a quick ball and it would be going to the other wing.

It caught them out. They never sussed what we were doing. Every player knew that when we got to a fourth defender on the way back from the touchline that was where we were playing.

We had shape in the middle off the centres, we had a shape in the outside channels with the wing, outside centre, blindside wing and full back – we had two groups of four but we communicated with just one word. We used animals, so the calls were Lions, Pumas or Tigers. Each one was a specific shape or part of the field we were targeting. Under pressure the players did not have to think or talk a lot. We repeated it in training so often that it became instinctive.

In 1997 we used what was called a 'piss off!' move. Sorry about the language, but I'm afraid there is no other way of describing it. Once we had got the forwards in place, if we called a move the forwards got the ball, but if we called the move and 'piss off!' after it, then the forwards didn't get it.

The ball went either behind them or in front of them, depending on what the shape of attack was. It just meant that the forwards didn't get in the way. They were always in the right position but it was up to the decision-makers either to use them or to play across or behind them. Basically I was trying to get the 2009 tour as close to the one in 1997 as I could, but it was not easy logistically, especially in the preparation phase. It is interesting that in the *Behind the Lions* book the chapter about 2009 is entitled 'Old School Values'. I do not necessarily agree with that. I would say it was just about sticking to some principles that pull people together. Having a beer together is not necessarily old school.

We did not do the sort of pre-tour bonding we had done in 1997. We did not have much time, but I was also mindful of what had happened before the 2005 tour. There, some of the bonding exercises had not gone down well. For example, everyone was asked to do some painting as part of a mural, as well as acting out television sketches in front of the rest of the squad. I know a lot of players felt very uncomfortable about this and could not see the point of it.

I could understand their viewpoints. It was not quite the same as in 1997, which had been all about working together, and I think the players could see how that had translated to the rugby field. I am not so sure they saw that in 2005. You must never force team-building, in my view. Also in 1997, this sort of thing was new; now everybody does it. I genuinely think it has run its course.

In 2009 we did have an activities day on the Thursday and had planned to go sailing on the Solent. What I had set up was the use of 10 40ft sailing boats. I had picked 10 teams of players and staff and we were going to leave Pennyhill Park early in the morning to get down to Southampton. We would have about three hours of instruction in the morning and then a series of races in the afternoon as each team took control of their boat.

But on the Wednesday night we had the tour's gala farewell dinner at London's Natural History Museum. It went on quite late and we did not arrive back at Pennyhill Park until 12.30 a.m. A short while after we got back, there was a knock at the door of my room. Standing there was Paul O'Connell and a group of players and indeed coaching staff, because I remember Graham Rowntree being there too. Paul told me that the players were tired after a tough week and asked if there was any possibility that the sailing could be cancelled.

I said to him: 'Is that the general feeling amongst everyone?' He said it was, so I said that I would sort it. Bear in mind it was now about 12.45 a.m., but I still felt that I could call Louise Ramsay and ask her if she could organise for everything to be cancelled. Even though it was obviously a hassle for her and it would also cost the Lions a lot of money, she just said: 'Leave it with me.' That was typical of her and her wonderful attitude.

The one thing I did say to Paul and the others, though, was: 'You have obviously been talking in the bar so I'm giving you 15 minutes to get any players not already in the bar into the bar and we'll have a few drinks together before we go to bed.'

David Wallace, the Irish flanker, is apparently a very keen sailor, so he was probably the only one who was a little disappointed about the sailing. But everyone seemed to enjoy a few beers in the hotel bar and a singsong with Jamie Roberts and England centre Riki Flutey playing their guitars. And the next day everyone had a day off, with some playing golf, some going to Kempton races and others just using the spa facilities at the hotel.

'At the next training session you could sense the team spirit straight away,' said Martyn Williams. 'We clicked as a group from then on. I think that was as close to the magic formula of the three tours [2001, 2005 and 2009] I was involved in.'

It was the best thing we could have done in terms of team-building. And when the tour had finished and we were all saying our goodbyes, Paul O'Connell mentioned the incident to me. He said: 'It was at that moment that I realised what a responsibility I had as captain and how important it was that I made the correct decision.'

Something similar happened on the actual tour, but on that occasion Paul made a decision with which he was not quite so comfortable. It was after the second Test in Pretoria. It had clearly been a devastating defeat and the series was lost at 2–0. For the Sunday and Monday there was already a safari trip to Entabeni booked. On the Saturday night after the match I said to the players: 'We are not training until Wednesday now. You can do what you want but when you arrive at training on Wednesday I want you ready to win a Test match because we are going to leave South Africa as winners.' I wasn't going on the safari drive because Judy had come out for the second Test and we had already decided that we would spend some time in Johannesburg.

There were two buses booked to go on the safari and they duly left on the Sunday morning. But some time after they had left, Paul started talking to those on his bus and it was decided that they should turn back. The other bus carried on and I am told they had an amazing time, staying in top-quality lodges, going on some stunning game drives while having some beers and singsongs in the evenings. As soon as the bus had turned around Paul questioned his decision. I know for a fact that he regrets it very much and that it actually kept him awake at night afterwards.

'Up until then there had been a real feeling of togetherness in the camp that wasn't quite there in New Zealand four years earlier,' he wrote in his autobiography. 'Friendships were made that I know will endure. As head coach Ian had done really well in making it work with a much smaller squad. I was sitting beside Stephen Jones, and our bus hadn't gone a hundred yards before I started doubting my decision. "Are we splitting the tour a bit here?" Stephen was a really good pro and he was asking himself the same question.'

It was not a big thing. Those who didn't go – about 12 of them – realised they had made a mistake and should have carried on. There was no break in the squad. Brian O'Driscoll has said publicly how much better it was than his previous tours in 2001 and 2005. 'Without a shadow of a doubt the 2009 tour was the happiest,' he said. 'It was the most enjoyable for sure. We had such a harmonious and tight bond.'

I have said already that we probably should have picked Simon Shaw for the first Test, but I think his recollection of waiting to be selected for the second Test demonstrates that we had the right environment and attitude on this trip:

Before the team was announced, my room-mate [the Scotland lock] Nathan Hines, who was also hoping to get the Test No. 4 jersey, was cited for what was deemed to be a dangerous tackle and banned for two weeks. Of course, you don't hope something like that happens, but a little bit of luck in your favour can create a huge opportunity. When Nathan came back from the disciplinary hearing, I said 'bad luck, mate', and he just congratulated me on my selection. I don't think I had ever spoken to Nathan before the tour and there we were sharing a bathroom . . .

It just summed up what is so great and special about a Lions tour. The friendships you make last a lifetime, particularly from a tour like the 2009 Lions.

Every one of the other second rows came up and shook my hand after the team announcement, and it showed just how much we were backing each other.

This kind of behaviour was a repeat of the 1997 tour and the 'Lions Laws' on it.

As ever when I was in charge, we had a players' committee on that tour in 2009, consisting of Paul O'Connell, Phil Vickery, Stephen Jones, Brian O'Driscoll, Martyn Williams and Ronan O'Gara. Hines was in charge of the room allocations. Mostly he would put every player's name in a hat, and down at the front of the team bus Gerald Davies or I would pick the names out and announce who was with whom. It caused lots of noise, suspense and mickey-taking. Sometimes they even did it by bingo calls or by numbers on a dartboard.

But it was good fun, and, on a more serious note, was all about feeling you were creating your own special environment. This can be done in different ways, but it is all about pulling in the same direction.

There were all sorts of other committees and responsibilities for players. For instance, the Harlequins and England wing Ugo Monye was the travel guide, so that he had to swot up on every place we were visiting and tell the rest of the squad all about it when we arrived. He was brilliant at it.

It was a role apparently taken up by the Welsh scrum half, Mike Phillips, who was superb for me in 2009 and was very close to my player of the tour, in Australia in 2013, along with the England prop Dan Cole. I hear that when the squad reached

Melbourne, Phillips grabbed the microphone on the team bus one morning to remind the squad that singer Kylie Minogue is from Melbourne.

'There was once a rumour that we went out together,' he said. 'It was huge global news at the time and a reporter asked Kylie: "Is it right that you go out with the rugby international superstar Mike Phillips?" To which Kylie replied: "I should be so lucky, lucky, lucky . . ." Very good.

Euan Murray had to tell a joke every day in 2009, while the Irish lock Donncha O'Callaghan and the Welsh No. 8 Andy Powell were the bus announcers and a laugh a minute at the same time. What a pair of characters. Riki Flutey and Jamie Roberts, as you would expect after their guitar-playing antics at Pennyhill, were in charge of the music, and the entertainments committee consisted of Simon Shaw, England flanker Joe Worsley, Lee Mears and Ireland wing Tommy Bowe.

There was a fines committee that collected an awful lot of money, about 40,000 rand in fact, which was about £5,000 then. There were simple fines for misdemeanours such as lateness (300 rand), wearing the wrong kit (300 rand), a mobile phone ringing during a meeting (300 rand) or a yellow card in a game (500 rand).

If you did not want to pay any money immediately, you could throw a dice (and I know this was repeated on the 2013 tour). So if you threw the number one your fine was scrapped. For number two you had a leg wax. For number three you had to grow a moustache, for number four you were given 300 rand in credit, for number five you had a spray tan, and for number six you had to pay double. I don't think anyone will ever forget what Paul 'Bobby' Stridgeon looked like after his spray tan. He did it himself! His back didn't look too clever!

The 'Bobby Cup' was something we had had at Wasps and it became a crucial part of this tour. As I wrote afterwards in my report: "The 'Bobby Cup" (a feature from Wasps) was the most popular meeting, by far.' Bobby is an effervescent character, whose party piece is to grab a lamppost with two hands and support himself horizontally. That takes some doing!

The cup was a metal camping mug bought in Bloemfontein and was presented to the person whom he deemed to have done something outstanding during the week. It always caused much hilarity, and I know it was a tradition that was continued on the 2013 tour, even if it was presented for on-field exploits then.

In 2009 the players chose to give the money collected in fines to two charities, but not before they had paid for a holiday for our kit man, Patrick O'Reilly, and his wife. I thought that was a wonderful gesture and further confirmation of the environment we had created.

As an overall operation, in the way everything worked together, this tour was the best in which I was involved. It was the perfect antidote to the troubles of 2005. Unity was the key word: it was about the players being the centre of everything, about them travelling together and being together.

In New Zealand in 2005 there had been two buses on tour, with the players split between them. In 2009 there were still two buses, but all the players were on one bus, and all the coaches and management staff were on the other. It was a crucial difference.

This was why we had Guy Richardson as logistics officer. It was the first time the Lions had made such an appointment, but I thought it was hugely important that we had someone like Guy, who could work 24 hours, or at the very least 12 hours, ahead of the rest of us. That was his job: to make sure that everything that could be collected was collected the day before. Lorries then drove across South Africa through the night with tonnes and tonnes of baggage and equipment.

This is what I am talking about when I say 'teams within teams'. In any organisation it is all about the people involved, at every level, and you have to trust them and trust them to do their jobs. We could do that. We had charter flights so that the buses would often pull up next to the planes on the airport tarmac and then there would be buses waiting for the plane at the other end.

When the players arrived in their rooms at that next desti-nation, their luggage and kit were already there. The luggage lorries would have arrived already. It was something we had begun in 1997. This was when we thought up the idea of two separate lorries, so that there was one set of kit and equipment where we were and another already on the way to the next venue. Wherever we went to train the field was laid out and the kit was there, all set out exactly as we wanted it.

Nigel Horton, the former England second row, who had been an uncapped Lion in 1977, was involved in that as a representative of Predator, the squad's training equipment manufacturer. With his expertise on scrummaging machines, he was involved again in 2005.

The players didn't have to worry about anything. All they were carrying was one bag, their hand luggage for the plane. That was when you would see them in hotel lobbies and airport lounges on laptops looking at some of the training or the games. It started to build conversations and camaraderie.

Everything was streamlined for the players. Everyone knows how tiring and stressful travelling can be, fretting about where bags are and whether they will arrive. But that was all taken out of the equation for the players. They did not have to worry at all. With Louise Ramsay also so efficient as operations manager, it made for a very slick set-up. As she had been on the 2005 tour, Louise understood what we wanted because she had seen the outcomes and ramifications of some of the things that had happened in New Zealand.

In 2008 I had travelled to South Africa with Gerald Davies to watch them play New Zealand, as well as look at all the facilities and hotels. Louise had compiled shortlists for hotels and other facilities that we looked at. I was still director of rugby at Wasps but it was really a sabbatical year so I could concentrate on the Lions and do some planning. I was meeting Louise and many of the other staff on an almost weekly basis in the build-up. That is how rigorous and detailed we were in our planning.

In fact we had two other visits to South Africa, the first when Wales were playing two Tests there in June and the last when all the heads of the various departments – coaching, medical, conditioning, analysis and logistics – were there. As I detailed in my tour report:

> I wanted, as well as meetings in the UK, three visits to South Africa, with each one having key objectives.
>
> *First visit (June 08)* – Follow Wales and Welsh coaches [Wales were playing two Tests there that summer] and initial appraisal of hotels and training options.
>
> *Second visit (August 08)* – Assessment of South Africa rugby (2 x Tri-Nations games) and second appraisal of hotels and training facilities – main choice made.
>
> *Third visit (January 2009)* – All heads of sections. A dry run of the tour with 'heads' to confirm facilities from all viewpoints. This was very successful and I believe vital.
>
> The main programme and travel were signed off by early February 2009.

In every hotel in South Africa I wanted a big room where the players could have their own base. That was our village, as it were. You knew that if someone wasn't in his room then that was where he would be. You ended up mixing more and more with players you did not necessarily know that well. If you wanted some privacy you went to your room and that was respected.

We got that big room in almost every hotel and we made sure that the team room was the heartbeat of the tour party. In each hotel it was big enough for us to eat together and to have everything else in there: televisions, computer games, dartboards, table tennis tables, plus all the equipment for physio-therapy and analysis. Everything happened in that one room. That had not always been possible in 1997 because the hotels were simply not big enough. Everything we talked about went up on sheets around the room. Whenever we decided upon something it went up on the wall on a sheet, and all those sheets travelled with us.

We also ensured that the press were welcome in our hotels. If they met players in the foyer or had a coffee with them, that was fine by us, it was not a problem. Alastair Campbell had said in 2005 that this could no longer be done. The game was too professional, he said, and a good number of the journalists agreed with him too.

But in 2009 we achieved it. The feedback from the press was very positive. Gerald Davies obviously helped in this regard because of his previous position in the press as a writer for *The Times*. The 1977 tour was an eye-opener for me in terms of the relationship with the press, and therefore I have always tried to accommodate them and get on with them, despite the obvi-ous changes over time.

In 2009 you would walk into a press conference and there would be some 250 people and 50 cameras in the room. Suddenly I was thinking: 'This is different, especially compared with 1989!' You could count the number of British press on one hand then.

Even in 1997 at the bonding camp at Weybridge I had made sure that we had had an open day with the press, and we got David Norrie of the *News of the World* and John Taylor of the

Mail on Sunday to speak to the squad about their roles and what the players could expect from them. I always thought it good that the players saw and heard the sort of pressures journalists work under. I think a lot of them struggle to see things from the journalists' point of view, and it was very educational in that respect.

So in 2009 we made sure that we knew what the press wanted, and that they knew what we wanted. Gerald, media officer Greg Thomas and I met with three or four of the more senior journalists before the tour to talk about how we could operate together, and we found a lot of common ground.

There was a good relationship between us on the tour and I think that was reflected in the fact that at the end of it I presented a Lions jersey and a raincoat, both signed by the squad, to Peter Jackson, who was retiring as the *Daily Mail* correspondent after many, many years of service.

On the Sunday that we departed for South Africa I had wanted all the families to be there with us at Pennyhill Park, so they had been invited for lunch and to spend the afternoon at the hotel before we left for the airport that evening. We also invited the press to be there for afternoon tea. We did about 20 minutes of formal interview stuff but then we made them welcome to hang around, mingle and talk off the record. Some of them could not quite believe it, I think.

Then on the second night in South Africa we put on a joint press and Lions management quiz night. We had food and beer together and it was a really good night. A tour environment is created by everyone on the tour, but what you have to remember is that not all the people there are Lions. It is not just about the Lions players and management, it is much wider than that, and the press is very much a part of it.

My view is that if you take any animosity out of the environment you are probably two thirds of the way to having the right environment. That has always been really important to me. It gave me a clarity – I felt I was doing things that gave the Lions the best chance of succeeding, because, if everyone is onside, then the Lions have a fighting chance of the wider environment being right. And the press were very important to that wider environment.

I come back to the concept of collective intelligence, where everyone can put forward their ideas, not just players and coaches. I had had separate sessions with the British press in 1989 and that was what I wanted to do in 2009. I wanted to be open, and I think I was. As I wrote in my post-tour report:

Staying flexible was, I believe, key, as was our collective honesty with the press and I am also convinced that the decision to allow press to share our hotel (this was so important a principle to me but I also knew it was a risk), but with Gerald [Davies] and Louisa [Cheetham] then working on a protocol, a level of trust was generated from the outset.

I am also aware another head coach might be totally against it.

Also the monthly meetings I had with Louise [Ramsay] and Louisa proved very important in establishing key tour working principles, from a rugby perspective.

There is no doubt Gerald being 'one of them' helped enormously because of the respect with which he is held.

I believe it is still worth evolving a SQUAD/PRESS protocol in the future.

Mixing coaches/management/players up for press conferences gives variety and takes the pressure off.

I am sure our less formal, but open approach leads to a stronger press relationship and in this vein – TEA with the LIONS – FAMILY & PRESS, I was keen to see work well.

We wanted to avoid what had happened in 2005, when it became a fight about who could get one over on the other. Clive Woodward did not want the media staying in the same hotels, so the media then saw it as a challenge to get into those hotels. It created an unnecessary division. It was a battle of wills all the time.

We tried to let the press know what was going on, so James Robson would do press conferences to give updates on injuries and other members of the backroom staff were always available for interview if required, even Dave Campbell, the chef.

Dave was a superb part of the set-up. He had been chef to the England team since 2001 and had been on the 2005 Lions tour. He was not only a brilliant chef – he was always cooking in hotel kitchens, which must be an interesting dynamic knowing the way most chefs operate – but a brilliant judge of a mood too. So if we had had a bad week he would open up what he called his 'Phat Phuckers' café and put on fish, chips and mushy peas for everyone, with a special chocolate biscuit for dessert.

It would change the mood in an instant. The chicken, pasta and salad were suddenly out of the window and you could see the players being lifted. As I said in my report: 'Dave Campbell became available at late notice, but was another key appointment. The menus were VARIED and TASTY and occasionally "Phat Phuckers". This again added significantly to the players' mental as well as physical well-being.'

Yes, there is certain food you need to eat for performance but actually one's frame of mind is twice as important. Dave recognised that. In an interview with Paul Rees of the *Guardian*, he said:

I served up fish and chips on Monday, and the biscuit, in which I am using the highest quality milk chocolate, is a treat many have been talking about for days. The good effects of the diet they have been on here has taken such a grip that allowing the players a few favourites – and not all of them take them up – as the tour nears its conclusion will not set them back in any way.

I did not want it to get too repetitive with the chicken otherwise they would have started sprouting feathers. I have given them ostrich five times this trip because it is tasty and healthy but I have drawn the line at cooking warthog, which is a popular dish here!

I always give them a large choice of salads and the emphasis is on flavour as well as healthy eating. A side-effect is that the management have all seen the benefits of the diet. They have all lost weight and Gerald Davies is 5kg (11lb) lighter than when we arrived.

My job is to ensure the food is cooked in the way the players are used to, because they do things very differently here in South Africa. For example, even in the coastal cities, fish does not feature highly and it is very much meat-oriented here.

I like to give the players as much choice as possible and I can truly say that this has been the best bunch I have ever cooked for. There have been no complaints and plates are left empty.

Campbell was doing his job and ensuring that the players not only behaved like professionals but also felt good about themselves.

Others had to go to even greater lengths to ensure that. For instance, when we went to Phokeng, near Rustenburg, for the first game of the tour, there were no facilities for gym work despite the fact that we had purchased our own equipment for the tour. There were just school gyms. Compare that to when the football World Cup was in South Africa in 2010 and the England team had use of a £2m centre in that area.

We were staying in a colonial hotel with huge lawns in front of it. So how about an outdoor gym there? Paul Stridgeon and Craig White, our two fitness staff, thought so. But not just that, they also decided to set it up themselves. So they got all the equipment delivered in a lorry and put it out on the lawns so that when the players walked to breakfast it was there ready.

There were no four walls but everything was there. That was what the strength and conditioning boys had done. It might not have been a state-of-the-art gym but everything that was on the lawn would have been *inside* a state-of-the-art gym. What the players could see was people being outstanding at what they were doing and ensuring that nothing was second best, and that had a huge, visible knock-on effect on them.

Everybody contributed in 2009. We may not have got the result of the series quite right, but we certainly got the environment right. In a way that made the tour successful, especially after the problems in 2005.

There was a comment from Brian O'Driscoll afterwards that particularly pleased me. He said that on a lot of other tours, he would often enter a room and be a little choosy about whom he sat next to. On this one he felt he could just breeze in and sit next to anyone because he knew he would feel comfortable. Or as Phil Vickery said: 'I can honestly say that I have never been on a tour with so many good men.'

I would have no hesitation in agreeing.

KEY WORDS

- Environment makes people, people make the environment
- Games within the game
- Manage disappointment
- Test players help midweek team
- Lions laws
- Collective intelligence
- Badge getting bigger
- Teams within teams

1997 South Africa, First Test
We worked hard in 1997 to ensure that the environment was right
and this was immediate confirmation that we had done just that.

HEROIC LIONS POUNCE LATE

South Africa 16 British Lions 25

Dazzling Dawson breaks Springbok hold

Stephen Jones at CAPE TOWN

TRY ON TRY, joy on joy. The Lions were trailing by a point inside the final 10 minutes of the win-or-die first Test. Then they erupted in glory, with a boom-boom of tries. The first was a wonderfully cheeky individual effort from Matt Dawson, titanic at scrum-half; the other an exuberant team try touched down by Alan Tait down the left wing when the match was in injury time. Tait ran around behind the posts in a wild arc of celebration.

He was not the only man celebrating. Cape Town is South Africa's most wonderful city, but last night the city was taken over by thousands of celebrating Lions supporters.

The solid blocks of red in the crowd, chequered with mini-forests of Union Jacks, won a decisive victory in the shouting stakes. They roared the Lions home and roared them off the field at the end as the celebrations began.

It was 16–15 to South Africa and the game clock had ticked around to 72 minutes when the Lions put down a scrum 22 metres out. Dawson seized the ball, sprinted clean past Ruben Kruger down a narrow blindside, and headed for the corner. The cover defence came across in numbers, Dawson held the ball up as if to flip a high pass inside, and his dummy rooted the cover to the spot.

Dawson held, ran on, treated himself to a little high-stepping routine and scored in glorious isolation, sealing a staggering few weeks during which he has risen from the ranks of fortunate selections to world class.

That made it 20–16 and the longest eight minutes in the career of any Lions player began to tick by. But here the thunder of the Lions' tackling took a hand. All match long, Tim Rodber and the back row, and Scott Gibbs and the inside backs, had dumped the Springboks back on the seat of their pants. Henry Honiball at fly-half was neutralised and Andre Joubert was given blind alleys in which to run. The pretty patterns that they tried to weave behind the scrum usually ended in a jolting tackle.

Having scented blood, the Lions

came again with the match in injury time. They almost pushed South Africa over for a try that would have turned rugby history on its head. But Rodber and Dawson set up a movement with a sniping burst close to the scrum.

When the ball came back, Gregor Townsend sent Gibbs blasting at the heart of the home midfield. The ball came back again and a high pass from Rodber sent Neil Jenkins on his way, to make the try for Tait. Game, set and Test.

South Africa will be back. They will fight like crazed rhinos on Saturday in Durban. Joost van der Westhuizen was masterly, especially with his wicked, teasing kicks. But, before the end yesterday, they were bedraggled and out of ideas. Their camp will come under intense pressure. The heavier Springbok pack had generally squeezed the Lions for possession, but in the final 15 minutes, the smaller Lions were shoving them back.

In this respect it was a triumph for the backroom. The Lions picked their fastest team. A fast game was never really on the cards once the weather broke and the wind howled around the stands and the surrounding mountains. But they took a tremendous risk with the choices at prop and lock. The Lions pack never dominated, there was never a stream of quick possession. But they held on with vast courage.

Tom Smith is so quiet that it takes a major effort for him to say boo to a goose. But he and Paul Wallace took the brunt of the massive home front row and were still strong in the loose.

The remarkable Jeremy Davidson, shorter and lighter than your average lock, soared. Martin Johnson was everything you could wish a Lions captain to be. Dawson was superb, blending deft skills with hard edges. Jenkins kicked good goals in a wicked wind and made up in skills for what he lacked in pace. The red-dressed passion warmed a cold and blustery Cape day, and warmed British and Irish hearts.

There were sticky periods. After 24 minutes, with the extra muscle of the home forwards beginning to tell. South Africa won a lineout through Mark Andrews, one of two dire home locks. Hannes Strydom and Os du Randt barrelled through the Lions pack in unholy tandem and the massive du Randt scored.

But the Lions fought back after the try. They were back at 9-8 ahead at half-time and Jenkins put them 12-8 ahead with his fourth penalty early in the second half, as hopes rose. Then came the one defensive disaster. Honiball ran a slowish ball to his left, but Gibbs mistimed his tackle on Gary Teichmann. The South African captain merely bounced out of the tackle and sent Russell Bennett over for the try. It was the worst time for the Lions to concede a score.

It could have been worse later in the half when Kruger and Andre Venter sent Bennett over again down the left. However, Mr Hawke spotted the forward pass and the move was recalled. There was only a penalty apiece until the momentous closing stages, and then came Dawson and Tait for the tries of their lifetimes.

The tour caravan moves on to Bloemfontein in midweek. then to Durban for the second Test. There is still so much to do, but a fervent spirit now with which to do it. Historically, Test wins by the Lions have always been rare. This was one to savour for years to come.

4

KNOWING THE OPPOSITION

'One minute,' the French referee Didier Mené said to the New Zealand captain Sean Fitzpatrick. One minute remained of the Test in Pretoria between South Africa and New Zealand in 1996. New Zealand were winning 33–26. This was to secure their first-ever series victory in South Africa.

The Springboks had a lineout in New Zealand's 22. 'They do not score,' apparently Fitzpatrick said to his team.

South Africa win the lineout and spread the ball right. It goes loose and right wing Justin Swart runs back across field almost to the touchline, where the lineout had been. Flanker Ruben Kruger takes the ball on. Then his back-row colleague André Venter does the same. Then prop Os du Randt smashes into the All Black defence.

New Zealand are under serious pressure. A converted try will tie the scores and the series as well. They concede a penalty. South African scrum half Joost van der Westhuizen takes a quick tap penalty and is tackled into touch.

The New Zealanders have certainly not retreated 10m. Penalty try? No. Mené says that the penalty should be retaken. Replacement hooker James Dalton takes the tap penalty, with all his South African forwards around him ready for the drive. This is it, the last chance, one furious last chance. They go once and then twice, before another replacement Wayne Fyvie picks up and goes close to the line. He is stopped and the ball cannot be played.

Mené blows his whistle. The All Blacks have won: the match and the series. It is their first series win in South Africa.

Some arms go up in the air and there are some hugs, mainly amongst the All Black backs. But lying on the ground are Fitzpatrick, Zinzan Brooke and Michael Jones, three truly great forwards who have given every last bit of their strength, stamina and resolve to win this match and make history for their country in South Africa. As Fitzpatrick had instructed, the South Africans had not scored, but it had taken one almighty effort to ensure that. 'I can remember lying on the bottom of a ruck just thinking "please blow that final whistle",' said Fitzpatrick in his book, *Turning Point*.

'Just look at them, they are absolutely shattered,' said the commentator on the television. They were; they were utterly spent and exhausted. It took them an age to get to their feet. Before he did so Fitzpatrick pounded the turf with his fist in his weary elation.

Ever since I first saw this I thought it was a magnificent scene, one that encapsulated so brilliantly how tough it can be to win a Test series in South Africa. So I showed this one-minute video clip to the Lions squad of 1997. Indeed it was one of the first things I did when we met up for training at Weybridge. I showed it again in 2009, too.

In 1997 the names and memories were clearer in people's minds. I told the players that that was what they were going to have to go through if they were to beat South Africa. These were the lengths they would have to go to, the lengths that the likes of Fitzpatrick, Brooke and Jones had gone to. I was just letting them know that this was what they were in for, this was the approach we would have to have, and in a way yet again I was also thinking again of that chat from Willie John McBride before the tour in 1974.

As previously touched upon, I had been out in South Africa during that All Blacks tour. I had been there checking out facilities for the tour but I was also lucky enough to spend time in the All Black camp and I spoke with coach John Hart and captain Fitzpatrick.

It was a vital part of the 1997 tour. I had never been able to make such a trip before. To spend time with the All Blacks was immensely helpful, and I was able to put together a 20-page report not just on the tactical approach required to beat South Africa but also on all the off-field requirements as well.

I got some great advice from Hart. It was from him, and Fitzpatrick as well, that I got the idea of taking 35 players on tour rather than 30. Fitzpatrick in particular pointed out how beneficial it was for someone like him as hooker, because it meant you could take another hooker on tour and it would allow him to have a match off, whereas before he would have been required on the bench.

And I also took from Hart the idea that you should take all your own equipment with you on tour. By that I mean your own scrummaging machine, rucking and mauling machines, tackle bags and pads, even drinks bottles. That is what New Zealand had done and that is what we did in 1997 in South Africa, sending it all out by container ship and then having it transported around the country by lorry, as already explained. It gave us complete control over what we were doing and also a reassuring independence.

Hart also pointed out that they had checked and vetted every hotel and training facility beforehand. We made sure we did the same, and the manager of the tour Fran Cotton went to South Africa on a 12-day trip to facilitate that.

As I wrote in my report of the 1997 tour:

I cannot emphasise too greatly the value of my visit. The meeting with John Hart and his coaches gave me a valuable insight into the best way to organise and structure the tour from the availability of equipment to the policy used by the All Blacks at every hotel. The most significant points were that we should be as self-contained as possible, keeping ourselves in total control of all playing and practice equipment and also operating with 35 players rather than 30 to alleviate the additional pressure and stress on specialist positions, e.g. hooker and scrum half.

Similarly, the policy for hotel management, from team rooms to laundry, was invaluable, as was the suggestion that we only accepted travel by South African Airways, as they were the only ones large enough to deal with the amount of equipment associated with a touring party.

Lastly, my most valuable insight was to the games themselves. Having watched a match in Cape Town and then one in Durban between South Africa and the All Blacks, it left me in no doubt as to what we would have to do and how we would have to play if we were to succeed against the Springboks.

The fact that we knew from the word go what the playing philosophy had to be gave us the basis for the selection policy, in that we could then select the best type of player who could have the best chance of successfully carrying out the game plan. Selection undoubtedly was very important in producing a uniformity of purpose throughout the touring party.

It was so gracious of Hart to help me and it was typical of New Zealand rugby that he should have done that.

I think that one of the prime reasons why New Zealand are so good as a rugby nation is the amount of information they share between coaches. It helps, of course, that all their players and coaches are centrally contracted so there can be a united approach and way of thinking, but it begins long before the professional game is reached and it also extends to sharing it beyond New Zealand, as Hart showed.

New Zealand rugby has always been the same. The key is that every player in the country understands the game so well, and that is why they are so difficult to beat. Sometimes you might have a better team but the All Blacks might have a better understanding, and that can be crucial.

New Zealand have an interconnected process so that the strength of their system is knowledge shared down and player information shared upwards at each level and between levels. It is a process that flows both ways. When you share knowledge like that, you have got a very powerful coaching base from which to work.

People are working together, coordinating the development of players through the schools system, to their provincial rugby, right through to the All Blacks at the very top. There is a big emphasis on skill, and less on tactics, especially in the teenage years. It is a totally integrated system. Everyone knows where they stand in it, how the talent is nurtured, how the knowledge passed on, and throughout this all the rugby is very, very competitive.

All Blacks are created by the system and environment, not just by pulling on the jersey. That is why I love being in New Zealand, simply because they are so open in their thinking and talking. As a player, I remember when the 1978 All Blacks played against the North of England and I got invited on the team coach back to the hotel. I found players like Graham Mourie and Bruce Robertson so easy to speak to. They wanted to hammer you when you were on the field, but off the field they were open and friendly.

There was so much you could take on board. It was the same when talking to Steve Hansen in 2005 during the Lions tour. We met for a coffee and just chatted about rugby. He was very willing to talk about what he was doing and how he was doing it.

Likewise the invaluable time I spent pushing salt and pepper pots around a table for hours while talking with the likes of

Jim Telfer, Doug Morgan and Derrick Grant during my time coaching with Scotland.

That is where you evolve your ideas. It was in the amateur days but there has to be a place for it today. We did it when I was at Northampton and at Wasps, and, to be honest, it is the thing I miss most now – having that chance just to chat rugby and talk through things.

It is the rugby equivalent of what used to go on at Liverpool Football Club in the 1960s and 1970s, where they would have their 'boot room' chats under managers Bill Shankly and Bob Paisley. Do the rugby coaches of today get enough of that? I certainly think we should encourage them and give them opportunities to do so.

There is certainly not enough of this in the northern hemisphere, especially in England where coaches are so reluctant to talk to each other, mainly because the Aviva Premiership is such a cut-throat league with the pressures of relegation and the battle for European places. You have got to be able to learn from others and then develop your own philosophies which you can carry with you when you put a side on the field.

I think people are sometimes scared of sharing notes, which is crazy. For example, this is what Warren Gatland said after he had been announced as the coach for the 2017 Lions tour and it had also been revealed that he was going to stand down as Wales coach for the season before the tour: 'Hopefully there will be a chance for me to go and spend the day with the other national set-ups,' he said. 'People from the outside sometimes get a bit paranoid and talk about spying – it's nothing like that.'

Of course it isn't. Nobody will ever develop someone's knowledge in the same way. Nobody can copy exactly what you do because they can't know the logic and the thinking. What it might do is spark an idea in their head of the lines they want to take, but they will inevitably take it a different way.

I have always said that once you become a head coach you have to be a 'benevolent dictator'. You listen to everyone and everything, enjoy the conversations, but ultimately that should just give you a clarity about where you are taking the team. You make the final decisions.

In terms of my coaching career I was lucky that I coached at club level for three years and in between I coached Scotland under-20s, Scotland A and then became assistant coach at Scotland before being made head coach. By that time I had eight years of coaching behind me. I was assistant to Derrick Grant at Scotland and Jim Telfer was a selector, and to have that experience around me was very important. I was able to have great conversations with the two of them, and that was critical for me.

I have always had a thirst for learning and new knowledge, and that is where my years of teaching stood me in such good stead for coaching. I always remember being told just after starting teaching: 'After 20 years make sure you have got 20 years' experience, not one year's experience that has just been repeated 20 times.'

That is so true. As a player I always liked to read about opponents to find out as much as I could about them. So I used to find as many newspaper reports as I could, even when on tour. I used to enjoy the New Zealand newspapers, especially the writing of Terry McLean, the doyen of New Zealand rugby writers. He was like Norman Mair and Vivian Jenkins, such good writers and so interesting to read.

I also used to buy books about the All Blacks to discover more about how they operated. It was just about trying to get a feel for them and pick up little bits about them. I remember on the Lions tour in 1977 being in Christchurch and going around the second-hand bookshops because they were stacked full of rugby books. I enjoyed browsing through them and buying some of them. It gave me a really good insight into the All Blacks.

Even then as a player I was keen on analysis, and when I became a coach that just grew and grew. The coaches today with their paid analysts poring over every detail with digital equipment do not know how lucky they are. I had to make up my own analytical system. And this was to analyse a game live without any video equipment.

Whether I was watching the game live or as live on television I would have a clipboard. And on that I had my own system of marking a game. I could write down in my own shorthand what had happened so that I could interpret it later. So at a lineout, for instance, I would mark down a plus or minus sign to signify whether it was our ball or theirs, and then various signs for where it went to in the lineout, whether it was caught or tapped back, where it went to next, where the first breakdown was, who was in it, where the ball went next, either left or right (so that was another plus sign if it was going in the same direction or a minus sign for a change of direction).

The upshot was that afterwards I could actually plot and track the movement of a team. I would circle players that kept on showing up in the analysis. I also divided the field length-ways so that I could see how often a side got into the outside channels, whether they went up the middle of the field, whether they kept it short and who were the key players. All that was done with a pencil.

I would like to think that I was looking at new ground here. At the time Liverpool University were one of the first places to do sports analysis. Allan McNish, a coach I often spoke to while in Scotland, knew what I was doing and his daughter was on this course at Liverpool. They asked if they could come across to Leeds and see my work.

They then produced an analysis format for being able to record sport in general and I think his daughter ended up getting a first-class honours degree. It was something completely new. They helped me because they shared their findings with me. For a while Liverpool University were actu-ally ahead of everyone else on the subject of sporting analysis.

In terms of analysing matches and players on video, the first I had seen of this had been when Bill Dickinson, the Scotland coach in the 1970s (or 'adviser to the captain' as he was called because again no one could bring themselves to call anyone a coach back then), showed the Scotland team some on his reel-to-reel tape machine.

Bill was an excellent coach. He had been a student at Jordanhill College, the Scottish School of PE in Glasgow, and then a lecturer there afterwards, and was therefore a very good communicator. After Scotland training on the back pitches at Murrayfield, we would often sit in the freezing cold in the back changing room of the stadium and watch as Bill operated his machine until the appropriate moment or incident in a match that he wanted to show us.

As a player I got a huge amount out of what he picked out. That was the first time I had seen my own performances and got a feel for what I could do and what I needed to work on. It also ignited a flame for analysis inside me.

By the time of the 1989 Lions tour I got together all the videotapes of Australia from their matches in the previous year. England had played two Tests there, then New Zealand had played three and finally Australia had travelled to England, Scotland and Italy. They had won four, drawn one and lost three (two against New Zealand and the England match at Twickenham), so there was plenty of varied material to work with.

I also got some footage from their 1984 Grand Slam tour when they beat England, Ireland, Wales and Scotland, with a wonderful side that included the likes of Nick Farr-Jones, Mark Ella, Michael Lynagh, Andrew Slack and David Campese. That was just background research for me rather than for the players.

But I did do some video analysis with the team, in a very simple way. It was simply using very old-fashioned video cassettes. It would often take me seven or eight hours just to go through one match, usually only to get about 10 excerpts to show to the players. You had to mark the numbers where you wanted to fast-forward to, and then how many numbers you were showing a certain clip for and then fast-forward to the next number. I had notes written next to each number on the counter about the point I was trying to make.

I don't think anyone else was doing this sort of video analysis at that stage, although in 1990 I think England were maybe doing a bit. It was around this time that Judy and I bought a new four-headed video recorder to use at home, where I could actually pause the action and see what was on the screen. You couldn't do that on the old machines because the frame would just shake too much. You had to look at the counter and wind it back to see what you wanted.

With the four-headed machine you could now pause the action and then move it forward slowly. You could still see what you were looking at. For me that was a big breakthrough. The problem was that you only got to work from the television coverage. What we forget is that there were not any cameras set up specifically for one team in those days. What you were taking was the television recording of the game, so whatever cameras they used and whatever action they chose to show, that was what you got.

In Scotland we had a camera put behind the goals that was bolted to the stadium roof so we could watch the games from end on. That was a good addition to the usual match coverage, but it was nothing compared to what they have nowadays. Once everything went digital, if you asked nicely the television company would give you all the output from all their cameras; at the big internationals they now have some 18–22 cameras.

You need that many because there is so much scrutiny with the Television Match Official and you need all the angles.

In 1997 I watched videos not just of the New Zealand versus South Africa Test series but of all of South Africa's matches in the previous two years and broke them all down. I tracked their patterns and looked at which players they played through. I wanted to see what they did when they got good ball and they were on the front foot. Where did they take it? Who were the players involved? What were the calls? Who had the highest game involvement? When they were playing well, which were the players who kept it moving, who kept making the good decisions? And then when they were under pressure, what was their option? Who took control?

I narrowed it down to eight key players, who were critical to the way they played. That was all of the exceptionally well-balanced back row - Gary Teichmann, Ruben Kruger and André Venter, the prop Os du Randt who could have some games where he absolutely destroyed the opposition front row, Mark Andrews in the second row for his lineout work, as well as scrum half Joost van der Westhuizen, fly half Henry Honiball and André Joubert at full back.

We tried to isolate van der Westhuizen, Honiball and Joubert. At full back Joubert always came late to a high ball so we put our kicks a little shorter and made sure that someone was always challenging him. As a result of this, he put a few high kicks down in the first Test.

Joubert had been part of a World XV that I had been asked to coach, with the All Black legend Brian Lochore as manager and the Australian Bob Templeton as my assistant coach, against New Zealand in 1992, as part of the New Zealand Rugby Union's centenary celebrations. We actually won the first Test of three, but were told we could not pick the same side again and so lost the next two Tests (New Zealanders don't like losing!), but there were a number of South Africans in the squad so it was a valuable exercise in terms of learning about their rugby psyche.

In 1997 I was mindful of the Natal link between the footballing No. 8 Teichmann and Honiball at fly half. Their coach was Carel du Plessis, who was inexperienced although he had been a marvellous player as a winger. I sensed he wanted his team to play a more expansive game but that was always going to prove difficult for him because that is not the Springbok way. They prefer to play through the forwards and around their half backs.

And that is what they ended up doing against us in 1997. Honiball was very powerful for a fly half and they looked to run some big runners like Teichmann off him. In our defensive strategy we needed to make sure that we were up very quickly on Honiball and also into the spaces around him. That was where Scott Gibbs was so good. We did defensive drills with bags positioned across the field. It was about going hard into the contact and then repositioning for the next play.

There were three waves: the hit wave, the near defence group and then the wider group. It was all about line speed. If we got at them we just kept pushing through. And in the end the defence undoubtedly won us that Test series.

As I have mentioned, at the time it was not something British teams were used to doing, but we did it superbly, so that every time Honiball looked for his runners around him all he saw were red Lions jerseys. We had done our analysis and it paid off. And Honiball was dropped for Jannie de Beer after the second Test.

For all sorts of different reasons that 1997 tour was a watershed. It was the first professional tour, of course, and that meant it came with many benefits in terms of preparation and analysis – from me going on that trip to South Africa with the All Blacks the year before and doing my report, to having Andy Keast there as an analyst.

What was also important was that we were able to use the *Living with Lions* cameramen from the company Worldmark to film the training sessions. They didn't use much of it for the final video, but it meant that we as coaches could sit down every evening and watch the training. It was the first time I had ever had training footage like that.

The three of us – Jim Telfer, Andy and myself – watched every training session and every player. We did not want to complicate matters by having extra people involved if they were not needed. We were able to transfer that clarity to the players because there were only three of us looking at the footage and two of us (Jim and I) delivering our judgement.

We would show the players the training videos as well as clips from the games. It wasn't digital then, but Andy was clever enough to cut tapes and shorten things up so that we had some brilliant footage for the players to look at and use. I have mentioned the time Andy put in but it was not just quantity; there was obvious quality in his work, too. When everyone came to a meeting they knew that work had been done and that it was relevant and meaningful.

Using the research I had done on South Africa in all their Test matches over the previous two years, each Lions player had a tape of his opponent and how he had played during that time. So, for example, hooker Keith Wood knew all about the South African hooker Naka Drotské long before they met on the field. It wasn't like today when players can call up such information on their laptops; it was a key summary for each of them.

In terms of tactics on this tour I was keen for one attacker to be joining the line late, so, instead of the usual two-on-one drills, we did 'two-on-one plus one' drills instead. In my post-tour report, I wrote:

Having learnt lessons from previous tours, I had agreed with Jim [Telfer] a group of core skills which we had to implement from the word go. These core skills would be the skills on which our game was to be based. There had to be no question, we had to do them in such a way that they became second nature and were done outstandingly well.

All these skills became part of every session during the first two weeks of the tour. They were repeated and repeated and repeated. We were producing the first part of what I called our 'trademark plays'. The two major aspects of this were off-line running (against everything in the coaching manuals), which I felt would be important to upset the very aggressive and channel-dominated defence of the South Africans, and defensive practices in which we would progressively become stronger and more offensive in our work when we did not have possession.

Even with the forwards, I was constantly stressing the need for a second wave of attack, setting up secondary targets to shift the big South African players around. Time and time again I emphasised that we needed to create this second wave from players who had been out of the game, either because they had been on the wrong side of the ball or because they had been returning to their feet having been involved in a tackle, ruck or maul situation.

In that report under a heading of 'General Coaching Principles on Tour' I talked about this second wave of attack, adding:

The ability of players to get in this second line position allowed us to create attacks in which initial front line runners of four suddenly became an attack of eight, and this late re-grouping again allowed us an advantage of players arriving into space late and isolating defenders.

In order for this 'team shape' to develop, we had to recognise there were various key things that had to be spot on. They were:

The angles of the midfield and the back three
The support lines of the back row

The second support line awareness of the front five plus any
player who was the wrong side of the ball as play was
re-grouping

In addition to this overall plan, the other major tactical areas around which every session and game were planned were as follows:

Defensive tackling and channels plus communication
Set-piece attack and defence with back row links
Kicking strategy in attack and counter-attack in defence

The key words in everything we did were 'COLLECTIVE INVOLVEMENT, INTENSITY, PATIENCE, ZERO MISTAKES, NOISY COMMUNICATION.

After five weeks I decided that the team were so proficient at the 'plus one' drills that it was time to move on.

One thing I pride myself on is that I have never repeated the same training session. Yes, I have core values and principles, and indeed core training drills, but I have never done the same training session from beginning to end twice. There might be the same wider framework, but there will always be little differences within it.

I keep notes from every session I have done and have always thought long and hard about what should come out of every training session. I also added notes in the margin of the page if the players in training had found a better way of delivering the tactics. But here I experienced something that I had never experienced before. A number of the players told me straight away that they thought we should not change anything.

'No. Don't change what we are doing,' they said. 'We can now do these drills and they are part and parcel of what we are. What they do is keep us honest because, if we are not thinking, they do not work. The reason they look easy is because in our minds we know what we are doing.'

It was interesting because on that trip I was very conscious of the fact that I did not want us to over-train. So we would have a big training session on the Wednesday before the Test, then a sharper session on the Thursday, which was still pretty full-on, but then crucially we would have Fridays off.

In my report I suggested that Wednesday fixtures be discontinued:

I would recommend that future tours play Tuesday and Saturday for the duration of the whole tour. The Wednesday games interrupt the coaching build-up to the game on Saturday. The following structure for a tour week would, I think, be more balanced:

Sunday: Train
Monday: Team training
Tuesday: Match
Wednesday: Heavy training for non-players
Thursday: Team training
Friday: Rest
Saturday: Match

The Test team would meet on the Friday for afternoon tea. So before the first Test in Cape Town, from our base near the Newlands Stadium we went to the Kirstenbosch Botanical Gardens. After a walk around the gardens we had some tea and scones. In Durban for the second Test we went to the Bird Gardens, where the people there laid on a special show with owls, vultures and eagles. We were only there for about an hour and a quarter but there was time to see the flamingoes on the lake, too. And then for the third Test in Johannesburg we went to a huge park with a café in the middle.

I know it doesn't sound like the great call to arms you might expect before a Test match but that would come nearer the time, usually that evening. What this did was let everyone take their minds off the game for an hour or so while still keeping everyone together. Key elements would naturally be discussed in casual conversations, and this helped to embed core thoughts and actions.

We were effectively giving the players 48 hours between the last training session and the game. A few hours before kick-off, though, we would run through all our set pieces and moves at the back of the hotel or somewhere nearby. That was just about picking up the detail before we went to the ground.

And the night before the first Test we did have something special for the players. First we had a team meeting in which we did little more than run through some key themes, but then I put a video on for the players to watch. It was made by Keith Lyons, an old contact who was working at the Cardiff Centre for Notational Analysis, where they had been taking sports analysis to new levels. He had a big and growing sports analysis department there that was much more sophisticated than my original stuff had been. Things had become very scientific and very clear in the elements you could record.

Keith had helped me to compile a lot of the videos before the tour, both as regards selection and the analysis of South Africa. I had shared my tactical thoughts with him about what we were trying to do on tour, so after every game he had analysed it and faxed me out his results (communication was not so simple back then!). Generally it was two A4 sheets of paper of what he had seen and his thoughts.

So on the back of that I asked him before the Test what we had looked like so far from the UK. 'Do not underestimate how well you are doing,' he said. 'You are doing so much good stuff.' And he said he would put a video together.

He did just that. He sent it out by air mail so that I received it on that Friday before the Test. 'I am really enjoying the quality of Lions' performance,' he said in a fax signalling the video's imminent arrival. 'The efforts you have put into a dynamic pattern in the context of a TEAM ethic are more and more visible and observable.'

The video was unbelievably good; so powerful and motivational. It was 12 minutes long, to music, and for the first six minutes we did not have the ball. We had been doing all this work on defence and Keith said that what was coming over was how good we were when we were not in possession of the ball, how hard we were working and how organised we were. It was what impressed him the most.

The second six minutes was all about our attack, and he had made sure that he included all 35 squad members in it. He had picked up the fact that we were using that extra runner, as practised in our drills, and how we were using a second wave of attack. He had highlighted all the good stuff from being in those sorts of shapes.

You could have heard a pin drop in the team room. The players thought it was incredible. For the next two hours every time I went into the room the video was playing. The players were just playing it again and again and again. It had an amazing impact. It was so important to know what we looked like back home. Mind you, after the tour I lent it to someone and never got it back!

You have to remember that this was before digital analysis had come in. That was what made it even more impressive.

By the time I toured South Africa in 2009 with the Lions, everything had changed in terms of analysis. In 2002 I had been alerted to a system called SportsCode, which was being used in Australia by some Australian Rules clubs. So when I went there on a pre-World Cup visit for Scotland, I decided to visit a couple of them, Sydney Swans and Brisbane Lions. These Australian Rules sides were way ahead of everyone in terms of analysis and were aligned with American Football, which is a game based on analysis and numbers. These two clubs introduced me to SportsCode and it blew me away immediately.

My philosophy with analysis was that I wanted a picture of what the other team were trying to do and which players were key to actually making it work for them. Once I had that information I was pretty comfortable with how I would train the players and tactically what we would do to combat the opposition's strengths. It was also about having a clear understanding of the tactical impact of training practices towards the overall plan. Those were my reasons for doing analysis right back in the early days when I was just using pencil, paper and a clipboard. SportsCode could now give me exactly what I wanted in an instant, and I found it amazing.

At the time Scotland were using a medical analysis system that had been converted to try to analyse rugby players. It was hopeless. I used to want to throw my laptop out of the window half the time because it was so frustrating. To be fair, when I came back from Australia the Scottish Rugby Union chief executive Bill Watson said that I could go for it and we introduced SportsCode straight away. We were the first in rugby to use it.

England were using the football system, ProZone, which mostly just measures the distances you run and how fast you run them. You needed about 12 cameras for that and all the data went to the company and they then sent you the results the next day. It was time-consuming and you were totally reliant on them reading it for you. And it was all about statistics.

With SportsCode it was so much more coach-friendly. You could stop and start it and it had a touchscreen facility. There were statistics but you could click on them and you could see the videos of those statistics. So, say, you wanted to see how effective a forward's carries had been, you could click on his number of carries and it would tell you how many of them had resulted in him getting over the gain line or how many had resulted in clean ball. And then, crucially, you could watch them as well.

You could set it up for whatever you wanted as a coach. It could be tailored exactly to your requirements. It was individual to every coach and I liked that. You could simply set the preferences to reflect your personality.

Every part of the game could be tagged – tackles, passes, rucks, mauls *et al*. – and then all the information was put together so that you could spot trends in a game. For instance, if a team was coming down the tight channels you would expect your players with one to five on their backs to make a lot of tackles.

Sometimes your tackle count would tell you where teams play. The great thing with SportsCode is that you could be told the number of tackles made in a game and when you clicked on that you could see where they were made and by whom. It gave you an immediate picture of where the tackles needed to happen.

I liked that sort of information but I preferred it to be relevant to the player and the game. I didn't like statistics for the sake of them. What I wanted was instant verification that what I thought I saw was right. SportsCode gave that.

As Rhys Long, our excellent analyst, said in an interview with the *Guardian* during the 2009 tour:

Studies have shown that the most a coach can take in of a game is 40%. Now, no detail is hidden from them or the players. There is no place to hide. The big danger is bombarding the players with too much information.

The beauty of a Lions tour is that you have time. With a national side or clubs you tend to have a couple of analysis sessions a week. That means getting players into a room and their attention span will start to drop after 15 minutes or so. With their own laptops, they can view data on their opposite numbers at their leisure, in their room, by the pool, on the coach or a plane.

I am careful not to bombard them with stuff. Analysis is a filtration process and it is about giving players and coaches pertinent information. We provide specifics for players: Paul O'Connell will get a lineout database while Brian O'Driscoll will have material on set-plays and patterns. It is all individually tailored so that players do not have to watch whole matches, but receive information that is relevant to them.

And in another interview with the *Sunday Times*, he said:

The SportsCode system can deliver between 4,000 and 10,000 items of information on a match. However, the devil is in the detail being delivered in a fast, user-friendly format, so that key tactics can be pinpointed and delivered to the players as clearly as possible.

It's like a filter process where days of work for the analyst are distilled into hours for the coaches and minutes for the players.

So in 2009, using SportsCode, we spotted that South Africa were competing very hard at the first two breakdowns. If we could be very efficient at those two breakdowns and get to, say, a fifth or sixth breakdown, we knew we were in business. This was the case throughout the tour.

In virtually every match SportsCode would prove its worth. I remember a game for Wasps against Leicester in 2006. I spotted that the alignment of Leicester's back-line was very narrow and deep whenever their forwards took the ball on. That made them susceptible to a counter-attack if we could turn the ball over. I got the message onto the field and I think centre Ayoola Erinle scored at the very next turnover. That was very satisfying.

It is a process I enjoyed being part of. It was about giving the players better information, about why something was not working or why it needed to be changed. I always got excited about that.

With SportsCode you could split the screen so that you could watch the game from behind and from the side at the same time, which is really useful. I always liked watching games from behind the posts because you are actually seeing the game that the players see.

By 2009 Rhys was using what he called 'accelerated adaptation'. As he said: 'Come match day in South Africa, we'll be using a technique known as "accelerated adaptation". My job will be to analyse events as they unfold and get messages to the coaching team that will effectively allow them to think quicker than the opposition. It's about getting inside their decision-making cycle before they get inside ours.'

In 2009 we had six laptops (red ones, too) running in the coaches' area in the stands at games. One of them was running with an 18-second delay. If we were watching the game and wanted to look at something again we just looked at that laptop in the middle. And using SportsCode we could also ask Rhys and Rhodri Bown to tag something that we might want to view at half time. Rhys had three laptops of his own (one for training, one for analysing the opposition, and one for matches) and every player and coach had one.

The lawyer on tour with us, Richard Smith, even had a laptop and he was looking at it to check on possible citings and other disciplinary matters. He was excellent on tour, always helping out, whether clearing things up or kicking balls back for the kickers. I always liked it when the management lent a hand in other areas, like Clive Rowlands helping the scrum halves in 1989. I come back to the matter of the touring environment and how it can be enhanced by little things like that.

I had persuaded the Lions to invest in a big television that we could have at the side of the pitch, so that the players could look at it and be shown clips using SportsCode. Then they could go straight out and put it into practice on the training field. The coaching wasn't done in a room, after which you would have to get on a bus, get changed and then try to remember what was said. It was done in an instant. It was a case of: 'This is what it looks like, this is what we want to change, let's go and do it.'

I was never keen on too many meetings anyway. In my 1997 tour report I had said:

I also felt it was important to cut down on meetings with the players, so we would not be talking about what we would be doing and become bored by it, but that we would establish our philosophy and tactics on the training field in action when we would then review and adapt as necessary.

It was, though, important to establish meetings with senior players for feedback as well as speaking to individual players at the end of each training session. Consequently, I established a procedure of a team meeting at 9.15 each morning so it was the same time, same place in the team room, in which any notices or information would be given out and I would give a brief 5 or 10-minute explanation of the training session – what we were going to do and why. We would then go straight from that meeting onto the bus and away to training.

In the northern hemisphere now virtually every team uses SportsCode, because the company has impressively kept evolving its system. We were using it at Wasps as soon as I took over there for the 2005/06 season. We were very lucky to recruit Rhys there as our analyst at the time; he really was very special. He had once been a Welsh Schools' No. 8 before a broken leg ended his career with Bridgend, but he threw himself into his new role, gaining a master's degree in performance analysis, and he became quite brilliant at his job, whether with Wasps, Wales or the Lions. It was a loss to the game when he left for the Football Association in 2016.

In those early years at Wasps I have no doubt that our analysis work was much better than most international teams'. Rhys was not only using SportsCode, but expanding it at the same time. There were always further possibilities. For instance, in 2009 in South Africa, despite Rhys and Rhodri Bown being there as analysts, I would be spending three or four hours a day on analysis of my own. It just showed that there was always more to look at, more to be done, as well as the importance of having tactical clarity in your own mind.

On the 2005 Lions tour I had originally asked Clive Woodward if I could use SportsCode just for the midweek team. For the Test team Clive was going to use the ProZone system that he had used with England, but he asked to see SportsCode when I mentioned it. I think he was as taken aback as I had been on my first viewing. He said that he could not believe that other countries were using something as good as this.

So he said, 'We'll use that on the tour full stop.' To be fair to him, he was open to it; he knew how good it was. It helped that one of the two analysts on that trip was Gavin Scott – the other was Tony Biscombe, who was an old school pal of mine – because he knew the system well from using it with Scotland.

The use of GPS (global positioning system) technology was also a big breakthrough. You could track everything a player was doing, such as distances run, speeds reached and their heart rates. At first GPS was just used in training – that was the case on that 2009 Lions tour – but gradually, through a small unit slipped into a pouch between the shoulders of the jersey, it has become the norm in games, with New Zealand and Australia beginning to use it from 2010 and everyone else eventually following. On the 2013 Lions tour to Australia it was used for the first time by the Lions in matches.

There is also an accelerometer, which means you can measure the force of the tackles and hits at scrummages; you can grade how much contact a player has taken in a game. They are excellent devices for managing the loads of players, especially in training. Nowadays you will see a member of staff sitting at pitchside peering at a laptop and monitoring how much work the players are doing. This is invaluable knowledge to have.

All this information is wonderful. As I say, it really excites me and it certainly improves and enlivens the game. But the truth remains that the coaches and analysts cannot play the game for the players. It's the players who have to go out on the field and perform. They have to implement the game plans devised for them, and make their own individual decisions.

What you want most, as a coach, is for your squad to understand exactly what you are trying to do. Once you give them the framework, everyone must buy into it so that all the players are doing the basics well, and as a result individual decision-making and talent can flourish. It is at that point that the players can almost take over themselves. You can feel very happy as a coach then.

On this subject, there is a famous story about Warren Gatland when he was in charge of Wasps. Before one of the many finals in which he was involved there (he won three Premiership titles, the Heineken Cup and the Challenge Cup!) he felt comfortable enough to stand back and allow the players to take their own training session. As he was standing on the touchline just observing, one of the girls from Wasps' office staff came up to him and said: 'I don't mean to be rude, but what is it that you do exactly?' Gats thought that was brilliant. He saw it as a real compliment. And it was.

I experienced something similar on the 1997 Lions tour. It was the third game of the tour when we played Western

Province, and we won 38–21. It was the first time our rugby had really clicked. We had got bits right before then, but only bits. At the time England were playing a very conservative game, but we were saying that we had to keep the tempo up because we knew that the South Africans would try to smash us.

As I've said, we wanted to shift the ball and bring runners in late. At the press conference afterwards the press asked Martin Johnson – it was his first game as captain because of his shoulder injury that we had kept quiet – why things hadn't been tightened up in the last 15 minutes. He said: 'Look, the rugby we need to play requires the players to play for 80 minutes and we have to have that mentality.' In my mind I was screaming 'Yes! Yes! The captain is saying exactly what I want!'

Johnno had nailed it and I knew we were in a good place as a squad. He had such an impact on the players as captain that you knew if that message was in his head we were three-quarters of the way on the journey. My tour report reflected that moment: 'That, more than anything, was music to my ears. We had the tour captain fully committed to the philosophy.'

It was a light bulb moment, for me and the Lions.

KEY WORDS

- Control all your own operations
- Share your knowledge
- Pre-tour visits
- Boot room chats
- Benevolent dictator

1989 Australia, Second Test
Again, we will come to this later, but this was an example of
looking at the opposition and deciding to change our tactical
approach to play in a different way.

TOTAL COMMITMENT BENEFITS LIONS IN BRUISING ENCOUNTER

Australia 12 British Isles 19

From David Hands Rugby Correspondent Brisbane

There will be no misconceptions at the third time of asking in Sydney next Saturday. The British Isles were caught napping in the first international with Australia nine days ago and, at Ballymore on Saturday in the second, Australia were similarly unprepared for the volume of the storm that burst about their ears as the Lions levelled the series with only their second win in three tours this decade.

It was, without question, their finest performance on tour but whether it would have been achieved had René Hourquet, the French referee, done his duty leaves an unwelcome query. Young, the Cardiff prop, should have been sent off just before the interval for kicking Cutler at a ruck, which would have left the Lions scrum in great difficulty. As it was, for all the positive aspects which happily dominated the second half, they did not take the lead until three minutes from time.

There is a fine line between the physical commitment acceptable in international rugby, and downright acts of violence. Four Australian players (both half backs, Martin and Tuynman) required stitches for cuts caused by punches or kicks, and Farr-Jones's face looked as though he had been involved in a fairground boxing booth. At times the Lions stepped over that line, such was their resolve to square the series and they were fortunate to have a French official, because I have no doubt Hourquet has seen far worse, week in and week out, refereeing in French club rugby.

"Commitment is everything in rugby," Calder, the Lions captain, whose own face bore the scars of battle, said. "It's a contact sport first and last. If you are more committed at the breakdown you win the ball." Ian McGeechan, the coach, expressed his belief that there was nothing vicious about the game though Australia, I suspect, will not agree. Asked if he felt more sinned against than sinning, Farr-Jones replied tightly, "Yes".

We had a battle royal only five minutes into the game, when Farr-Jones pushed Jones out of the way before a scrum and the little Welshman – continuing a disagreement which began in the New South Wales game last month – laid into him. Both sets of forwards joined an unedifying melée and the Lions were lucky that Lynagh missed the resulting penalty – as he did after the Young incident which was seen by Keith Lawrence, the touch judge.

Indeed, since Lynagh, who passed 400 points with his first successful kick and has averaged over 13 points a match for his country, missed three penalties and two dropped goals, it is pertinent to wonder whether the gash over his right eye put him off his goal-kicking; at the same time Andrew missed a conversion and two dropped goals and Gavin Hastings two penalties, so those points missed were almost equal.

There was, though, so much to commend in the Lions' victory by a goal, a try, two penalty goals and a dropped goal to a goal and two penalties. I doubt if Teague and Moore have played better internationals anywhere, Richards was – as usual – immense and both locks had marvellous games. It is no coincidence that all concerned are English for the presence of so many England forwards permitted the Lions to vary the lineout at will; added to the driving zest of Sole and Calder the stage

was set for the half backs to produce a telling tactical display.

There were times – his second missed dropped goal for instance – when Andrew might have run the ball and twice Scott Hastings cut back when he might have released Guscott. Given the Lions' limited approach in previous matches, however, it was not surprising that we had to wait until the final quarter (when the touring side's fitness showed to great advantage) before Guscott announced his coming of age as an international.

Given space the Lions backs suddenly looked far more dangerous than ever they did in Sydney. On three occasions desperate defence kept them out, the best attack coming in a break from their own 22, when Guscott glided through, fed on to Scott Hastings and Underwood, supporting faithfully, made a marvellous pickup off his toes only for Farr-Jones to intercept his pass.

Australia had opened with a well-constructed try by Martin and led 9–6 at the interval. Lynagh's second penalty made it 12–6 and the Lions were denied a try from a five-metre scrum when Australia heeled and Teague lunged for the touchdown, ahead of Farr-Jones. The referee decided, correctly, that he was offside but awarded the Lions a penalty for a collapsed scrum; the disappointment was assuaged subsequently when Andrew persuaded over a penalty.

The turning point came shortly after: Lynagh, from 32 metres, hit an upright with a penalty and the Lions, dominating the rucked ball as they did all afternoon, came bustling forward. Scott Hastings was held out by Campese two metres short, Underwood rounded Williams on the left and finally Moore cleared a ruck, Calder lobbed a pass to Andrew and Scott Hastings, who may have dreamed of moments like this as a child at home in Edinburgh with brother Gavin, scuffed out a pass which the full back gobbled up off the ground, handed off Maguire, and gave his side the lead.

The best was yet to come. Campese, in a display of fallibility which only shows we are all human, twice dropped high balls; Calder thundered forward and there was Moore again to play scrum half for Andrew. Guscott, as though he were playing towards the clubhouse at Bath Recreation Ground, dabbed forward a little grubber and collected the bounce to score at the posts. But the publicity posters were right: it had been jungle warfare.

5

WEEK FIVE

Jason Leonard is my ultimate Lion. I have always said so.
Why? Because his attitude in 1997 summed up what being a
Lion should mean, and it is an attitude that you have to carry
with you if the Lions are to have any chance of success.

In 1993 in New Zealand, he propped on both sides of the
scrum when required, to make it all work – actually to help us
out because we had not selected particularly well at prop. He
just delivered whatever we wanted. So because of that and
the fact that he was the most experienced of the England
players, everyone presumed he would be a Test starter in
1997.

But he was not. He was on the bench, as we chose Tom
Smith at loosehead and Paul Wallace at tighthead. Was he
disappointed? Definitely. He was a competitor so it must have
hurt him not to be picked, but he hid it very well.

Instead, he made sure that the chosen props had everything
they needed to perform in the Test match. I marvelled at the
way he talked to them and the way he talked about South
Africa; they just spoke as a group about what the props needed
to do. He was a complete part of the preparation. When you

see that as a coach you think: 'This is why this tour is being successful.'

When you see how someone like Jason reacted, that to me is being the ideal Lion. You can be a Test Lion, that's easy. But to be like Jason Leonard, to hide your disappointment and help the cause: that's the ultimate. You might not be on the field the whole time to win a Test match but you can help create the environment that helps win that Test match.

That is one of the Lions' many great attractions and challenges. As a Lions player, you are asked: 'Just how strong a character are you? You happen to be a rugby player. Fine. But are you strong enough to do whatever the situation requires?'

As Leonard himself has said: 'I am as competitive as the next person but Lions tours are different. I knew I wasn't going to make the Test side so I decided to try and help the other front-row players as much as possible. I did everything I could, whether it be scrummaging sessions, lineouts, or rucking or mauling sessions. On the 1997 Lions, it really felt like it was our small, close-knit group of players and managers against however many millions of people there are in South Africa. It felt like us against the whole world and you felt as if there was a role for you whether you were playing in the Tests or not.'

I spoke to the 2013 squad in Australia before the first Test, having handed out the jerseys to the Test team, and I mentioned Jason and about him being the ultimate Lion. So I was interested to read that captain Sam Warburton later mentioned it in his tour diary when discussing the omission of Brian O'Driscoll from the last Test and how he handled it. 'It may be that Jason has a rival for the ultimate Lion,' he said. That was good to hear.

There are others who have behaved in a similar way. Donal Lenihan on the 1989 tour was an example I have already mentioned. It might surprise some if I mention the name of Austin Healey for his behaviour on the 1997 tour. Now, he could be a character but he was another who stayed true to our reasons for being on that trip.

Graham Rowntree was magnificent on that tour, too. He was sharing a room with Jeremy Davidson after one of the Test victories, and Davidson had a few too many to drink and couldn't find his room so he slept in someone else's room. We had to be on the bus at 9 a.m. the next morning and when Jeremy eventually relocated his room, there was nothing there. All his kit had gone. He thought somebody was playing a joke and got to the bus in a bit of a state but Wig, as everyone calls Rowntree, was there waiting for him and reassured him that everything was OK. He had packed all his stuff for him and it was already on the bus.

'How can I thank you?' said Jeremy. 'You already have,' said Wig. 'You won a Lions Test yesterday for us.' That is some collective impact.

In the final week of the tour Rowntree played against Northern Free State on the Tuesday and then on the Wednesday he had to take a full part in a scrummaging session because Tom Smith, who was going to play in the Test, was ill. Was Wig miffed that he was not in the Test team? Of course he was. Did he complain, though? Did he heck. He scrummaged as vigorously and enthusiastically as he always would.

Allan Bateman, the Welsh centre, was exactly the same in his attitude. He was there at that training session holding the tackle bags and encouraging everyone as he had done throughout the tour. He came off the bench in the third Test to win a Lions Test cap but I have always thought that he was one of the most unlucky players on that tour. He was brilliant. On many other Lions tours he would have been a certain Test starter.

In 2005 I was in charge of the midweek side so I saw this type of character at close hand. And there were two who stood out in particular: the England fly half Charlie Hodgson and the Ireland lock Donncha O'Callaghan. I thought Hodgson was exceptionally good on that tour. His tactical decision-making was quite superb. The more I saw him, the more I appreciated his awareness and how good he really was as an attacking fly half. But both were very good characters, with Donncha again proving that in South Africa in 2009 with his bubbly, humorous and sometimes madcap personality.

In 2009 there was also Welsh No. 8 Andy Powell. He was certainly different as a character, and madcap might be a good word to use again. He worked hard but he was a joker as well; he lifted the whole atmosphere. If Powelly was around, people had a smile on their faces. You can often underestimate the impact of that on a tour.

I always liked to take an uncapped or young player on a Lions tour, so in 2009 I selected Ireland's centre/wing Keith Earls. I thought he deserved it. He only had two caps then, and one of them had been off the bench. He was 21 and had not been involved in the Six Nations that season, but I had been particularly impressed when he played for Munster against the All Blacks and had tracked him after that.

The older players tend to look after a youngster. When I gave him the job of looking after the toy Lion (called Lenny on that trip and handed over by Earls to 20-year-old Leigh Halfpenny when he arrived late on the tour after injury) the players would try to hide it from him. That fun-loving, caring quality helps with the general atmosphere.

There is a reason why I have mentioned these names and talked about how they dealt with disappointment, and that is because on every Lions tour there is a moment when those characteristics become vital, when they stand out because the tour reaches its pinch point, when it's necessary to make the biggest calls: to decide at last the side for the first Test.

I have always called it 'week five'. Tours have obviously altered in length but that description is still pretty close. It is the week leading up to the first Test. If there are any problems, whether it is amongst the support staff or the players, they will come out in week five.

Suddenly you have a challenge that you do not have with an international side – all this talent has been playing for five weeks and now you have got to tell half of them that they are not playing in the Test match. If the tour is run as it should be, all the players will have had the chance to wear a starting Lions jersey in the first three or four games of the tour. There will have been no midweek team and no Test team for those first five weeks.

Until the first Test it's one Lions team wearing a Lions jersey. If it's done properly there is no way that any player can be disappointed by a lack of opportunity, but that does not mean he will not be disappointed if not picked. The psychology is very powerful and demanding. As a player who might be first choice in his country and not used to being left out, it asks him questions he may never have been asked before.

All of a sudden he is told that he is not going to be on the pitch, he may not even be on the bench and instead he could be sitting in the stand and watching the game in his blazer. Is he big enough to handle all that?

In 1974 I had seen every single player who was not selected deal with disappointment in an appropriate manner. There were some phenomenal players like Andy Ripley, Tony Neary, Mike Burton and Roy Bergiers who did not make the Test side, but Syd Millar had given them all the opportunity and they all still gave everything to the cause. They kept training and stayed competitive. I didn't expect to make the Test side and I learnt as much from them as I did from the more established players.

The impact players can have on each other cannot be overstated. As outlined in the chapter about the environment, I have always thought that you can never have a bad Test team on a Lions tour, but you can have a bad environment if the non-Test players are not pulling their weight. They set the environment. If a Lions tour is not right, it is generally because of what is happening away from the Test matches.

Therefore I have never had any truck with players who are not prepared to behave in the same way as those players in

1974 who were not in the Test team. I had seen what that non-playing group had done and what they had delivered. At no time did anybody go off tour. It was a magnificent example to set, and it was set over three months and four Test matches.

There was always someone at your shoulder saying: 'If you want to do some more training I am here.' It made for a phenomenal environment, and none of that changes in the professional era. There is no reason why any player cannot deal with it.

But, of course, things are never quite that simple and that is why I always think that week five is the tour's barometer. For that is when you realise how unique the Lions are. You don't own the jersey, you just carry it for seven weeks; that is the legacy. Each tour will reflect the group of players on it and the next tour will be completely different. You are wearing the same jersey but you have got different experiences and a different environment. That is the uniqueness.

There is no other environment when so many different strands come together during a critical period of four or five days. It is a reflection of what has gone on in the four weeks before that, a culmination of everything you have been doing and everything you have got in place.

We are back to talking about the environment again, the off-the-field behaviour. More than with any other international team, it is about what that group has become off the field. That will have an impact on where the players take their rugby on the field.

So how does it pan out? There is often a midweek game on the Tuesday. I always insisted we meet on Tuesday night for Test selection but that we would not confirm it until Wednesday morning. We would not rush it. We would look at it, sleep on it just as we always did with the initial squad selection, and then we would challenge ourselves with what we had actually seen, which for me is still the most intense pressure I have ever felt.

Making that call for the first Test group is so difficult because you need to take into account what you have seen, which players are performing well and also ensure you get the partnerships right within the team. A lot goes into it from a coaching perspective, which is why I would always talk it through with the captain. I would also talk to the medics, so you would get a real feel for where players were, physically and mentally, and they would give me warning if they felt, for instance, a player might be struggling emotionally with the weight of the tour.

That was why in 1997 we raised the issues surrounding selection for the first Test with the players. Everybody had to be part of the solution; it couldn't be something we left and only considered when we came to it. I always thought it was very important that we planned for it by having a very open discussion about how best to manage the emotional and mental pressure that comes during those days leading up to the first-Test selection. And in 1997 the players decided that they wanted to receive letters under the door to tell them whether they had been selected or not.

John Bentley was a tremendous character on that tour and giving him the mini video camera for the *Living with Lions* video made for some entertaining viewing, but the truth is that he did not take the news well that he was only on the bench for the first Test on that tour. He filmed the build-up to receiving the letter from Samantha Peters, but he did not film the reaction because he was so disappointed. 'I was crushed,' he has said. 'To make matters worse, the letter started "Congratulations" so I thought I was in until I read the rest of it which told me I was a substitute.'

Indeed, he did not film anything for a couple of days. As he has also said: 'I was sulking, which was totally out of order. I was bitterly disappointed because I thought I had done enough to make the side but we had discussed back at Weybridge how we would handle that moment when it arrived and I had preached professionalism. When the moment came I did not show it.'

But at least because of the way we had decided to handle it, players could come to terms with not being picked in private and then be ready to show up and keep the support going when we were into training and in the public eye again. Finding out in a meeting can be brutal, especially if you are just posting the names up on a board. I never liked that idea.

In 2009 Warren Gatland and I between us spoke to every player not in the 23 before the first-Test announcement. Then we did the same as in 1997: there were congratulations all round, then we were pretty much straight on the bus to training before the dinner out in the evening.

We went with Alan Tait and Ieuan Evans on the wings for that first Test in 1997. Bentley had played well against the Gauteng Lions (previously known as Transvaal) when he scored his famous individual try, forever now known as the 'Bentos moment'; it was an exceptional score and certainly ranks up there amongst my favourite Lions tries. It began when Neil Jenkins collected a kick just outside our 22 and passed from left to right to Bentley. The winger glided past a couple of defenders to go beyond halfway before he stepped off his right foot twice to beat two more defenders and then veer towards the posts, holding off two more defenders, to score.

It was sensational stuff and it was such an important moment because it sparked us into life and gave us a 20–14 victory, which we badly needed after losing 35–30 to Northern Transvaal at Loftus Versfeld, a game in which Bentley had not been at his best. So while we had been hugely impressed by that try, we still had some concerns about Bentley. Yes, his running had been spectacular, but we felt that he needed to work on his kick-chase work and his positioning in defence.

Evans was hugely experienced and was an excellent reader of the game in both attack and defence, which meant he was a prolific try-scorer but also that he rarely got caught out in defence, however big his immediate opponent was. As for Tait, we liked his defensive work as well as his superb work-rate, and it should also be said that England's Tony Underwood was close to selection, too. He played as well as I ever saw him on that trip and some of his work in defence against Gauteng had been very good. As it was, Evans was injured for the second Test, so Bentley got his chance after all.

The most difficult conversation I ever had to have on a Lions tour? Probably with Will Carling on the 1993 tour when I

Will Greenwood was so good in 1997 before he was injured.

With my old mate Jim Telfer in 1997.

Gregor Townsend against Western Province in 1997. He was one of the
most talented fly-halves I ever coached.

Will Greenwood was so good in 1997 before he was injured.

With my old mate Jim Telfer in 1997.

Gregor Townsend against Western Province in 1997. He was one of the most talented fly-halves I ever coached.

Doctor James Robson treating Tim Rodber in 1997. Robson deserves as much praise as any Lions player.

Chatting with Gregor Townsend, who always had plenty of good ideas. It has been no surprise that he has become such a good coach.

Mike Catt showed himself to be an excellent player when called up in 1997.

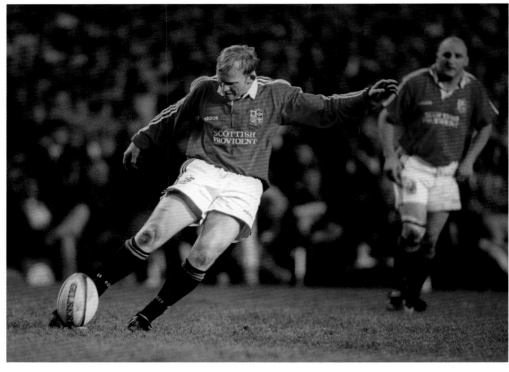

Neil Jenkins in 1997. We could not have won without his kicking.

What a try this was from Matt Dawson in the first Test.
One of the most famous Lions' tries ever.

Jeremy Davidson winning valuable lineout ball in 1997. He was a revelation on that tour.

Martin Johnson trying to steal South African lineout ball in 1997.

Ah, that drop goal from Jeremy Guscott. Some players just know when to turn it on.

Lawrence Dallaglio could genuinely play anywhere in the back row. He was a special athlete.

The third Test may have been lost but the series had been won.

John Bentley proved to be one of the great characters in 1997.

dropped him for Scott Gibbs for the second Test. He was the current England captain after all. As a coach you must then give the player your reasons why and give him something to work at or something different to look at so that he stays in contention.

There have always been big decisions to make, but this was a bit like the one Warren Gatland made with Brian O'Driscoll in 2013. As a coach, when you are in the mix and you are seeing the players train all the time, you get a definite feel for where the players are. So although it might look like an extraordinary decision outside the circle, within the Lions group it is not as extraordinary. Will was struggling with the whole environment. It was affecting his game hugely, whereas Gibbs was taking it all in and just getting better and better.

The hardest selection? I sweated on all of them! In 1989 we had to make some big calls for the first Test but we had injuries as well. It was about trying to get the balance in the back row right. I'd have to say that we didn't get it right. That and the midfield just didn't work, and we lost 30-12, conceding four tries to nil, so we ended up having to make some massive calls for the second Test. We changed the whole midfield – 10, 12 and 13 – for that match.

The back row in that first Test was Derek White, Finlay Calder and Dean Richards. We played the Scotsman White because we felt we needed size for the lineout in order to counter Steve Cutler and Bill Campbell. We didn't select another Scotsman, John Jeffrey, and he was playing well. Mike Teague was injured.

In the second row we went for Paul Ackford and Bob Norster. Norster was a good lineout man but he just wasn't big enough. We wanted physicality so we brought Wade Dooley in for the second Test. Teague was fit for the second Test too, so he came in.

In the first Test Craig Chalmers was at 10, with the Irishman Brendan Mullin paired with the Welshman Mike Hall in the centre. We swapped that for Rob Andrew, Jerry Guscott and Scott Hastings in the second match. We wanted Hastings' presence and a bit of guile from Guscott if Andrew got it right. Bringing Jerry in was a big call, definitely the biggest call I had to make on that tour.

The week five in 1993 was probably the hardest I had to deal with, simply because some players who were not near the Test team very quickly went off tour and started drinking heavily. They still trained but the two or three per cent difference in achievement appear then. That was hugely disappointing for me. In 1989 and 1997 we had some good nights out but the whole squad never lost the focus of why they were there. That is the Jason Leonard example. But 1993 was different, and all the worse for it.

In 1997 there were some big selection calls again for the first Test: as previously mentioned the bolters like Jeremy Davidson, Tom Smith and Paul Wallace. There was much debate, too, about Tait, Gregor Townsend at 10 and Matt Dawson at nine. I knew those players really well from either Northampton or Scotland and I was confident that under pressure in the biggest environment they would deliver.

With Gregor I knew how good he could be, and he was outstanding on that 1997 trip. He was a hugely talented player – that pass he gave to Gavin Hastings when Scotland won in Paris in 1995! – but he was so good there because he showed discipline in his game too. He was playing with talented players around him – something he sadly did not always have with Scotland – and he responded superbly.

That had a knock-on effect because his performances for Scotland in 1997, 1998 and 1999 were the best of his career. He was at a different level. He stood very flat on the line, he had good feet, he could get inside or outside the defender, and he could dummy or just shift.

Will Greenwood played superbly off him on that tour. His running lines and ability to come off the ball carrier late were well suited to Gregor's style. They hit it off immediately. That was another good example of chemistry when good players react to good players. It was such a shame that Will got injured.

In 2009 the one selection we got wrong for the first Test was Simon Shaw. Gats and I should have known better because we knew him well. As I have said, he is one of the most under-rated players and a natural ball-handler. Another big call was at full back where we went with the Welshman Lee Byrne, who had played well in the build-up. But under the intense pressure of the first Test we discovered that some of his decision-making could be a little suspect.

Ireland's Rob Kearney was coming through on the tour and he was duly selected to start the last two Tests, having come off the bench in the first. I thought those last two Tests made

Kearney as a player; he came of age. His progress as a player was a classic example of the momentum of a Lions tour, where you were watching a player in training and you could see him improving before your very eyes; he grew and got stronger as the tour progressed. You could just see that he was ready for a Test match by that second Test.

Tom Croft at blindside flanker was the interesting selection in that first Test. He had not been picked in the original group, but Ireland's Alan Quinlan got banned and Croft got his chance. Quinlan was there originally because he was a grafter and fighter. He had the natural respect of all the front-five players. I spoke to all the other countries and to Paul O'Connell, and there was a respect for him as a tough man. That was what we needed in South Africa.

Croft just missed out even though we thought he was probably the better rugby player. As it transpired, Croft got his chance and just got better and better as the tour went on. He has got a massive engine so his running ability is fantastic. I told him to use that engine to get into the outside channels, but I said: 'Don't do what you do at Leicester and stay out there. Work your way back in and then work your way back out again.' In the first Test he scored two tries. His positioning on the shoulders of the centres was incredible. He was undoubtedly another very good example of someone coming through during the tour and taking his rugby to a different level.

If we had Croft we probably couldn't have the Welshman Martyn Williams in the side as well. That was why we went for Ireland's David Wallace at seven. Williams was a clever player.

In the third Test he at last got the Lions Test start he deserved and he was outstanding. He had a knack of being in the right place at the right time and getting his hands on the ball. Sometimes you ponder over whether to play a tough man or a rugby player, and when you put the rugby player in you discover he is a tough man anyway. That was certainly the case with Williams.

Once the Tests are underway the midweek side becomes what is known as the 'dirt-trackers'. I am not entirely sure where the name originates from, neither am I a huge fan of the term (we have seen that Fran Cotton did not like using it in 1997), but it probably goes back to a time when tours were much longer. As a coach, you have to manage the disappointment of those midweek-side players. Good coaches do it well. It either leads to a stronger environment or one that divides, so getting it right is vital.

In New Zealand in 1977 when I was a player, there was a group of players who went off tour, and that was a long, long tour. It was 26 games long, in fact. The weather was poor and it was such hard work because that group of about half a dozen players were just out there then for a good time. It's amazing how quickly it can change the atmosphere. We should have won that Test series, but that group didn't help us one bit.

It was the same in 1993 when some of the players couldn't handle the pressure in New Zealand. It is harder in New Zealand and South Africa than Australia, I think. Because it is their number one sport they are always challenging not just as a team on the field but also as a nation as a whole; there are no easy times.

Mentally you have got to be really tough. Often the mental strength comes from that disappointment in week five and that is where the really good tours kick on. You can see it in the way the dirt-trackers handle it, the way they challenge in training, the focus they keep and the determination they show not to lose when they play their next game in midweek.

The 1974 trip was like that for the whole tour. There was a gap of either two or three weeks in between Tests so everyone was challenging all the time. That was a big lesson for me as coach; you have to keep the training competitive. You have to keep those who have not been picked involved and those who have been picked on their toes. It is a reciprocal arrangement; the respect flows both ways. This creates a positive and dynamic environment, which actually gets stronger once the Test series starts. It is not about processes, it is about people and the environment you create.

So often a tour is about momentum, and the midweek side can play a huge part in that. For instance, in 1997 we had lost 35–30 to Northern Transvaal and in the next week we faced two very tricky assignments against Gauteng Lions and Natal in the lead-up to the first Test. Those were the 'Big Three' and to play them in the space of eight days was always going to be tough.

Losing the first one of them was a blow, and when we returned to the hotel that night I made sure that I spoke to the players in the team room, reassuring them that I still thought they could win the Test series and that, if they were the group I thought they were, they would respond accordingly, both in training and in the matches.

They did. The midweek team won 20–14 in Johannesburg, and then we won 42–12 in Durban against Natal who were Currie Cup champions and had got to the semi-final of the Super 12 competition, as it was then. Our analyst Andy Keast had coached at Natal and therefore had plenty of contacts to tap up to assess the mood in their camp. The message we received was that unsurprisingly, despite the absence of their Springbok players, they were highly motivated and highly confident that they could show themselves as South Africa's premier province.

It was highly pleasing, therefore, that we played so well and won, scoring three tries, with the last of them from Lawrence Dallaglio being an absolute cracker, with Neil Jenkins kicking 24 points. The only downside was the shoulder injury suffered by Rob Howley that put him out of the tour.

We then played against a Springbok jersey for the first time on tour when facing the Emerging Springboks in Boland, and we put 50 points on them. Then there was the first Test victory, before the outstanding rugby against Free State that I have already mentioned, and finally the second Test and with it the series triumph.

There was a momentum shift after the Northern Transvaal game. It was a collective swing that happened because all 35 players delivered in that set of games. It was not the isolation of a Test match; it was a playing momentum that grew from game to game. Without the non-Test players delivering, that momentum would never have been there. People like Neil Back, Allan Bateman, Tony Underwood and Rob Wainwright were all vital in this. There were some big performances that made the whole thing work and come together. That gives you the one or two per cent extra that matters.

There are other ways in which the midweek side can help. For instance, in 1989 when the game was still amateur it was by selling some unwanted Test tickets at the gate to make a bit of money for everyone, and it was then shared around. It was the non-Test players driving that, especially John Jeffrey and one or two others.

I said to Clive Woodward in 2005 that I would take responsibility for the midweek side because I felt I could make a difference. I thought that if the team could feel that they had a purpose and an identity then they would not go off tour. And they didn't, to be fair. I also thought that if I could get that right, it would keep the Test side in good shape. My job was to keep my group positive, intent on delivering and not losing, which ultimately we achieved.

The Test series was lost 3-0 but the only other match that resulted in a defeat was the 19-13 loss against the New Zealand Maori; a defeat that caused much panic. It was only the fourth match of the tour (including the match against Argentina in Cardiff before we left), we only lost 19-13 and it was against good opposition that included such fine players as Marty Holah, Carl Hayman, Luke McAlister and Carlos Spencer. It cost some players their chances of a Test place and it also meant that we as the midweek coaching team were suddenly asked to oversee three matches on the trot – against Wellington, Otago and Southland – because Clive then wanted the Test team to concentrate on the first Test.

The Otago match in Dunedin, which we won 30–19, was actually one of the best performances of the tour, with the Wales No. 8 Ryan Jones, who had just been summoned from Wales' tour of Canada, really impressing and scoring one of three tries. We clearly made a statement because their captain Craig Newby said: 'They cheated like buggery and good luck to them because they got away with it.' My reply was: 'If they're now worried how effective we are at the breakdown we must be doing something right.' I was pleased, and allowed the players to have a good night out in Dunedin. They deserved it.

But what pleased me most on that tour was the game against Auckland in the last week of the tour. We knew that was our own Test match. And the group delivered, they were fantastic.

Auckland were going very well at that time, and were looking at a third consecutive win over the Lions. To add to the sense of occasion, my old pal and mucker from Northampton, Pat Lam, was coaching them. The atmosphere around that game, with a crowd of nearly 47,000, was absolutely superb. We won 17–13 after a try from Martyn Williams and to walk into the dressing room afterwards was wonderful. We could all say that we had done nothing in the midweek matches to hamper the Test team.

'You could see there was desperation to put the tour back on track,' said Lam afterwards. 'I thought Matt Dawson was outstanding. He was a real pest. It'll give them a lot of confidence going into the third Test.' That was no use, as it happened, because the final Test was lost 38-19. But the 'Midweek Massive' could have done no more.

The difference on that tour was that there was a physical separation from the Test team in training. A division was created because of this and also some of the tactical thinking was split because there were two separate coaching teams. This should not happen, and has not happened since.

But in terms of attitude and approach, that midweek side was absolutely spot-on.

KEY WORDS

- Ultimate Lion
- All play in first three or four games
- Badge gets bigger through attitude and actions
- Chemistry changes performance
- Every job has a responsibility and purpose
- Unselfish actions transform an environment
- Dirt-trackers

1997 South Africa v Natal
This was a classic example of the effect the midweek side can have
on the Test side, creating both momentum and group dynamics.

RAMPANT LIONS ROAR A WARNING

Natal Sharks 12 British Lions 42

Nell Drysdale at KING'S PARK

WE'VE had our fair share of false dawns in the past, so over-optimism should always be avoided. But what the hell! This was the afternoon when British rugby proved it CAN compete with the Southern Hemisphere countries, and only the most negative observer could forbear to cheer the quality of the Lions' display.

Oozing commitment, the much-criticised pack never creaked, with Keith Wood providing a barnstorming 80 minutes as the cornerstone of the front row, while their backs made hay, courtesy of a masterly show of flair and fluidity and, yes, the occasional *faux pas* from Gregor Townsend. Ultimately, it was altogether too heady a brew for Natal, who were brushed aside with almost contemptuous ease the longer the contest progressed.

South Africa will offer a sterner challenge when the three-Test series begins on Saturday, but the greatest compliment we can pay the Lions is that Jim Telfer, Ian McGeechan and Fran Cotton will have an incredibly difficult job on Tuesday evening when they sit down to pick their team for Newlands.

The proceedings marked an unhappy farewell for John Allan, late of Scotland and South Africa, who ran out alone for his final game with Natal to a rapturous welcome, and the cosmopolitan atmosphere was reinforced by the United Nations line-up in Lions' colours.

While it would have been unthinkable a month ago to forecast that only four Englishmen would figure in the ranks a week before the first Test, the determination of the so-called second-string players has consigned all prediction to the scrap heap.

How little Natal's proud pedigree and impressive credentials mattered once the whistle blew. Scott Gibbs and Allan Bateman flung themselves ferociously at their opposite numbers, Wood inflicted serious damage to Robert du Preez's ego with a juddering tackle which floored the Springbok, and the Lions were in the ascendancy, bolstered by a Welsh-dominated midfield and the myriad ploys of Townsend.

It was no surprise, therefore, when Neil Jenkins established an early lead with the simplest of penalties, but there were worrying signs as Rob Howley struggled with a shoulder injury and delivered a terrible pass to Townsend, which presaged a swift Natal riposte and Gavin Lawless levelled matters.

So far so equal, but, although Howley trudged off disconsolately to be replaced by Matt Dawson, the Lions roared on, with Alan Tait producing a thrilling foray, only for the referee to ignore a blatant obstruction on Townsend.

However, even at this stage, it was an exhilarating performance from the tourists and, despite Lawless briefly establishing a 6–3 lead for Natal, the Lions surged forward at a remarkable rate of knots and often left their opponents clutching at shadows.

The consequence was a spate of points for the Britons. First, Townsend landed a sweetly-stuck drop-goal, and the No 10 then pounced on Wood's deft chip to embarrass Lawless in scoring a fine opportunist try. Jenkins duly converted for a 13–6 cushion and, amid the maelstrom, we barely noticed that Martin Johnson had temporarily departed the field for treatment to a cut.

Natal responded with their own onslaught, but Tait, Gibbs and Bateman were pillars of strength in defending their lines, Natal's only profit a third penalty for Lawless. But, all the same, the Sharks were hanging on desperately as if awaiting Robert Shaw's arrival and, with Johnson re-entering the fray and Townsend bristling with purpose, the tourists extended their cushion through Jenkins on the stroke of the interval and were worth every inch of their 16–9 advantage.

Upon the resumption, the momentum flowed relentlessly in the Lions' favour, a spiralling up-and-under from Townsend inducing panic in the Natal ranks and allowing Jenkins another easy penalty. Such was the inherent confidence that Bateman even attacked from within his own 22, and you began to wonder whether the South Africans had the spirit, let alone the creativity, to claw their way back.

A wonderfully aggressive surge from their pack soon answered that question and André le Roux nearly grabbed a try, but frustration crept in and, despite a morale-boosting Lawless penalty, it was immediately cancelled out by another two from the metronomic Jenkins. You could see the Springbok shoulders drop as the match slipped inexorably away from them.

By the final quarter, the Lions were truly in command, and the crowd's recourse to the Mexican wave testified to their lack of interest in the one-sided tussle as the Lions emphasised ther superiority with a try from replacement Mike Catt after an inch-perfect kick ahead by the ubiquitous Townsend.

The climactic scenes were glorious to behold as the demolition was completed in a flurry of exciting continuity rugby with a touchdown for Lawrence Dallaglio

OK, the message might be chauvinistic, but let's recite it regardless; bring on the 'Boks!

6

THE TESTS

I love walking, as does my wife Judy, and we spend a lot of time in the Lake District. As a coach I also liked walking, but then I was on my own – either walking from home with the dog or from the team hotel in some faraway land. It was the time when I could think best. This was especially important on the morning of a match, because I could then prepare what I wanted to say to the players before kick-off.

People often ask me when I began preparing my pre-match speeches and the honest answer is that I only ever started thinking about them when I began my morning walk. That was when I could clear my mind, get a feel for where we were as a group and decide what I wanted to say. I would make some notes when I got back, mainly key words around a basic frame-work. I always tried to speak from the heart, and I always tried to speak clearly and slowly so that my thoughts were clear.

I have never been more nervous addressing a group of Lions than when asked by Warren Gatland to do so before the first Test in Australia in 2013. As an outsider who was not part of that tour – remember that it is the group that makes every Lions tour – it made me feel very uncomfortable.

But I was also nervous on the afternoon of 28 June 1997. We were in Durban. It was about two hours before kick-off in the second Test. We had won the first Test and we could now win the series. We could become only the third side, after the 1974 Lions and the All Blacks the year before in 1996, to win a series in South Africa.

The stakes were huge. The Test players gathered in the team room at the hotel. Fran Cotton had taken the non-Test group to the bus. John Bentley was smiling, but it looked like a nervous smile, Lawrence Dallaglio was juggling some tennis balls, but generally it was quiet, with only a few whispered voices piercing the silence.

I stood before them and this is what I said:

There are days like this that many rugby players never have, never experience. It is special. Jim [Telfer] and I have been involved in rugby a long time. I can tell you that these are the days that you never believe will come again. It has. And I can tell you that I have given a lot of things up. I love my rugby. I love my family. And when you come to a day like this you know why you do it all. You know why you have been involved.

It has been a privilege. It is a privilege, because we are something special. You will meet each other in the street in 30 years' time, and there will just be a look, and you will know just how special some days in your life are.

We have proved that the lion has claws and has teeth. We've wounded a Springbok. When an animal is wounded, it returns in frenzy. It doesn't think, it fights for its very existence. The lion waits and at the right point it goes for the jugular and the life disappears.

Today, every second of that game we've talked about what they are going to do or everybody else has. We go for the jugular. Every tackle, every pass, every kick is saying to the f****** Springbok, you're dying. Your hopes of living in this Test series are going. And on that field sometimes today all that will be between you is a look, no words, just a look that will say everything. And the biggest thing it will say is that you are special. You are very, very special.

It has been and is a privilege. Go out, enjoy it, remember how you got here and why. Finish it off and be special for the rest of your lives.

Good luck. Go for it.

In the dressing room just before the players departed for the field I was even more passionate. Martin Johnson was saying a few words, but the likes of Keith Wood, Scott Gibbs and Gregor Townsend were whipping the boys up into a frenzy, with myself and Jim Telfer chipping in with the odd comment.

Every second of every minute of every play [I shouted] let them start looking at the floor, let them start looking down. There isn't one man there you should be frightened of. There isn't anything you should be afraid of doing. Whatever it takes.

You are in places no British player has been in before.

What's behind that badge, who are you playing for? Who does it matter to? Everybody here, whoever it is. Think about it.

The emotion was taking over, I'm afraid, but those last words were always very important to me and were at the heart of most of my speeches to the Lions players. The journey to becoming a Lion should never be forgotten by any player.

I know what my parents had given to allow me to become a Lion, particularly in my late teens. When I played at Headingley I will never forget my father putting a fiver in my pocket on a Saturday morning so that I could stand my rounds at the bar after the game. I was the secondary modern kid and he did not want me to be embarrassed around all the middle-class grammar-school boys. A fiver was a lot of money in those days and it was not until after my father had died of lung cancer that I discovered it was actually a quarter of his weekly wage. He ended up walking to work. What a sacrifice that was; what a motivation for the rest of my life.

I had so many people to thank. I was very conscious of the fact that many of them had given up a lot of time – without expecting any thanks – and had provided me with opportunities to thrive. There were people like my maths teacher at West Park School, Ken Dalby, who told me to go try my luck at Headingley rather than playing for West Park Old Boys. Eight of us from the school went and joined the Colts. Within 12 months I was in the first team, playing for them on a Saturday afternoon, having played for the school in the morning.

There were others like Ivor Lloyd and Pat Donovan at Headingley, who would come to wherever the school was playing in the morning and then drive me to play for Headingley in the afternoon. There was Bernard White, a lecturer at Carnegie College in Leeds, who was a great influence upon me as a coach because he was so far ahead of everyone else in his field at the time.

When I was speaking to the Lions players I knew we all had our own stories, our own timelines. At every key decision or moment in my career I could see a face here or a name there to signify that step – people like Ken, Ivor, Pat and Bernard. That kept me honest. I had to keep making sure I did those people justice.

And that included my wife Judy. She spent hours and hours on her own with the children, and often even when I was at home I was in a different world. Then there was all that extra training she helped me with when I was a player. To be honest, it is only when I look back now that I appreciate the sacrifice she made and the responsibility she took.

I have always wanted to keep the players honest about what they would have to give out on the field, so that is why I used to draw on the things that were important to me. My speeches came from the feelings that I had had as a player, and I had been in a privileged position, too, as a coach.

You don't own a Lions jersey – you just try to add to it and then it is passed on. It is never the finished article. That is the unique challenge of the Lions: to take up the jersey every four years and try to add to what is already there. Each tour is different, it reflects the players and the staff on that tour. This is something I have emphasised throughout the book, I know, but I have done so again because it was always the essence of what I was trying to say in my speeches. It was about where we were but also about placing it in the greater Lions picture.

I am an emotional person and this was no better demonstrated than after my final speech to the Lions as their coach, ahead of the final Test in South Africa in 2009. Despite playing so well and so heroically, we were 2-0 down in the series. I knew this was my last involvement as a Lions coach. It was such a good group of players and I was just desperate that they should get something out of that third Test.

A series result of 3-0 would have been really harsh for the players. There aren't many tours where the Lions have won the last Test match. Indeed, it has only happened nine times in 28 tours. Even in 1971 and 1974 the last Tests of the tour were drawn.

All this led to me making this speech:

They've said there is nothing to play for, that it is a dead series. I will remind you what Gats [Warren Gatland] said on Wednesday – I think we have everything to play for. Because today will determine what we are. It will say everything about us. The biggest thing about what you earn in this jersey is a respect and a reputation and to any person that is the biggest thing you can ever have for what you do and what you stand for.

We can leave a legacy in this last game in this jersey for the players to pick up in four years' time. And for four years we can leave something that makes sure when people think about the Lions they think good. They'll think about you, they'll think about this performance and they can live with it for four years.

Some of you might be there to pick up the next jersey in four years' time, some of us won't be.

Please, please, give them something to play for and something to understand.

Good luck. But play for everything that we want that jersey to be and everything you have made it so far. All the best, boys.

The players filed out of the room slowly and I picked up my bag, slung it over my shoulder and went to follow them. But I had been struggling to keep my emotions in check during the final part of the speech and now suddenly they came flooding out. I went to the corner of the room and began crying. Graham Rowntree, the former England and Lions prop and now part of the coaching team, came over to me and hugged me. I began sobbing loudly.

The reality that this was my last time with the Lions had hit me. It meant so much, and I knew it was the end of a very special chapter in my life, an involvement spread over 35 years. You can see that moment on the *Living with the Pride* DVD of that tour. I agonised for a long time whether to give the go-ahead for that clip to be shown. The producers had to come back to me two or three times before I gave my permission. It was a very personal and emotional moment for me. But I eventually cleared it, reasoning that it was part of the story.

It is also part of my story, I suppose, because I have always believed that emotion is crucial in rugby. You have to love what you're doing and hate losing. Rugby has got to be emotive, it can't be pure science. And for me there is nothing more emotive than a Lions Test. For the Test matches are the games that really matter.

Yes, I have talked a lot about the environment and the midweek matches, but all that is preparing for one thing: the Test series. You do not go into the tour with your Test team but, as I have touched upon, you do go into it with your Test-match principles, thoughts and tactics. You need to know the type of rugby required and therefore the type of player required to deliver it.

In 1997 at the very first training session I told the players that we were going to have to play a brand of rugby that surprised the southern hemisphere. It was based around winning the Test series and having players capable of playing a game that we were not playing in the northern hemisphere but one that we needed to beat South Africa.

That was the biggest lesson learnt – that by the first Test our house had to be in order. And in each game along the way what we had to be doing was ticking off things that we thought we had to be good at and accepting that certain things would not be in place in the early games, but that the key ones would be building internally towards that Test-match performance. You could see it coming together in training.

The big thing for me was that South Africa did not think northern hemisphere teams defended particularly well. That was why I had spent time at the St Helens rugby league club before the tour, just talking to them about what they did, and I had also spoken to Mike Slemen, the former England winger, who had done some defensive work with England. I said to the players that we had to be so well organised that it would be difficult for the South Africans to pick us off.

As I observed in my post-tour report: 'Another important feature of all our early work was that we were already gearing our practices to playing the Springboks. I wanted to use every provincial game as a build-up to playing Test-match rugby. Consequently there was concentration on work with the half backs, back row and inside centre to tactically play in such a way that nullified the South Africans' strengths and patterns of running and support.'

It was the same in 2009. It means that even if you have to make changes to your Test team through the series, you do not have to re-educate those coming in. They will know what to do. I think this is one of the biggest lessons I learnt, because early in my Lions coaching career I was thinking about winning individual midweek games by certain methods. There has to be one way and one message throughout the tour. For example, in 2009 we made seven changes for the final Test but the rugby was still the same.

Essentially it boils down to what I have previously referred to as 'world-class basics'. Winning Test matches is not about fantastic tactics, it is about doing the basic things time and time again under pressure in order to put your game on the field in better shape than your opponents' game. It is about ensuring that the game you want to play in the first Test is taking shape in those early matches. If you lose the odd game it will not matter as long as it is obvious that progress is being made in the game plan and that you can hit the first Test running.

The key for me was learning from previous tours. As a player I was on such long tours that you literally did prepare for every opponent. There was time to do that. So when I first started coaching that was the only thing I knew, and therefore in 1989 and 1993 we were looking at opponents game by game and working out specific tactics.

In 1989 one thing I wanted to do was take on Australia up front, so in my head I had some idea of the sort of rugby we were going to have to produce to win the Test matches, but it wasn't as clear as it was in 1997, where I went out of my way to get the tactics right, to know the South Africa Test players inside out and then to look for the right players within our own group of players to look at the best delivery of those tactics. That was why 1997 was such a watershed tour in a number of ways. One principle I kept to was that I would not pick the Test team until Test week because I wanted to give every player the opportunity. So if you are doing that then some of the tactics evolve strategically.

In 1989 we were unbeaten up until the first Test but we had adapted to the teams we played along the way. And we had learnt some tough lessons when we played Queensland in the third match of the tour, only winning 19–15. It was a pretty brutal match, dirty even, with a lot of off-the-ball hits and one disgraceful incident when the Queensland flanker Julian Gardner kicked the Wales centre Mike Hall time after time, so much so that Hall's shirt was shredded.

We nearly got caught out with the physicality. So even though that aspect of the Test matches, which descended towards brutality and violence at times, became a big issue and it was said that we started it, actually the lesson was shown in that Queensland match at Ballymore.

Queensland had started it through Gardner. 'Dai Young clocked him and the mood was set,' said Hall. I remember speaking to the players after that game and insisting that we should not take a backward step on the tour from there on in. I was not advocating some sort of 99 call like in 1974 and I was not saying that we should start any trouble, simply that we should finish it if it did start. As the tour wore on and we lost the first Test that thinking had to be channelled towards the second Test, otherwise the series was over.

In the first Test I tried to get some of the footballers like Brendan Mullin to carry but essentially we were just too loose in that Test and lost 30–12. We turned over far too much ball and allowed their half backs Nick Farr-Jones and Michael Lynagh to control the game too easily. But for the second Test I looked at the Australian side and realised we had to get more physical. We had to attack their pack, because I did not think it was as good as I originally thought.

So the training that week and the selection reflected that. I have mentioned selection for this game before, but Mike Teague being fit and Wade Dooley coming in made a huge difference. It was about dominating Australia up front and putting the half backs under intense pressure so they couldn't have a back row that was free to run into the open spaces or run off the shoulders of the centres, which is what they had done in the first Test.

We collectively trained like that and on the Friday before the Test Roger Uttley and I took the half backs Robert Jones and Rob Andrew to the Ballymore ground in Brisbane. All the other players had taken the opportunity to go out and do some shopping because they were buying some cheap coats. But Jones and Andrew wanted none of that; they wanted to go to Ballymore.

So we did just that and the four of us spent an hour walking the whole of Ballymore. We covered almost every blade of grass on it. We talked about every place on the pitch, the decisions we would make, the lineouts we wanted, where we would play next, what we would call when we got to the halfway, what we would do inside their 22 left and right, how we would do it in our own 22. We spent an hour going through all the alternatives and all the tactical calls we would make in every area of the field.

I wrote most of this down so that later that night Jones and Andrew could stand up in front of a chart and talk the rest of the team through it. By the end of it every player knew the options for the backs and forwards, not just their own department. We did it as a group.

I did something similar, although not quite the same, in 1997 when we wanted to give the players 48 hours off before the Test, so we finished the last 15 minutes of the training on Thursday as we wanted to start the first 15 minutes of the Test match on the Saturday. We mirrored it. We then met for cream scones on the Friday. But that tactical clarity in 1989 came out of needing to stay in the series. In the other games we had had variances in approach.

When I look back now, the fact that we lost the first Lions Test I coached actually did have an impact on what came afterwards. That second week and what we planned, I kept it in my head. The third week was just a continuation of that.

That second Test will forever be known as 'the Battle of Ballymore' because of its often violent nature. And I do blame myself for some of that because I wound up Robert Jones rather too much. He began the 'argy-bargy', as the great Bill McLaren, would have said. He stood on Farr-Jones' foot at a scrum and all hell broke loose. Not long afterwards Dai Young kicked Steve Cutler at a ruck, instigating another huge brawl. That was out of order and Clive Rowlands and I told Dai as much after the game.

But we won. We won 19–12 and were back in the series thanks to tries from Gavin Hastings and, most memorably, Jeremy Guscott, who chipped ahead and collected his own kick to score. Our forwards, with Dooley, Teague, Dean Richards and Paul Ackford standing out, were magnificent. But afterwards I remember that I did not want to single anyone out because in truth they had all been superb in one of the most satisfying wins of my career as player or coach.

It remains one of my favourite Lions Tests because we didn't go ahead until about 10 minutes from the end. What I was watching was a team that knew exactly what it was doing and why. We got control of the game eventually and we took that control into the third Test. That was a big breakthrough moment in our thinking for me as a coach and also for the group.

Those big forwards had just got bigger as the second Test went on. We had limited the space Australia had and had then ground them down and tired them out until some space came for us, and then we had taken our chances.

The aftermath was messy, with the Australian Rugby Union issuing a press release in which it said it was preparing a video to send to the four home unions showing certain acts of violence during the match. Farr-Jones, who ended with a battered face full of stitches, said before the third Test: 'I think the third Test could develop into open warfare. As far as I am concerned, the Lions have set the rules and if the officials are going to do nothing about it then we are going to do it ourselves.'

It was typical of some of the stuff that was said and written at the time. It was all getting out of hand so I knew that I had to do something about it. I decided to meet with Bob Templeton, the highly respected and regarded Australian assistant coach. We talked like friends rather than enemies and agreed that, even though we both knew that the final Test was going to be every bit as aggressive and physical again, we could not let it descend into the sort of 'open warfare' Farr-Jones was talking about.

And it didn't. But we won again, this time by just 19–18, with the crucial moment coming in the second half when David Campese made a horrendous error behind his own line, opting not to touch down, throwing an awful pass at full back Greg Martin and therefore allowing Ieuan Evans to pounce and score.

Again, the forwards were outstanding and even though a couple of penalties from Michael Lynagh brought the score to 19–18, we were able to hold them out fairly comfortably at the end. The celebrations were loud and raucous. Clive Rowlands was in tears. It had been a magnificent achievement.

To think that some people had not been keen on this tour taking place at all, because it was a trial of sorts, a means of testing Australia out as a proper Lions venue. Some like J.P.R. Williams had even said that these were 'not real Lions'. They were real Lions, believe me. They stood up for themselves in the face of some massive intimidation both on and off the field.

In 1993 in New Zealand there was the issue of the way the squad was selected. That clearly militated against an obvious philosophy running throughout the tour, and so I tried to make sure we were in the right shape to win the provincial games. As I have mentioned, I still believe we were robbed in the first Test that we lost 20–18. I didn't realise until I was searching through my possessions for this book that in my report of that tour I had written detailed reports of every single game.

For that match I wrote:

It was quite amazing to think that New Zealand had originally said that they would run us off the park, but now they were commenting about scrummaging us off the park and playing us through the set pieces. It was a significant change of approach. We knew our lineout work had to be of the highest quality and that the extra scrummaging we had been doing should give us a tightness in the scrums, which would not result in the All Blacks gaining any significant advantages from the set pieces. If we could ensure this then I was convinced that we, through the backs, could run at their defences and create enough second and third plays to disorganise.

At the time I was emphasising to the players the need to play 'ninety-second rugby'. In other words, if we could go through the phases for longer than ninety seconds then spaces would appear in the defence and there would be opportunities for us.

In the event two crucial decisions, one in the first 60 seconds of the game, and the other in the last minute of the game, meant that we lost a match I felt we should have comfortably won [I wrote]. Both sides were nervous and tentative, although we did not significantly develop enough attacks from chances gained. The forwards played exceptionally well, particularly in the second half against a significant wind, and it did give them a lot of confidence to realise that they could match All Black rugby, particularly in the phases which they always assumed they (the All Blacks) would have superiority – i.e. the breakdown phases of the game.

Needless to say we were all desperately disappointed at the end of this game, not only because we felt it should have been ours, but also because we now knew we had to produce an outstanding performance in the second Test and again in the very last match of the tour.

A feature of our after-match routine was to have a quick review and thoughts from the players on the way the game had gone. This time we did not pursue that because of their disappointment. We got some general comments, but I felt it was more important that they relaxed, did not harbour thoughts of what might have been and now concentrated very positively on getting hold of the opportunities we still had in the remaining games.

On that tour there was a two-week gap between the first and second Tests, which meant we played Auckland on the intervening Saturday, losing 23–18 against a team that was full of All Blacks – 'effectively the fourth Test match of the tour', I wrote in my report. Then in the week of the second Test that was to be played in Wellington, we played Hawke's Bay in Napier and lost 29–17.

'It was probably the most disappointing Lions game I have ever been involved with,' I wrote. 'I would say Hawke's Bay were probably the second poorest side we played on tour. In every way this was a very unsatisfactory performance.'

In my book, *So Close to Glory*, I went further. 'We hit rock bottom,' I said. 'There was the unmistakable sound of the scraping of the barrel. We could sink no lower. I'm afraid it was just one of those dismal displays which defies description.'

For that second Test we had to make sure we had certain things in place tactically, and we had to do something I never wanted to do on a Lions tour. As I explained in my report:

I now felt that if we were to achieve success in the Test match I had to divorce the Test 21 [as it was then] from the others in the group and almost make scapegoats of the performance in Napier simply to focus the Test team onto the priorities of beating New Zealand and use that result as a means of example and motivation.

On arrival in Wellington I had a separate meeting with eight senior players from the selected Test team in which we discussed the tactical changes I felt we had to make and then we wanted to organise not just the sessions but the whole build-up to the game.

Following a general session in Napier before we left for Wellington, the main session was to take place privately in Wellington on Thursday, and here I changed completely the structure of the programme. I wanted completely different lineout variations as well as codes, speeding up of driving and collective hits on packs both in attack and defence. We had to take the game to New Zealand and we could not let them settle.

Because of the tactical input the session lasted over two hours, but was not physically hard. The good weather allowed us to stop, talk, practise from various areas, develop, look at alternatives and work through all the changes we wanted to implement. And the players were involved in all these variations.

The session concluded with the forwards working on 30 to 40 live scrums. There was a very good feeling at the end of this session.

These tactical changes were again worked through on the blackboard on Thursday evening, and more and more we just talked collectively about how we wanted to attack the game.

We ended up with a record win of 20–7 for the Lions over the All Blacks. The Lions have only beaten New Zealand on six occasions in 38 attempts, and only in Wellington in 1971 when they won 13–3 has there been another victory margin of 10 points or more.

But our win was more piecemeal because of the selection in the first place. We made significant changes for that Test, bringing in Martin Johnson at lock and moving Jason Leonard to tighthead prop to replace Scotland's Paul Burnell, even though Jason hadn't really played there since school. If the tighthead is in trouble at the scrummage it is the hooker who is affected most, so we brought in Brian Moore instead of Scotland's Kenny Milne and he was very happy to have Leonard alongside him. And in the backs, of course, we made the huge call of dropping Will Carling and replacing him with Scott Gibbs.

The game as a whole had moved on since 1989 so it was not as easy to win playing the kind of simple, physical game we had in the second Test in Australia, but we still needed to get our fundamentals right. And we did, with the lineout going particularly well. We now had four genuine options in Martin Bayfield, Johnson, Ben Clarke and Dean Richards, with Bayfield having the game of his life, while the half backs Dewi Morris and Rob Andrew tackled more than any half-back combination I had ever seen before.

They also kicked superbly, not kicking to touch but down the touchline, keeping the ball in play as we had talked about. We also decided to play into the wind and indeed the sun when we won the toss, in contrast to the first Test when we had played with the elements behind us. Often sides take too long to get going and do not take full advantage of the elements in the first half. Here, we were able to turn around 9–7 ahead at the break, having shown great discipline not to concede one kickable penalty for Grant Fox, their esteemed goal-kicking fly half.

Centre Eroni Clarke scored a first-half try that Fox converted, but New Zealand did not score another point, and this was the first Test for five years in which Fox had not kicked a penalty. Gavin Hastings had dropped a high ball to concede that try but it was his only mistake and he was a huge influence as captain; there had been considerable doubt during the week whether he would play because of a hamstring injury.

I had been absolutely desperate for him to play because of that influence and had actually said to him that it did not matter if he only lasted one minute in the game. I just wanted his presence as the leader in the build-up. 'I felt it was imperative that he did play even if it was only for one minute,' I wrote. 'Because it was difficult to over-estimate his influence as a captain during the build-up and on the attitude of the other players.'

It took some persuasion. 'With help from Jeremy Guscott and Rob Andrew he was convinced that he would not be letting the side down if he had to leave the field in the first minute,' I wrote. 'And that was more important in these next 24 hours he played a significant role. Having agreed this he was a changed man, and took everything in his positive style.'

He played and it was a famous win, with England's Rory Underwood scoring a memorable try after a lovely delayed pass from Guscott. The photograph of Underwood diving over for that try is one of my favourites, not least because it shows a huge advertisement for Scottish Life on the hoardings in the background. I was working for them at the time and that pleased their chief executive, Malcolm Murray, no end!

We lost the last Test in 1993, because in truth it was a game too far, but the following tour in 1997 to South Africa was when everything changed in terms of the tactical preparation for a Lions trip. It was the first time everything was geared to a Test-match performance. Clive Woodward had gone the other way in 2005 when he tried to pick a Test-match team early in the tour and keep it together and build it that way. But by doing that you cannot see the players who are growing in the Lions environment. It is a completely different pressure and it is about how the players react to it.

Whenever people ask me about the Lions Tests that stand above all others for me, I can never look beyond the 1997 tour. The first Test was just so memorable because so many people thought we would lose the series 3–0. As Jim Telfer said in that speech of his: 'They don't respect us.'

Some of the rugby we played in that Test was incredible, especially the off-loading and the speed at which we played. I think that surprised South Africa. I thought we were very good and just got better as the game went on. Defensively we harried them, and Scott Gibbs just grew and grew as the defensive leader of the team. We showed we were fit and that we had that collective strength to keep playing.

We had talked about ensuring that we were still in the game with 20 minutes to go and though we were 16–15 down with 10 minutes to go, we still fancied our chances, and that was when Matt Dawson scored his wonder try. Then Alan Tait scored too and it was all ours as we won 25–16.

In Durban in the second Test we got stronger and stronger as the game went on. Yes, we were fortunate that they didn't kick their goals, with Henry Honiball, Percy Montgomery and André Joubert all having a go and missing six attempts between them, but Neil Jenkins kept putting them over for us – such is the pressure of this sort of match. As Keith Wood said: 'People say they didn't have recognised kickers, but they did. They had really good kickers but they crumbled under the pressure of the series. Whatever it is about the Lions, there is crazy intensity, crazy. And things happen in that sort of pressure.'

The way we responded after being 15–9 down at the hour mark was quite remarkable. We had conceded three tries and certainly two that we should not have conceded, with Montgomery and Joubert scoring, firstly when Tait coughed the ball up and then when John Bentley went too high in the tackle. The way we came back even surprised me a little. The courage was enormous. Jenks kicked two more penalties so that it was 15–15, before we created the position from which Jeremy Guscott was able to drop the winning goal.

Jim Telfer and I were sitting in the main stand and as the ball went between the posts we leapt in the air and screamed in celebration. It was a hostile crowd that evening and we were right in the middle of it, but we did not care. It was a special moment.

There were some jitters then before the end, of course. South Africa threw everything at us but somehow we stood firm, with some crucial interventions from the likes of Neil Back, who was on for Richard Hill, when he made a vital turn-over and Austin Healey, who was on for Tait, when he helped Jenks stop a try.

When the final whistle went it is still probably my favourite rugby moment of all time. Winning a Grand Slam with Scotland in 1990 was special, as was playing for the victorious Lions in 1974, but this beats them simply because we had defied the odds so spectacularly. We had been written off, and even in this clinching game in Durban we had not played that well, and had only had about 30 per cent of the game, but we over-came all that to win.

It was the sweetest of moments.

KEY WORDS

- Emotion is part of performance
- A badge is its people
- The look
- The journey
- Game plan for Tests not midweek games

1974 South Africa, Second Test
As I said, the final whistle in Durban is still my
favourite moment in rugby.

SOUTH AFRICA 15, BRITISH LIONS 18: TOURISTS ABSORB SPRINGBOKS' PRESSURE AND

It's mission accomplished

STUART BATHGATE In Durban

THE Impossible Dream has become implausible reality, and with a match to spare. The Lions will go to Ellis Park on Saturday looking for a 3–0 whitewash in the Test series, but they have already done what they came here to do and what few people really believed they could do. In winning the series they have not only shown how quickly a bunch of talented individuals can become a coherent fighting unit, they have also restored the reputation of Northern Hemisphere rugby.

By contrast the Springboks, who started the series as 1–5 favourites, are in utter disarray. The South African *Sunday Times* ran a phone-in poll yesterday asking if the national coach, Carel du Plessis, could be sacked – and this after just three matches in charge.

Du Plessis, dubbed the Prince of Wingers during his playing career, is now in danger of becoming the Clown Prince of Coaches. He will surely be allowed to stay for the Tri-Nations series, but with New Zealand looking unstoppable and Australia recently formidable against France, more grief for Du Plessis seems just around the corner.

What lies in store for his Lions counterpart Ian McGeechan is less certain. He can name his price now, having shown himself to be the most inventive thinker in world rugby. The harmonious triumvirate he has formed with Fran Cotton and Jim Telfer, has displayed an adaptability utterly at odds with the reputation of the European game – and with the reality of the way in which the English national side frequently play.

And all this without Robert Howley, Scott Quinnell and Doddie Weir – three men who had surely played themselves into the Test team before injury ended their tours. Ieuan Evans, who played in Cape Town but was ruled out of Saturday's second Test in Durban because of groin strain, was another who had looked to be an automatic Test selection.

In other words, a squad already regarded over here as second rate had four of their best players removed yet still triumphed. It is an extraordinary testament to the unity of this squad, and to their never-say-die spirit.

They certainly needed that at King's Park. If the first Test had been close, this was a real skin of the teeth job. At Newlands the Lions had gone 2-0 down on the try count, but ended up at 2-2 after the late scores from Matt Dawson and Alan Tait. On Saturday they went 3-0 down on tries, failed to amend that position, yet still won.

You are not supposed to be able to do that in modern rugby – and, to be fair, the Lions would not have succeeded in doing it had the Springboks possessed a halfway decent kicker in their side. While Neil Jenkins sent over five out of five. Henry Honiball, Percival Montgomery and Andre Joubert were unable to score one out of the six they attempted between them.

Yet, even given that demoralising deficiency. South Africa came close. As the match entered its last quarter, the Springboks, already 15-9 ahead, entered the Lions' 22. "I think they've given up on this one," said the man next to me of the British and Irish XV. Then, as the teams waited for a lineout, the massive visiting support took up the refrain: "Lions, Lions, Lions."

It is not quite in the Noel Coward league when it comes to lyrical subtleties, but it sent a shiver up the spine, and succeeded, too, in stiffening the Lions' back bone.

The danger cleared, the tourists inched up field. Penalty: 15-12.

Then, with seven minutes left, the same thing again: 15-15. Finally, with only three minutes showing on the stadium clock, Jeremy Guscott collected a pass from Dawson, dropped a goal, and the match was won – well, once the small matter of a chase for the Lions' line, thankfully won by substitute Austin Healey, was out of the way.

"The ball was at the base of the scrum, Dawse [Matt Dawson] looked for Gregor Townsend, but he only saw me – and there was panic on his face," said Guscott after the match.

"But he sent a sweet pass to me, and the ball sailed between the posts. Three points, Test series won, thanks very much."

While the Lions managed those nine points in the last quarter, their opponents failed to score in the final 25. Again, one was reminded of what Telfer had said on the eve of the first Test; if we can stay in touch with 15 or 10 minutes to go things could get interesting.

Staying in touch was easier said than done in the first hour, though. The South Africans were far more co-ordinated than they had been a week earlier, and threatened throughout that spell to run away with the game. Their first try, scored by Joost van der Westhuizen, on the verge of half-time, was a big fillip, sending them in at the break just 6–5 behind.

The score by Montgomery, who apart from his kicking had a competent debut, took the Springboks into the lead for the first time at 10–6, but by the time Joubert shrugged off the attention of John Bentley to take his team's tally to 15, Jenkins had slotted another penalty, so that the Lions were still, after being on the ropes, just six points behind.

"We weathered the storm, and were never more than a score away from them" said McGeechan.

"The last 15 minutes we played quite cleverly, and started to move the game around a bit."

Moved around a bit? The game, in the wider sense, has been shaken to its foundations and then rebuilt anew by the Lions, these history makers, these architects of excellence.

7

TEST-MATCH ANIMALS

It was the morning after New Zealand had beaten Ireland in Dublin in November 2016 and I was reading what the All Blacks' head coach Steve Hansen had to say about his team's 21–9 victory. Ireland had sensationally beaten the All Blacks a fortnight before, triumphing 40–29 in Chicago, and apparently Hansen had used the word 'character' at least 10 times in his post-match press conference in Dublin to describe his side's performance.

'You can't coach character, you can't teach it,' he had said. 'It's got to be there. It's called a Test match because it is a test of your mental strength and your character.' I found myself nodding my head in agreement at these words, and I also thought: 'He is talking about Test-match animals here.'

That is the term I have long used – I think I first employed it in 1997 when I also referred to 'putting a marker down', which seems to be quite popular these days too – to describe players who can thrive above others in Test-match rugby. And I thought that it was good that Hansen recognised that even though he has all that talent in his All Black squad, New

Zealand won that match because of the Test-match mentality of his players.

What is a Test-match animal? Well, he is never prepared to be second. He knows what is required and he does it again and again and again, and he does it in such a physical, determined and focused way that he is never going to be beaten. His instinct is just that little bit more ruthless than others'. You can be a good international player but what a Lions Test does is find out something more about a player.

It is about that animal instinct. He is there not just for survival but also for control. He has an instinct to do the right thing that makes a difference. It is not in every international rugby player, but it is in every successful Lion.

At international level it's an ability to say: 'My head is going in there, and this is going to make the difference whether we win or lose.' It is about playing on the edge, but with intelligence and awareness. That is why the Test-match animal is so efficient and effective: he is a combination of execution and decision-making.

You can have all the skills and techniques from training. You can build experience from playing. But the instinct to do the right thing at the right time is inside you; that is the difference. To have that animal bravery, to know what you are doing is probably stupid, but to do it anyway with the conviction that it will tilt a game, is a special gift.

You need an open mind as a coach. That animal instinct is what you are looking for in training; it is what you ask other coaches about when you are selecting a Lions squad.

Test-match animals are as competitive at training as they are in matches; on the 1974 Lions tour there were a lot of fights in training. And I remember hearing that J.P.R. Williams had scrummaged in the front row in training on the 1971 tour, but he tried to do it again in 1974 and came back a couple of minutes later, saying: 'I'm not getting stuck in there again!'

That 1974 pack was unbelievable. You always knew that you had back-up, that there would be players around who would not back off from the difficult stuff. You knew that these players would be grafting to be in the best and most effective places. I was so lucky that that was the Lions environment I was introduced to. I first saw this animal instinct in the likes of J.P.R. and Gareth Edwards on that tour. They were just so hugely, hugely competitive.

Gareth was a prodigious talent but it was the edge that he had that stood out for me. In the big situations he would still go for it and back himself and get it right. Gareth was simply phenomenal; he was an angry man if things were not going his way. That had a big impact on me. When you are on the field with such a player and the team is under pressure, like during the third Test on that 1974 tour, you understand what animal instinct is.

My wife Judy always says that if I ever lose at snakes and ladders I will throw the board across the room. Test-match animals are not good losers. You can accept it afterwards, but you hate every single moment of what it feels like.

Of those I coached, the greatest example of a Test-match animal was Martin Johnson. He didn't talk a lot but if something needed picking up he always said the right thing. In training if it needed a lead he would take it. Under pressure he was brilliant at assessing the right call.

For instance, he barely called any lineouts to himself in the first Test in 1997, because he knew that Jeremy Davidson had the beating of the South Africans and that his winning of the ball in the middle would have a greater bearing on the game. A lot of people would have just called them to themselves to say: 'I am the captain and I am in charge.' Johnno just did the right thing rather than trying to look good for the sake of it.

I still believe that despite all the talent England had in their team in 2003, they needed Martin Johnson there to win the Rugby World Cup. Without him I am not so sure they would have triumphed.

I have always loved the things forwards do to turn matches and Johnno did that for England time and time again. Take when they were down to six forwards against the All Blacks in Wellington in 2003, when Lawrence Dallaglio and Neil Back were in the sin bin. Who had his hands on the ball most for the next 10 minutes? At the lineout, on the carry? It was Johnno. When England had to scrummage, it was Johnno's head disappearing up his own backside, but he knew that was what he had to do. All he knew was that he couldn't succumb, even though, physically, it was probably hurting him an awful lot.

He just did what he had to do to make sure the game was not lost at that time, and for me, that is the difference: the understanding and instinct that there are times in a game where you cannot win it, but you could definitely lose it.

Johnno's attitude and influence extended to things beyond the field. He was actually a bit of an anorak in how he prepared. Before the 1997 tour he did some preparation with the media, for instance, because he had not done that before. He took himself out of his comfort zone because he knew that was what he had to do.

I have the utmost respect for him as a player and as a man, and that was why I was so disappointed for him when things went so wrong for him as England manager at the 2011 Rugby World Cup. I really wanted to speak to him in the aftermath, take him out for dinner and talk it through, but I understand that he was too devastated to do so. Whatever happened there will never change my view of him. He remains the ultimate Test-match animal.

I think the term resonates with the players. And I think they know who the animals are, even if sometimes it comes as a surprise to those on the outside and even to some coaches who might be looking for the wrong signs. For instance, Matt Dawson was a good example when he came into the Test side after Rob Howley's injury in the build-up in 1997 – and you have to remember that Rob was playing exceptionally well and it was thought at the time that it would be a crushing blow to the team.

You are then making a call on the next man in and not necessarily looking just at Dawson's ability. You are backing your own judgement and your own experience. Dawson had not been England's scrum half in the Five Nations that season – Andy Gomarsall and Austin Healey had been the starting scrum halves. But I knew all about Dawson the rugby player and the character because in the previous two years I had coached him every day at Northampton. I knew that under pressure he was the ultimate competitor. He had that animal instinct to keep the pressure on, to keep playing the right way, to not be afraid of taking opportunities and be ruthless about not missing those opportunities.

And, blow me, if ever a player saw an opportunity and took it, it was when he scored his try in the first Test.

I was criticised for picking him for the tour in the first place but I knew that I could totally trust him in that environment. He was a Test-match animal, and he showed it.

When I think of others I coached, I look at the side in Australia in 1989 and immediately identify the likes of Brian Moore, David Sole, Dai Young, Finlay Calder, Mike Teague, Wade Dooley, Paul Ackford and Dean Richards. Yes, there are eight players there, and, yes, that means the whole pack is included, but that was the pack that turned the series around and won it for the Lions.

I would include Ieuan Evans and Rob Andrew in my list. For me, Andrew was undoubtedly a Test-match animal. That might surprise some people but I am very clear in my mind that he was. Hugely competitive, he was also more skilful than most people gave him credit for. He had played first-class cricket and was a natural sportsman; that was why he got picked in 1989 and 1993. Being with him every day you could see what he could do and that in different company he could add to what he had shown before. His game evolved simply because of the company he was with in a Lions shirt.

He was able to see what had to be done in order to change a game at the critical moment. Some players get that wrong and some others might get it right seven times out of 10, but the Test-match animal gets it right when his decision will make the crucial difference between winning and losing.

I would put Gavin Hastings in that category, too, even though he did miss one kick in front of the posts for Scotland against England in the 1991 Rugby World Cup. He had taken a nasty bang on the head from Micky Skinner beforehand and should not really have taken that kick at all. As I have mentioned previously, the respect Hastings engendered in New Zealand, where they once rated him the best full back in the world, speaks volumes.

I remember a moment in Scotland's 1990 Grand Slam campaign that was critical. Playing against France at Murrayfield with a huge wind blowing, we had only managed to get ourselves 3–0 ahead at half time with the wind at our backs. At the start of the second half France kicked long so that the ball went behind our own line. They doubtless expected a short clearance and to stay in our 22 for the rest of the half. Gavin picked the ball up and produced one of the best kicks out of hand I have seen. He sent it into the wind and up to the halfway line, which was a huge distance in the circumstances. The French could not believe it; I'm not sure they recovered. We won 21–0.

His brother Scott was a Test-match animal, too. Indeed, that whole group in 1989 knew just what to do to beat Australia.

It wasn't fancy rugby that was required; they knew that, or they certainly did in time for the second Test. They were such a strong group in that respect. Some of them were still there in 1993, but there were others who proved themselves to be proud Lions and Test-match animals on that tour as well.

Take the England flanker Ben Clarke. He had a series and a half, a simply outstanding tour. He was a big man, a ball carrier and he could make some big hits. I remember him making one in particular in the second Test that we won when he crunched John Kirwan. It was a crucial moment, a game-defining moment. Throughout the tour Clarke got a lot of respect from the New Zealanders for the way he played, which says it all really. After that tour he was highly influential for England, too.

It was an all-English back row for all three Tests, with Clarke at six, Peter Winterbottom at seven and Dean Richards at eight. All were supreme Test-match animals, as was the bean-pole lock Martin Bayfield, who played so well in that second Test, and behind them Dewi Morris proved as much at scrum half.

Ireland's Nick Popplewell surprised a few people too and played exceptionally well. I can still recall in my mind the smile on his face as he left the field after we won that second Test. He was positively beaming, and rightly so. He had played his part in a famous victory.

Then in 1997 there were players like Tom Smith, a quiet man but who never accepted that he was beaten; he was always challenging. Keith Wood was a bit more flamboyant but he knew what to do at the right time – for example, when he kicked the ball upfield before Jeremy Guscott dropped that decisive goal to win the second Test and the series. So much of the build-up to that drop goal was a case of people making key decisions and doing things they were not necessarily that good at. That is the difference.

Guscott had actually won a turnover at the start, and I thought at the time it might have been the wrong option for Wood to kick because there were players outside, but South Africa fumbled the ball and we got the lineout. Jeremy Davidson soared high and we drove on. It was then that Gregor Townsend proved himself a Test-match animal, carrying the ball hard towards the try line on a sharp angle. He had fast feet and great hands and he would usually have used them as his go-to options, but he knew what was needed at that precise moment and instead went with that running line. We recycled the ball and Matt Dawson found Guscott, who landed that famous goal.

Guscott. Now, there was a Test-match animal. A lot of people looked at him in a different way from me, but he was hugely competitive. He didn't like some aspects and admitted it – for instance, he didn't like defending but he knew that he had to do it. You look at all his Lions Tests and, if there were critical tackles to be made, he was making them. It wasn't all about his silky runs.

We challenged each other right from the start, but he always had the confidence to say 'Give me the ball', as well as the confidence to say 'I don't want the ball'. He would look at the forwards and tell them: 'It's not good enough. I don't want it yet.' It was a kind of arrogance, I suppose, but it was likeable, and he could play. Boy, could he play. That drop goal was all about what I mentioned before: right person, right place, right time. And you can add 'right decision' to that.

What about his centre partner, Scott Gibbs? Now, there was another hugely competitive animal. And then you had the England flanker Richard Hill, the players' player, the coach's player. After Martin Johnson, he was the next name on the team sheet because of what he did. He simply stopped any advantage going the opposition's way.

Alongside him you had a more natural extrovert like Lawrence Dallaglio, but what a competitor and a winner he was. I got to know Lawrence well at Wasps, but I first came across him in 1997 when he was still relatively young. He had only made 10 starts for England when he played in the first Test that year.

His main attributes were his ability to carry ball and his high work rate. He was all over the field. He was injured in 2001 and 2005, so sadly these were the only Lions Tests he played, but in 1997 he became one of the senior drivers of play. Along with Richard Hill at openside and No. 8 Tim Rodber he helped form an incredible back row in the first two Tests. It was one of the best back rows I worked with. Some people had been a little concerned about Tim and the inconsistency he sometimes displayed, but I knew him from Northampton and I was convinced that he would rise to the challenge of the Lions, and he did. He was magnificent.

I think he was just what Lawrence and Hilly needed at that stage of their careers. They were younger and he provided that experience for them, but he also had a real swagger about him that Lawrence in particular loved and picked up on. I thought Lawrence became very much like him as he got older.

The funny thing is that Ireland's Eric Miller had been the original choice at No. 8 instead of Tim. It had been an incredibly tight call and it also meant that Back missed out at openside because we did not feel that we had enough weight in the back row with both Miller and Back there. But Eric went down with flu and was ruled out almost immediately, giving Tim his chance. It just goes to show that selection is not a perfect science. You do all your research, weigh up all the pros and cons of the players and the opposition they might be facing, but sometimes you have to concede that you would happily play either player. That was shown here.

Lawrence was the carrier in that side, though. If the pack needed a bit of momentum he provided it. If you had half a yard of advantage you knew that Lawrence would always be there making the most of it. He was young but you could see that he was willing to learn tactically and would always listen and take it all in. I remember that we were looking at a flip chart before the first Test, just talking things through with Jim Telfer, we discussed using the blind side and Lawrence actually playing like a No. 8 even though he was at blindside flanker, so that if there was any free ball or free hands he would be the first carrier. He got that, and performed the role excellently in the first two Tests – he actually played at No. 8 in the third Test, with Rob Wainwright at blindside and Neil Back at openside.

I think one of the main reasons the England World Cup-winning side were so strong was the fact that they had Lawrence alongside Martin Johnson as his lieutenant. At Test-match level Johnno was definitely the right leader. And while Lawrence was an outstanding leader at Wasps, I do think that position alongside Johnno as the other voice, usually the louder voice, was where he sat best. He would deliver in the back row, whereas Johnno was delivering in the front five. It was a superb partnership, where one fed off the other and they both had huge respect for each other.

Lawrence was hugely competitive. When I coached at Wasps latterly, he had slowed down a bit but the main reason Wasps did so well was because he simply hated losing so much. He talked to players, referees and opponents, and just never stopped. He would never accept being second best or admit that he was doing anything wrong.

And if things were not going well he would tell people. There was an edge to everything he did or said, but it was always for the right reasons. Nobody could rest on their laurels with Lawrence around. That is a Test-match animal for you. Even when things were not going well on the field, he was always still scrapping to try to ensure that the opponents did not gain significant advantage.

So in 1997 we had Johnno, Lawrence, Hill's work rate and then we had Scott Gibbs in the centre, who was telling the South Africans exactly what was going to happen to them if they came his way. At one point Gibbs picked Lawrence up off the floor and said to him: 'Come on, we need you here again.'

That is some combination of competitive spirit you have got there – a mix of personalities who have a huge impact on the game environment, not just beforehand but during it too. That helps others; it draws them in.

I'd put Jason Leonard in there, too. Whatever was needed he would put everything he had into the mix. The Test-match animal grows in the environment and he shows it in different ways. The outcome is on the field when you win Test matches.

Neil Jenkins is another. When you have to put every kick over from every angle to win a Test match, and indeed a Test series, and you do it – what a player that makes you. Yes, we lost some attacking edge by playing him at full back rather than his usual position of fly half, but without him we would not have won the series. What he did was convert into points all the things the likes of Martin Johnson and others were doing. And he did it under pressure, which the South African kickers at the time found too intimidating.

Then you go to 2009 and the first name that comes into my head is Paul O'Connell. And the next is Brian O'Driscoll. And what about Phil Vickery? He had that infamous trouble in the first Test when Tendai Mtawarira, or the 'Beast' as he is known, caused him problems at the scrummage and we had to replace him early in the second half. Vicks admitted that it was the lowest point of his career, and when we introduced Wales' Adam Jones, as well as Wales' Matthew Rees for Lee Mears at hooker, our scrum was much more stable. But Vicks was also unfortunate in the way that New Zealand referee Bryce Lawrence interpreted events, often penalising him unfairly, and indeed later Lawrence confessed to Vickery that he had got some decisions wrong.

I have already expressed my admiration for Vicks. He had been told that his career was over because of neck problems and I knew I was taking a risk by signing him at Wasps, but I also knew that it was worth it. He was a remarkable player and is a remarkable man. I made him captain for the match against Western Province a week before the first Test and the way he handled himself then was superb. Conditions were awful for that game, with the rain lashing down in high winds at Newlands, but we showed some character to win 26–23, with three tries from Martyn Williams, Tommy Bowe and Ugo Monye, and a long penalty from James Hook to clinch it, but a lot of that was down to Vicks' leadership.

We had to make changes for the second Test, so Jones and Rees both started in the front row along with the retained Gethin Jenkins at loosehead. But Jones was injured in that Test so we recalled Vicks for the final Test, and I had no qualms about that. Ireland's John Hayes was another possibility but I remember saying to Warren Gatland and Graham Rowntree: 'Vicks is playing, not John Hayes. Vicks is starting.' I knew he would respond and make amends for what had happened in the first Test, and he did.

Indeed, the way he set about making sure he did what he had to do in that Test was quite phenomenal; sometimes it is about how you react to a setback and what your mental approach is. The way he took the Beast on in that Test was incredible. We won the match 28–9 and I said afterwards: 'All 15 played out of their skins and it was a truly unforgettable effort. The skill level was astonishing. It would be wrong if I didn't single out a handful of players. First and foremost has to be Phil Vickery. He suffered in the first Test – he was heroic in the third Test . . .'

There were so many others who proved themselves as Test-match animals on that trip, too. Jamie Roberts and O'Driscoll could not play in the final Test because of injuries but I think they were the best centre partnership in world rugby at the time because of what they did on that tour. That is what the Lions can do to players.

Roberts had only been a professional for a couple of years and was still studying to become a doctor. Initially there had been some debate about his best position as he had won his first two caps for Wales on the wing and at full back, but there was little doubt in my mind that he was an inside centre, and not just the charging battering ram that some see him as today. He has much more skill and awareness than that, and in combination with O'Driscoll he was devastatingly good.

I can name so many more. Tom Croft, even though I nearly got it wrong with him. Shane Williams, Rob Kearney, Simon Shaw, Mike Phillips, Stephen Jones, Gethin Jenkins, Martyn Williams, Tommy Bowe, Joe Worsley and Jamie Heaslip: they all proved themselves as Test-match animals. Riki Flutey, the New Zealand-born England centre, who formed a makeshift centre partnership with Bowe in that final Test and performed magnificently. Some of those guys who had been peripheral really stepped up in that third Test.

It was why I was so disappointed that we lost the 2009 series. The animal instinct was there and was part and parcel of everything the players did. They were outstanding but they didn't get what they deserved. At least they won that last Test, though. In order to prove yourself as a Test-match animal you have to do it for the Lions, and they had.

There are Lions and there are winning Lions. They were winning Lions in that Test.

KEY WORDS

- You can't coach character, you find it
- Clear decisions under pressure
- Instinct is character
- Make a decision to make things better, not to look good
- Instinct
- Intelligence
- Martin Johnson

2009 South Africa, Second Test
We may have lost this match, but so many serious Test-match
animals stood up. It was such a physical and intense Test.

LIONS HAVE TO LIVE WITH REALITY OF DEFEAT

South Africa 28 B & I Lions 25

By Mick Cleary in PRETORIA

YOU can twist reality all you like, but you cannot rewrite history. No matter how aggrieved the Lions are about Schalk Burger's despicable act of gouging, no matter how much they felt that a dismissal would have turned the game inexorably in their favour and no matter how frustrated they were by the mass exodus of key players through injury in the second-half, the record books will show that they lost the series.

There's no comeback, no mitigation, no right of appeal..

Few remember that the Lions were comprehensively outplayed in the 1997 series in South Africa. Jeremy Guscott's winning drop goal has acquired legendary status in much the manner that Morne Steyn's 53-metre soul-destroyer will resonate down the years for South Africans. The Bulls fly-half might well have swung his right boot into the groin of every single Lions player for the upshot was the same – they slumped to the turf, the life drained from them in one ball-breaking act.

All these thoughts will be swirling round their heads as they wake at their game reserve at Entabeni. As they get stuck into 24-hour R and R it will not yet have crossed their minds just how on earth they can gather themselves for the final Test in Johannesburg on Saturday. Getting the series to 2-1 is the least they deserve but, regrettably, it is the most they can achieve.

Are the Springboks that much better? No. However, they have proven superior in one key area – finishing. In the two Tests the Lions had the greater number of opportunities, yet South Africa had the killer instinct when it came to putting away what was created. They certainly did at Loftus Versfeld.

The first try the Lions conceded was a soft one, rookie Ireland wing, Luke Fitzgerald at fault as his opposite number, JP Pietersen shot through from a set move off a line-out. But there was to be no denying the excellence of the other two tries. Bryan Habana timed the arc and arrival of his run to exquisite precision for the first in the 63rd minute.

The piece de resistance was the last one, touched down by Jaque

Fourie, a score only confirmed after deliberation with television match official Stuart Dickinson, the Australian who was also involved when ruling against England's Mark Cueto in the 2007 Rugby World Cup final against South Africa in Paris.

Fine lines, indeed, but they are what count. The Lions came up short in that regard.

Yes, they were unfortunate, noble and courageous as well as inventive and clever. But they didn't make the most of what they had, particularly in the first Test. They were not helped by being obliged to go to uncontested scrums for most of the second half of the second Test when props Gethin Jenkins and Adam Jones were injured in quick succession.

It will be no consolation to them that they participated in one of the greatest ever Test matches. It was a game of noble stature, one that revealed, and, in some cases, exposed character, one that soared to dramatic heights.

And in the play of Simon Shaw, Rob Kearney and Brian O'Driscoll in particular, it delivered performances of Wagnerian dimensions.

Springbok scrum-half, Fourie de Preez and, for his coup de grace, Morne Steyn, have claim to that standing as well.

The Lions will arrive home next week without the spoils.

But they will return better players as well as better people, and that is no mean feat in itself. But something even more profound has taken place over the last four weeks. The Lions have ensured their future. If they had been wiped out they would never have been seen as a serious force again.

Saturday's defeat was their seventh in succession, their worst losing streak in history.

That is not a ledger of which to be proud, but nor should too much be read into it. The two Tests lost in Australia in 2001 were epic contests, as have been the two Tests here in South Africa.

McGeechan has restored the credibility of the Lions.

They needed to show that they can compete on the field with the southern hemisphere giants. These matches, and especially Saturday's, will take rightful place in the annals.

This was sport of the highest order. The Lions have meaning and significance once again.

They might still have an interest in the series, too, were it not for Ronan O'Gara's gaffe at the death. The substitute fly-half, who was also bumped out of the way as Fourie thrust for the line, had no need to be so reckless as he leapt to contest his own high kick with Fourie du Preez. O'Gara was dazed, but even so. His anguished face as the penalty was awarded told its own wretched tale.

Kearney took his try splendidly in the 10th minute, the Lions profiting from Burger's absence, and Stephen Jones kicked five penalties, a drop goal and a conversion. It had looked to be just enough to keep the Lions in the hunt for another seven days. Then Steyn swung and the dreams of thousands turned to dust..

8
THE LEGACY

'B.I.R.U.T. tours must continue.' That was Clive Rowlands in his report in 1989.

'Let's ditch the negativity now. A Lions season is truly special. Let's embrace it and enjoy it.' That was what I said in my *Sunday Telegraph* column in 2016.

Why? Well, there appears to be an ever-present question mark over the Lions. It seems we have always had to justify them. Whenever there is a Lions tour there is always some-one, somewhere who wants to criticise it and ponder the merits of its continuing existence.

I just do not understand this. If the Lions concept was not working, then I might do, but it *is* working. Yes, there have been some rocky moments, notably in 2005 and also when the game went professional – which was why the success of the 1997 tour was so vital – but it has survived them and thrived.

Take the 2017 tour in New Zealand. The three Tests there were sold out in no time, even though the host nation has clev-erly scheduled two of the Tests at its biggest ground, Eden Park in Auckland, which holds 50,000 spectators. No doubt the cruise ships will be there again in the harbours acting as temporary hotels due to the influx of some 30,000-plus Lions supporters. There will doubtless be so many replica shirts sold that every other rugby fan walking down the street here and in New Zealand will appear to be wearing one.

That is some impact for a team to have, and it should be acknowledged and recognised. It is something very different and very special.

So how can people say that the Lions have had their day? They haven't. On every single front they are a success. Quite simply they are the flagship side of northern hemisphere rugby, both in terms of the finance they generate and as a pinnacle for the players. The Lions have just got bigger and better as a business while others have fallen away. I hate to use the word 'brand' but that is very much today's word. Maybe 'badge' is better. What we can say is that the badge is stronger than it has ever been.

It is not as if the rugby itself has been a failure. Yes, the last tour of New Zealand in 2005 was disappointing, but in South Africa in 2009 although we lost the series we won four of the six halves of rugby, and in 2013 in Australia we again won four of the six halves, this time to win the series. The Rugby World Cups are the first things that go in rugby's calendar, but the Lions tours should follow straight afterwards. That is how important they are. I go back to that interview with Steve Hansen in 2014 that I mentioned at the start of the book when he said how excited people were about the Lions coming in 2017. And they still had a Rugby World Cup to play in the meantime!

If the Lions are that important, they deserve more respect from administrators in other parts of the game. They must be given more time and space by all the relevant authorities at international and domestic levels. Everybody benefits if there is a good Lions tour. World Rugby and all the unions need to recognise that in a Lions year the Lions are the biggest team rugby union has. The Lions and the All Blacks are head and shoulders above anyone else.

Part of it is the history and part of it is that so many people, especially sponsors, want to be associated with them. It is a challenge because four countries are merging into one team, but it is the characters that come from the four countries that help make the Lions unique. As my 1989 tour report says: 'The concept of the Lions must continue every four years between World Cups. The Lions are unique and there is a special magic attached to their appearance. There is too much to lose by phasing them out.'

Of course, there is a problem with scheduling at the moment which I am not sure will be alleviated by the new schedule announced in March 2017. But that is not a Lions problem, it is a rugby problem. It is not right that in 2017 the first match of the tour will take place in Whangarei just seven days after the Aviva Premiership and Guinness Pro12 finals, but it was just as wrong that in 2014 England played the first Test of their New Zealand tour with a weakened team because they were without the players who had taken part in the Premiership final the weekend before. It was no different in 2013 when the Lions played the Barbarians in Hong Kong a week after the domestic finals.

But here we are in 2017 and the Lions are still the most important thing to the players, sponsors and supporters. The administrators have to respect that. Everything is in place: it is all there, you do not have to find it. You do not have to sell the Lions.

So the challenge is not for the Lions, it is for World Rugby and the other governing bodies. They have to find a better fit for it. I know tours will probably only ever consist of 10 games or even fewer from now on, but a little bit of space is needed, just to give whoever is playing and coaching the chance to prepare and to ensure that the Test series remains competitive.

That was the worry in 2005. The Lions have to be Test-match competitive; if they are, people will always go. In 2005 they were not competitive. To ensure that they are, there needs to be some planning and leeway. The point should be made: 'Here is a window every four years that has been allocated for the Lions and their preparation, as well as their tour.'

This is not a new issue. Here is what I said in my 1993 tour report:

> If we are to prepare properly and have the players in the correct mental and physical state for such an intense tour, then consideration has to be given to presenting the Lions preparation programme at least 18 months before the tour and asking each of the home unions to organise, for that season only, a change to some domestic fixtures. It seems ridiculous to me that we were finally at the mercy of the clubs as to how we could organise our preparation. Realistically the players should also have at least two to three weeks' break before having to attempt a tour of this intensity.

I do think that it is better now that the Lions Board is made up of the chief executives of the home unions rather than having a separate Lions committee. As decision-makers, they must be involved. I know it is difficult in England because they have Premiership Rugby as well to contend with, but both sides have got to be big enough to talk to each other. The Lions will say that they do not have to speak to PRL because they are not a governing body, but they should do.

Mark McCafferty, PRL's chief executive, made some interesting comments when talking in 2016 about the Lions' schedule for 2017:

> Personally I don't know why that was signed up to. To play 10 games over that period of time, I think, is a lot. It's a punishing schedule. For sure there's going to be a difficulty for players coming back off that tour into the Premiership for 2017–18. The stats will show you that countries that have had a very large contingent of Lions players – and Wales were the most recent – tend to suffer more injuries in that following season. It does have an impact.
>
> Just to be very clear, the Lions is a fabulous brand and an important part of the economics for the southern hemisphere and it should carry on. But it's one of the elements that's not sustainable to think that players can go through a club and international season and be involved in that scale of a tour and then be in shape for the following season as well.

PRL can do something about this. To be playing a domestic final when you should be preparing for a Lions tour is plain wrong. Professionally it is extremely short-sighted. There are ways of adjusting the season as long as everyone is prepared to sit around a table and there are open minds discussing the issue in a logical way.

> We've got to sit down and have a look at that [admitted McCafferty]. It will not be until we've sat through that and understood how crucial it is to the financial picture in the south that we can decide what might be done.
>
> Do you need to play that amount of midweek games? All the economics are driven off the back of three Tests in the main. I know there are views and counter-views but it would helpful to sit down.
>
> People behind the Lions need to listen to some of the other aspects to it. No one's operating in a vacuum.

Well, I think you do need the midweek games. I think that much should have become clear throughout this book. Otherwise it is impossible to give players the chance to create the unique Lions environment. As a Lion you must become a part of the country you are playing in. You need to get a feel for the culture, the communities and the vibrancy in a rugby context. You can only do that if you play the midweek games as well. And then if you understand the country, you have the best chance of beating them. Also the country has to get the chance to know the Lions, to bring them to their doorstep.

In 2005 in New Zealand under Clive Woodward the Test team stuck to three main centres – Auckland, Wellington and Christchurch – and flew in and out of other places as quickly as they could without pausing to embrace the cultures and communities. I have previously described it as 'antiseptic' and I think it was. I wanted to do it differently with the midweek side on that tour, so I made sure that at the various venues we stayed the night before and then the night after the games.

For instance, we went out for drinks after the game against Otago in Dunedin, but we also did some training and community stuff on the Sunday morning afterwards. By going out for a drink you get a feel for how many supporters there are and their mood. It is about understanding the environment that is growing around the tour. You can feel it growing, and it is obviously more substantial the nearer you get to the Test series. It is a good thing to experience. Players don't go over the top any more, but they can have a social drink and go out for team meals.

As for the criticism of a 10-match tour, and the talk in 2016 and early 2017 about the players being smashed by playing so many games, that is misleading. Not every player will play in every game. As I have stressed already, what is important is that Warren Gatland ensures that all of his squad start in the first four games.

According to the principles I have come to see as essential, I think Warren will have the confidence and nous to know that he can play around with those early games. It is about ensuring that the game he wants to play in the first Test is taking shape in those matches. If they lose the odd game it will not matter as long as it is obvious that progress is being made in the game plan and that they can hit the first Test running. This is where the Lions can have an advantage: they can reach that first Test in better shape because of the time they will have spent together. It is often the host side's first Test of their season.

What do I think should happen in terms of the season's structure? I would change the season in a Lions year. Would it be so bad if the Premiership and Pro12 were different just for two years in four (it obviously also has to be different in World Cup years)? There must be a way of playing fewer games. Maybe you could have a play-off at the end of the season involving eight teams rather than four as there currently are? Possibly there could be a split after all teams have played each other once into odd and even conferences with a Grand Final to finish? Or you could just remove or reshape other competitions to get to a 24-game season, with some financial balance from the Lions. There are ways, I am sure, with discussion and 'open minds'.

You never know, people might like it; it might throw up some different ideas. All you need is for the season to finish two weeks earlier and for maybe something to be put in place so that the Lions players can rest a little longer than the others after the tour. It could be as simple as shifting the beginning and end of the northern hemisphere season by two to four weeks, and the Lions Board getting agreement from the southern hemisphere that the tour can start a week later.

It will not cost anyone anything because the finances will be covered by the Lions tour. With new contracts to be settled for 2021, that represents a huge opportunity.

Everyone will benefit. The Lions are such a big business that they should be paying for the time it takes to prepare. And preparation is everything.

The captain and management team in 2009 – Rob Howley, Shaun Edwards, myself,
Paul O'Connell, Gerald Davies, Graham Rowntree and Warren Gatland.

Brian O'Driscoll was quite magnificent in 2009.

Jamie Roberts was man of the series in 2009, and rightly so. He and O'Driscoll were the best centre partnership in the world at the time.

Ireland No. 8 Jamie Heaslip in action in 2009.

Paul O'Connell was a quite remarkable leader in 2009.

Rob Kearney just grew and grew as a player on the 2009 tour.

Gethin Jenkins was so good in 2009. Few props have ever been so effective over the ball.

Stephen Jones was a clever fly half, a wonderful organiser and thinker. Another who has slipped easily into coaching.

Training hard in South Africa in 2009.

A delightful off-load from Stephen Jones in 2009.

Simon Shaw in 2009. What a player he was. Simply world-class.

Coaches Graham Rowntree and Shaun Edwards answering the questions.

Martyn Williams passing the ball. The Welsh flanker was a superb
reader of the game and link man.

With Mike Phillips in 2009. What a competitor, a true Test-match animal.

Coach Warren Gatland and captain Sam Warburton in Australia in 2013.
That relationship is so important.

The squad celebrate in Australia in 2013. The Lions can win!

Everybody involved has got to change the season. It is so important for players, coaches, fans, media and sponsors – it is just simply massive. If the administrators can't see that then they are small-minded people. They have to recognise the great respect given to the Lions in New Zealand, South Africa and Australia. It is something that PRL can't deliver, Ireland can't deliver, Scotland can't deliver, Wales can't deliver and England can't deliver.

They have to have respect for the bigger picture and what the Lions represent. They have to show that they are prepared to change things to keep the Lions. You don't have to sell the concept to sponsors or fans because they are already on board. You don't have to sell it to the players because, as Paul O'Connell has said, they would do it for nothing; the jersey sells itself.

That is the size of it. And they need to understand how important it is that the preparations are in place. Everybody should be saying: 'What gives us the best opportunity to win? What can a season look like in preparation?' It is in everyone's best interests that the Lions reach the first Test in good shape, and the itinerary leading up to it should reflect that.

For example, in 1997 and 2009 the South Africans tried to make it difficult for the Lions. They scheduled a game at altitude in Bloemfontein in between the first two Tests, which were at sea level. And in 2009 the first Test was in Durban, then there was a midweek game in Cape Town, both places at sea level, before the second Test in Pretoria at altitude.

Scientists say that you have either got to be at altitude for a week or for no more than 24 hours. So in 2009, although the

South Africans did not like it, we stayed at sea level and did all our training in Cape Town. We then did not fly to Pretoria until the day before the match and at a time later than the kick-off time the next day. We had a week until the last Test at altitude. All this we had to manage ourselves.

The Lions stopping off en route to Australia to play the Barbarians in Hong Kong in 2013 was crazy, as was the match against Argentina in Cardiff in 2005. The problem in 2013 was that they needed another warm-up game because Australia could not deliver it; they simply do not have the sides there to do it. So it was the lesser of two evils to get a game on the way out, where the conditions were very difficult and the Barbarians did not provide strong enough opposition. They would have been better off picking a team from the rest of the southern hemisphere, from the Pacific Islanders and some other New Zealanders and Australians, because in the end that game, which the Lions won 59–8, was no use in a rugby sense.

The Lions could easily have disappeared when the game went professional, so we should not underestimate the impact of the 1997 tour. There could not have been a better tour to begin the professional era; it was almost the perfect storm. It was in South Africa, and we won the series. Fans could get there in 12 hours; you could go for the weekend and watch a Test. All that, as well as Sky Sports being involved and the *Living with Lions* video, took the Lions to a different level.

If there is one worry I have, it is about the commercialism of the Lions. I was interested to read an article in the *Rugby Paper* in late 2016 in which Donal Lenihan said: 'It has become overly commercialised. I was there when they won the series in 2013. It was fantastic, but there were so many people with Lions blazers on out on the field waving at the fans, people who had never played rugby in their lives, and I thought: "This isn't right." I go back to my own travails with the Lions. You fought so hard to get that blazer and you see this circus now. The Lions as an entity need to stand up for themselves far more.'

I will admit that I had some concerns about this in 2009.

There was a stage when HSBC, as the main sponsors, were getting a little intrusive. So I had to make the point to chief executive John Feehan: 'Just get the balance right, please, John. It has to be more than 50 per cent rugby.'

If it is less than that, then it is wrong. I said it had to be 60–40, rugby to sponsors, at the very least. Each week has to be planned from a rugby perspective; then, quite rightly, there are commitments and obligations to the sponsors. As I wrote in my tour report: 'I still believe the rugby must come first with balanced sponsorship requirements. The Lions must be competitive in the Tests. A decision for the Board is how much profit is necessary from a Lions tour?'

Then you understand that the real reason everyone is going there is for the rugby. It is the rugby that makes the badge unique. What the sponsors should be able to do is feed off that and keep the balance. Actually, once we had clarified that balance, HSBC became a very good and strong sponsor, as did all the other sponsors on that trip.

I think that it helped that on the first of the three visits to South Africa before the tour – in June 2008 – all the sponsors were there and they had a two-day conference on how they would bring the sponsorship together as a team. I was asked if I would speak to them and I talked them through the preparation I was doing in terms of the travel, accommodation and training and also about bringing the four countries together. It was then that I think they grasped the idea of coming together as sponsors behind the one Lions badge. They were putting ideas on the table where they might share marketing ploys to use on the back of the Lions. I think the sponsors got a lot out of it.

I believe my remarks in the tour report summed it up:

SPONSORS

In the end, the balance of sponsors' requirements was manageable.

USE THIS TOUR AS A TEMPLATE

HSBC managed well – just!!
Good links and atmosphere with all main sponsors. The sponsors' day and dinner out in Johannesburg in June 2008 worked very well.

I do think that the best method is to involve the head coach with the sponsors so they can work together and get the balance right. In the lead-up to the 2017 tour I did some work for the main sponsors of that trip, Standard Life. I gave a presentation that was essentially an insight into the rugby part of the Lions business. In fact, it was probably a distillation of the principles in this book. I entitled it: 'The Lions, The Challenge, The Best of the Best.'

I used some powerful photographs to back up my points and I replayed the speech I made to the players before the first Test in Cape Town, South Africa in 1997, in which I emphasised the importance of the badge and remembering those who helped every player become a Lion:

> That badge we've always said represents four countries. I think it represents something else. You carry one on your own jersey. That is a very personal thing. What goes into that is your own country and three others. But what also goes into it is you.
>
> You should be carrying that badge for people who have put you in that position. It might be a schoolmaster, mother, father, brother, sister, wife, girlfriend. Whatever's special to you, the people who have brought you to this place, that's who you should be wearing it for. That's who you should be playing for. Because in the end they're the ones who matter. They matter to you. And if it matters to you, it will matter to all of us. And if it matters to us, we will win.
>
> Go out, enjoy it, but play for everything that's in the badge. For you personally, for all of us collectively. Good luck. Let's have a win, let's frighten them to death. Let's go.

I also quoted Alf Ramsey, the England football manager who guided his team to World Cup glory in 1966: 'Players never remember the team talks, players never remember the practices, what they will always remember is how you made them feel.'

And then to finish my presentation: 'Getting the basics right under pressure . . . there is no better feeling than being world class . . . a Lions tour is a totally unique environment. It is about people and relationships, about support and trust through the entire Lions' group, from support staff to coaches to players. The aim for all is to help create the "Test-match" environment.'

I think it gave those business people an understanding of what the Lions are like and what a massive influence they have on the rugby world and therefore on the business associated with it – for they certainly have that.

And I hope this book as a whole has given you, the reader, an understanding of that too, of what the Lions mean to me, how special they are, but just as importantly what a Lions tour is like and what it should be like for all those associated with it – the host country and supporters, as well as the tour group.

There is simply no sporting expedition like it. Indeed, there is simply no sporting team like it.

The Lions must continue.

KEY WORDS

- Strength of the badge
- Understand the country you are touring
- The country needs to get to know and respect the Lions
- Preparation is everything
- Remember the feeling
- The jersey sells itself
- Lions – a challenge for World Rugby
- Commercial/Rugby Balance

2009 South Africa, Third Test
If there was ever a test that proved beyond doubt that
the Lions must continue.

SHAW BANNED AFTER LIONS RESTORE PRIDE

South Africa 9 British & I Lions 28

By Mick Cleary and Gavin Mairs

ENGLAND lock Simon Shaw yesterday received a two-week ban for dangerous play, drawing a line under a Test series that the British and Irish Lions doctor, James Robson, described as the most physical he had ever witnessed.

The sanction took the edge off the celebrations of the Lions' rousing third-Test victory, and was indicative of an undercurrent of violence that at times brought equal measures of drama and shame to a series described by the tourists' coach, Ian McGeechan, as "the most outstanding" he had been involved with.

Shaw was found guilty of striking Springbok scrum-half Fourie du Preez with his knee just before half-time. He received a yellow card for the offence from Australian referee Stuart Dickinson, but was cited for dangerous play and suspended at a disciplinary hearing yesterday.

The 35-year-old Wasps player's ban — deferred to conclude at midnight on August 22 — made Shaw the fourth player to be suspended during the course of the bruising tour. Given that the Guinness Premiership does not start until Sept 5, Shaw will not miss any competitive matches because of his punishment.

The Springbok players could also be in the dock, facing charges of bringing the game into disrepute for their protest over Bakkies Botha's ban.

The International Rugby Board has launched an investigation into the protest after the Springboks sported white armbands with the message 'Justice 4 Bakkies'.

The lock was banned for charging dangerously into a ruck in the second Test. The incident left Adam Jones with a dislocated shoulder which requires further surgery today. The Wales prop is expected to be out for at least six months.

Whatever the outcome of the disciplinary cases, on the field there was finally justice for the Lions. Sport does not always reward deserving cases, but if the Lions had returned empty-handed it would have been a travesty.

This victory, which might have been by a record margin but for the ball toppling off the tee as Stephen Jones attempted a conversion, was a fitting send-off for some mighty Lions such as Shaw, Phil Vickery and Martyn Williams. Moreover, it was an appropriate riposte to the arrogance of an opposition coach who cheapened the fixture by making 10 changes.

The Lions should not be denied their moment in the sun. Few teams beat South Africa at Ellis Park, France being the last in 2001. However, it is worth remembering that this was a dead rubber. No one bothers to recall the outcome of the third Test in 1997, won 35-16 by the Boks after the Lions had clinched the series. That said, there was a different feel to this occasion. There was a sense of good guys getting due return, palpably so when you consider that they enjoyed an 11-point advantage over the three Tests, outscoring the Springboks by 74 points to 63.

There was a monumental display from No8 Jamie Heaslip, some defiant defence from centre Tommy Bowe and hooker Matthew Rees, another all-enveloping showing from scrum-half Mike Phillips and genuine spark from Rob Kearney, Shane Williams and Riki Flutey.

The last two of those combined brilliantly for Williams's second try in the 35th minute, Flutey chipping and chasing hard before flipping the ball inside as he collided with Zane Kirchner. Williams had earlier shown that he had rediscovered his scoring instincts when tracking Heaslip's spirited churn forward to be on hand for the decisive pass.

The Lions survived Shaw being sent to the sin-bin, conceding only three points while he was off the field. Monye pounced for a 75-metre interception try, Stephen Jones rattled off a couple of penalty goals before a diving tackle by Bowe prevented a try by Odwa Ndungane, a decision referred to the video referee, Bryce Lawrence. It was a tight call, but the right one, rather like the entire series.

9

THE BEST

A bit of fun to finish off with. No, I am not going to select my greatest ever Lions team, because I always think that is an impossible task when you have not seen certain players in the flesh. Comparing players from different eras is difficult enough when you have seen them, but when you have not, there is just too much guesswork involved.

So instead I have decided to pick two Lions teams. The first is from the players I played with on Lions tours, the second from those that I have coached on Lions tours – or rather when I have been head coach; I am not including players from the 2005 tour. I am just looking at those who played in 1989, 1993, 1997 and 2009.

The first team is simple. It is the 1974 Test team for the third Test *en bloc*. So it reads:

15 J.P.R. Williams
14 Andy Irvine
13 Ian McGeechan
12 Dick Milliken
11 J.J. Williams

10 Phil Bennett

9 Gareth Edwards

1 Ian McLauchlan

2 Bobby Windsor

3 Fran Cotton

4 Willie John McBride (capt)

5 Gordon Brown

6 Roger Uttley

7 Fergus Slattery

8 Mervyn Davies

What a team, what a group of men. I need say no more.

Now things start to get a bit more tricky. But let's give it a go and hope that those omitted understand how marginal some of the calls were and that, as I have said before here, sometimes you can be happy whether you have to go with one player or the other. The problem is that you can only pick one player in every position to start.

My team is:

15 GAVIN HASTINGS (SCOTLAND)

He played in two Lions Test series in 1989 and 1993. He was a series winner in the first and captained the other, so he does have some rather decent pedigree.

He was strong under the high ball, could kick the ball a mile and was really strong in contact, where you could play off him. He was the sort of full back that you knew was reliable at the back but also when he came into the line he was difficult to stop, which meant you were always over the gain line and could then play off that position.

He was actually very similar to J.P.R. On the 1974 tour that was the first time I came across a real Test-match animal, and J.P.R. really was an animal at times. His competitiveness, his bravery and the fact that he could counter-attack as well stood him apart from other players I had seen and played against. Gavin reminded me of all that.

Neil Jenkins was a contender for this position because he played there in 1997. He needs a mention because if he had not played in that series and kicked like he did, I do not think that we would have won it.

It was rather like Leigh Halfpenny in 2013 in Australia. He was the same. If you kick the critical goals they give you momentum in the Test matches.

The other one who was close was Ireland's Rob Kearney, who came in for the last two Test matches in South Africa in 2009. He was excellent there, but Gavin was the most outstanding Lions full back I coached. Oh, to have a player who could blend the strengths of J.P.R., Andy Irvine and Gavin. That would be some full back.

14 IEUAN EVANS (WALES)

A favourite of mine who went on three Lions tours in 1989, 1993 and 1997. Like all the Welsh wingers, and most especially Gerald Davies, whom sadly I never toured with as a Lions player, Ieuan had a very good sidestep which he could also combine with searing acceleration. He was a lethal finisher, especially in tight situations.

You also have to consider England's John Bentley and Scotland's Alan Tait from the 1997 tour, but Ieuan takes it.

13 JEREMY GUSCOTT (ENGLAND)

This was an extremely difficult choice and Ireland's Brian O'Driscoll is very unfortunate, but I have already stated my liking for Guscott as a player and a person.

He was a runner but he had a toughness too, and his combination with Scott Gibbs worked well. Gibbs would make Jerry work hard in defence, which made him a more complete player.

Wales' Jamie Roberts and O'Driscoll were magnificent for me in 2009 and they were certainly close to Gibbs and Guscott as a partnership – they were that good. I would have loved to have seen O'Driscoll play alongside Gibbs, though.

12 SCOTT GIBBS (WALES)

He made a huge impact on opponents and indeed on his own side when he was marshalling the defence, always screaming at people to get into position. He knew what made others tick and when to say something that would make a difference. There are not too many backs who have total respect from the forwards, but Gibbsy was one of them. His physical work was huge.

11 TOMMY BOWE (IRELAND)

I originally put England's Rory Underwood here and I did consider putting Guscott here too to accommodate O'Driscoll in the centre.

Underwood was a classic finisher like Evans, but I was so impressed by Bowe in 2009 that I just had to select him.

Yes, he is more of a right winger and his four Lions caps as a winger in 2009 and 2013 have come on the right wing (he played centre in the final Test in 2009 and he was outstanding there, too); he has played on the left for Ireland and I would have no hesitation in picking him there.

His influence on the games in 2009 was massive. He has speed and power, and of all the wingers I have seen he cuts the best lines and he does it so late, too. He does not just look to beat his man on the outside. If the opposition defence is drifting he has the instinct to cut back on a sharp angle at the very last moment and slice through the defence simply because of the angle he has taken.

Wales' Shane Williams deserves a mention, too. He proved that he could be a match winner in 2009.

10 GREGOR TOWNSEND (SCOTLAND)

I have gone for the ball player. He was one of the most talented fly halves I ever coached. But I will admit that England's Rob Andrew was close to him. He really showed what a good sportsman he was in a Lions jersey, certainly more so than he did in an England shirt. He had a huge effect on the 1989 tour.

Gregor thrived on the 1997 tour when he had so many good players around him. That set him up to play the best rugby of his career for Scotland afterwards.

Wales' Stephen Jones was very good in 2009. He controlled the game excellently, kicked his goals, attacked the line and brought his wingers in on his inside. He was a great sounding board for me as coach, too; I always liked talking to him tactically after games. Like Gregor, it was little surprise to me when he became a coach after finishing playing. You could see that thinking was there in both of them.

9 MATT DAWSON (ENGLAND)

Such a tricky choice. Again I changed my mind at the last moment here; I had originally gone with Wales' Mike Phillips.

I have mentioned how I knew that I could trust Daws in 1997. He was such a competitor but he was also so clever. And Daws was a natural breaker, as he showed with that wonder try in the first Test.

I have always thought that he was the reason why Jonny Wilkinson played so well for England, simply because of the type of ball Daws gave him and when he gave it to him. It was the same with Gregor in 1997 – Daws really helped him. He managed the possession so well.

I always say that nines make tens, and this showed itself to be true again. You could always see that in the fly halves who played outside Gareth Edwards. Barry John and Phil Bennett were magnificent players, but they were also indebted to Gareth for making them look so good.

Nines make forwards look good too and that was why Gareth was so exceptional in 1974, always bawling at the forwards. They then knew that they had to respond to him. If he made a break they used to hare after him because their first instinct was to protect him. That was their job.

I really liked Phillips because he was a genuine Test-match animal; he was immensely competitive. His power around the breakdown was phenomenal and it reminded me of Gareth. Phillips was not as quick as Gareth, but he was as powerful. He was always a threat, which meant that the back row always had to keep an eye on him.

He could also pass a ball two metres further than anyone else, which put his fly half outside the opposition back row. That in turn meant that the wingers running off the inside shoulder of the fly half could isolate the back row coming in to defend. People didn't always credit Phillips for his passing ability.

Wales' Rob Howley was unfortunate that injury ended his 1997 tour before the Test matches, and his only Lions Test caps came in 2001 in Australia when I wasn't coach.

Rob Jones was also brilliant in 1989, as was Dewi Morris in 1993. Both were superb competitors. Jones might have been small but his contest with Nick Farr-Jones set the tone for the tour, stopping a world-class player playing. And Dewi was a revelation in New Zealand. His tactical kicking in the second Test that we won in Wellington was quite outstanding.

The truth is that in every successful Lions tour the nine has been a hugely influential player and has had plenty of competition for his place.

1 DAVID SOLE (SCOTLAND)

This was another hard decision. I had three names written down at the start: Sole, his compatriot Tom Smith and Wales' Gethin Jenkins.

They were (and Jenkins is still going) all ball players. I went for Sole because he is a natural leader as well and quite a strong personality. When he played his three Lions Tests in 1989 alongside Brian Moore and Dai Young and then captained Scotland to the Grand Slam in the following year, I remember saying that he would be the prototype for the modern-day prop with his skills and mobility. That has definitely proved to be the case.

England's Jason Leonard was in contention too and he would definitely be on my bench were I picking one, and not just because he could play on both sides of the scrum but because of his personality and what it would bring to the environment.

2 BRIAN MOORE (ENGLAND)

For me it was a straight choice between him and Ireland's Keith Wood. Both of them had two Lions series. There is little to choose between them, but I went for Brian because of his huge competitiveness and the fact that his throwing was so accurate.

That is not to say that Woody did not have either of those char-acteristics – he could seemingly throw the ball onto a sixpence in 1997 – and he was probably the more natural rugby player and carried a bit more, but Brian just edges it for, if you will excuse the pun, his edge. He was a ferocious competitor.

Another contender was the Welshman Matthew Rees, who did so well in South Africa in 2009.

3 DAI YOUNG (WALES)

Again, this was a close call, this time between Young and his compatriot Adam Jones, who really surprised me in South Africa in 2009 by how good he was. His scrummaging was superb and, like Dai, he was a good ball-handler too. But Dai was a real tough nut and he was outstanding in Australia in 1989 when he was still so young.

I have mentioned Phil Vickery already and how he responded so well in 2009 after the travails of the first Test, and he too was a good ball player. This is now a common requirement for all tighthead props and it just shows that these three, amongst others, were way ahead of their time. And they all showed that for the Lions.

4 MARTIN JOHNSON (ENGLAND, CAPT.)

I am not sure that I need to say any more than I have already said in this book about Johnno. I just put his name down and moved on. It was as simple as that.

I do, though, have to mention England's Paul Ackford. In 1989 that was the first time I had really seen ball won properly at the front of the lineout. He was undoubtedly a game changer in the way he performed there. We won a brutal game against Queensland on that 1989 tour, mostly thanks to him. We had huge problems at the middle and tail of the lineout but Ackers managed to win every single ball thrown to him at the front. He was outstanding.

5 PAUL O'CONNELL (IRELAND)

I was very torn here between O'Connell and England's Simon Shaw. Those two performances from Shaw in South Africa in 2009 were so good, when he came in and just nullified Victor Matfield and Bakkies Botha.

But I have gone for O'Connell because of his leadership qualities, even though I know that of these three – Johnson, O'Connell and Shaw – Shaw was the most skilful with ball in hand. As I have said, he should have played so much more for England. In that 2009 series you just saw how good he was; he was world-class.

There was, of course, also England's Wade Dooley to consider. He proved an immensely physically dominant figure in Australia in 1989. He was a hard man, but he could also carry the ball and he had a very good understanding of the game.

Honourable mentions, too, for Ireland's Jeremy Davidson and England's Martin Bayfield. Davidson was very different and probably a little too light in this company but nonetheless played a huge part in our 1997 success, and Bayfield played his own considerable part in winning a Test in New Zealand in 1993. Not many can say that.

6 MIKE TEAGUE (ENGLAND)

He simply had a huge impact in 1989. He only played two Tests on that tour (he came off the bench when we won in Wellington in 1993) but he ended up being man of the series, so that just shows what he did and what an effect it had. He might have been a quiet man off the pitch but he was quite phenomenal on it. He was a big man whose fitness training was ahead of its time and he was a natural ball carrier.

7 RICHARD HILL (ENGLAND)

He was just incredible in 1997. Yes, you could say that he was not an out-and-out seven, but he was so competitive and such a good reader of the game that he was always there near the ball. As I've said, he was a players' player. You might have had to play alongside him or to coach him to realise how good he was, but once you had you were certainly in no doubt.

You could see in 2001 that Australia went for him. They knew how important he was to the Lions and it was shocking how they took him out of the series illegally. Had he not been injured, I think the Lions would have won that series.

Peter Winterbottom was close, too. I knew him from when he was a six-year-old at the Headingley club, where his father John was a club stalwart. It is not a natural selection for England to pick a genuine seven, but he bucked the trend – Bedford's Budge Rogers had been another – and was really competitive over the ball. I organised for him to play at Hawke's Bay in New Zealand and they rated him very highly. As I have said before, respect out there is hard to come by but he had it.

Neil Back was another in that mould, who made the 1997 tour. He was not just competitive over the ball. He could also hold up the ball well at the back of mauls, he was always on the shoulders of the midfield to run off them and was an excellent link player who was always comfortable in the open spaces.

Wales' Martyn Williams was like that too and he was brilliant in the third Test in Johannesburg in 2009.

8 LAWRENCE DALLAGLIO (ENGLAND)

I was considering him at six but could not leave Teague out so have gone with Lawrence at No. 8, where he did play in the final Test in 1997. He could genuinely play at six, seven or eight, which made him so valuable especially on a Lions tour.

Dean Richards was clearly a strong contender here. Like Teague he was quiet but he never gave ground and was always there when you needed to stop a ball or be over a ball, or pick one up, or whatever it was. He had the intellect in high-pressure situations to do the right thing. As I have mentioned, in 1989 and 1993 he was my sounding board for how training was going, which is why he has always been a favourite of mine.

Tim Rodber was another No. 8 whom I knew well and liked, and he came of age in South Africa in 1997. He was underrated in an England jersey but he shone for the Lions on that tour. And we should not forget Ireland's Jamie Heaslip, who was huge in South Africa in 2009. Indeed, all these players reflect the quality of player that has worn the Lions No. 8 jersey. They are all winners.

There were many difficult decisions here, but what I am certain of is that I would not have minded coaching this side. But then again I loved coaching all my Lions teams.

It was always an honour and a pleasure. I have been very lucky.

BRITISH AND IRISH LIONS STATISTICS

1888 Australia and New Zealand

Captain: Rob Seddon (Swinton and England), Andrew Stoddart (Blackheath and England)
Manager: Arthur Shrewsbury (England)

Tour Record:	P 35	W 27	D 6	L 2	F 292	A 98

1891 South Africa

Captain: Bill Maclagan (Edinburgh Academicals and Scotland)
Manager: Edwin Ash (England)

Tour Record:	P 20	W 20	D 0	L 0	F 226	A 1
Test Series:	P 3	W 3	D 0	L 0		

1896 South Africa

Captain: Johnny Hammond (Richmond)
Manager: Roger Walker (England)

Tour Record:	P 21	W 19	D 1	L 1	F 310	A 45
Test Series:	P 4	W 3	D 0	L 1		

1899 Australia

Captain: Rev. Matthew Mullineux (Blackheath)
Manager: Roger Walker (England)

Tour Record:	P 21	W 18	D 0	L 3	F 333	A 90
Test Series:	P 4	W 3	D 0	L 1		

1903 South Africa

Captain: Mark Morrison (Royal High School FP and Scotland)
Manager: Johnny Hammond (England)

Tour Record:	P 22	W 11	D 3	L 8	F 213	A 138
Test Series:	P 3	W 0	D 2	L 1		

1904 Australia and New Zealand

Captain: David Bedell-Sivright (West of Scotland and Scotland)
Manager: Arthur O'Brien (New Zealand)

Tour Record:	P 19	W 16	D 1	L 2	F 287	A 84
Test Series (Aus):	P 3	W 3	D 0	L 0		
Test Series (NZ):	P 1	W 0	D 0	L 1		

1908 Australia and New Zealand

Captain: Arthur Harding (London Welsh and Wales)
Manager: George Harnett (England)

Tour Record:	P 26	W 16	D 1	L 9	F 313	A 201
Test Series:	P 3	W 0	D 1	L 2		

1910 South Africa

Captain: Dr Tom Smyth (Newport and Ireland)
Manager: William Cail (England)

Tour Record:	P 24	W 13	D 3	L 8	F 290	A 236
Test Series:	P 3	W 1	D 0	L 2		

1924 South Africa

Captain: Dr Ronald Cove-Smith (Old Merchant Taylors' and England)
Manager: Harry Packer (Wales)

Tour Record:	P 21	W 9	D 3	L 9	F 175	A 155
Test Series:	P 4	W 0	D 1	L 3		

1930 New Zealand and Australia

Captain: Doug Prentice (Leicester and England)
Manager: James Baxter (England)

Tour Record:	P 28	W 20	D 0	L 8	F 624	A 318
Test Series (NZ):	P 4	W 1	D 0	L 3		
Test Series (Aus):	P 1	W 0	D 0	L 1		

1938 South Africa

Captain: Sam Walker (Instonians and Ireland)
Manager: Col. Bernard Hartley (England)

Tour Record:	P 24	W 17	D 0	L 7	F 414	A 284
Test Series:	P 3	W 1	D 0	L 2		

1950 New Zealand and Australia

Captain: Karl Mullen (Old Belvedere and Ireland)
Manager: Surgeon-Captain Leslie Bartlet 'Ginger' Osborne (England)

Tour Record:	P 29	W 22	D 1	L 6	F 570	A 214
Test Series (NZ):	P 4	W 0	D 1	L 3		
Test Series (Aus):	P 2	W 2	D 0	L 0		

1955 South Africa

Captain: Robin Thompson (Instonians and Ireland)
Manager: Jack Siggins (Ireland)

Tour Record:	P 25	W 19	D 1	L 5	F 457	A 283
Test Series:	P 4	W 2	D 0	L 2		

1959 New Zealand and Australia

Captain: Ronnie Dawson (Wanderers and Ireland)
Manager: Alf Wilson (Scotland)

Tour Record:	P 33	W 27	D 0	L 6	F 842	A 353
Test Series (NZ):	P 4	W 1	D 0	L 3		
Test Series (Aus):	P 2	W 2	D 0	L 0		

1962 South Africa

Captain: Arthur Smith (Edinburgh Wanderers and Scotland)
Manager: Instructor-Commander David Vaughan (England)

Tour Record:	P 25	W 16	D 4	L 5	F 401	A 208
Test Series:	P 4	W 0	D 1	L 3		

1966 New Zealand and Australia

Captain: Michael Campbell-Lamerton (London Scottish and Scotland)
Manager: Des O'Brien (Ireland)

Tour Record:	P 35	W 23	D 3	L 9	F 524	A 345
Test Series (NZ):	P 4	W 0	D 0	L 4		
Test Series (Aus):	P 2	W 2	D 0	L 0		

1968 South Africa

Captain: Tom Kiernan (Cork Constitution and Ireland)
Manager: David Brooks (England)
Coach: Ronnie Dawson (Ireland)

Tour Record:	P 20	W 15	D 1	L 4	F 377	A 181
Test Series:	P 4	W 0	D 1	L 3		

1971 New Zealand

Captain: John Dawes (London Welsh and Wales)
Manager: Dr Doug Smith (Scotland)
Coach: Carwyn James (Wales)

Tour Record:	P 26	W 23	D 1	L 2	F 580	A 231
Test Series:	P 4	W 2	D 1	L 1		

1974 South Africa

Captain: Willie John McBride (Ballymena and Ireland)
Manager: Alun Thomas (Wales)
Coach: Syd Millar (Ireland)

Squad

Fullbacks

A.R. Irvine	Heriot's FP	Scotland
J.P.R. Williams	London Welsh	Wales

Three-Quarters

R.T.E Bergiers	Llanelli	Wales
G.W. Evans	Coventry	England
T.O. Grace	St Mary's College	Ireland
I.R. McGeechan	Headingley	Scotland
R.A. Milliken	Bangor	Ireland
A.J. Morley*	Bristol	England

C.F.W Rees	London Welsh	Wales
W.CC Steele	Bedford and R.A.F.	Scotland
J.J. Williams	LlanellI	Wales

Half-backs

P. Bennett	Llanelli	Wales
G.O. Edwards	Cardiff	Wales
C.M.H Gibson*	North of Ireland	Ireland
J.J. Moloney	St. Mary's College	Ireland
A.G.B Old	Leicester	England

Forwards

G.L. Brown	West of Scotland	Scotland
M.A. Burton	Gloucester	England
A.B Carmichael	West of Scotland	Scotland
F.E. Cotton	Coventry	England
T.P. David	Llanelli	Wales
T.M. Davies	Swansea	Wales
K.W. Kennedy	London Irish	Ireland
W.J. McBride (capt)	Ballymena	Ireland
J. McLauchlan	Jordanhill College	Scotland
S.A. McKinney	Dungannon	Ireland
A. Neary	Broughton Park	England
C.W. Ralston	Richmond	England
A.G.Ripley	Rosslyn Park	England
J.F. Slattery	Blackrock College	Ireland
R.M. Uttley	Gosforth	England
R.W. Windsor	Pontypool	Wales

*Replacements

| Tour Record: | P 22 | W 21 | D 1 | L 0 | F 729 | A 207 |
| Test Series: | P 4 | W 3 | D 1 | L 0 | | |

15 May	Western Transvaal	Potchefstroom	W	59–13
18 May	South West Africa	Windhoek	W	23–16
22 May	Boland	Wellington	W	33–6
25 May	Eastern Province	Port Elizabeth	W	28–14
29 May	South Western Districts	Mossel Bay	W	97–0
1 June	Western Province	Cape Town	W	17–8
4 June	SAR Federation XV	Cape Town	W	37–6
8 June	**SOUTH AFRICA**	**Cape Town**	**W**	**12–3**
11 June	Southern Universities	Cape Town	W	26–4
15 June	Transvaal	Johannesburg	W	23–15

18 June	Rhodesia	Salisbury	W	42-6
22 June	**SOUTH AFRICA**	**Pretoria**	**W**	**28-9**
27 June	Quaggas	Johannesburg	W	20-16
29 June	Orange Free State	Bloemfontein	W	11-9
3 July	Griqualand West	Kimberley	W	69-16
6 July	Northern Transvaal	Pretoria	W	16-12
9 July	Leopards	East London	W	56-10
13 July	**SOUTH AFRICA**	**Port Elizabeth**	**W**	**26-9**
17 July	Border	East London	W	26-6
20 July	Natal	Durban	W	34-6
23 July	Eastern Transvaal	Springs	W	33-10
27 July	**SOUTH AFRICA**	**Johannesburg**	**D**	**13-13**

First Test

8 June, Cape Town
South Africa 3 The Lions 12
HT:3-3 Att:45,000

South Africa: I.McCallum, C. Pope, P. Whipp , J.Oosthuizen, G.Muller, D. Snyman, R. McCallum, T.Sauermann, P. van Wyk, W. Meyer (capt), K. de Klerk, J. Williams, B.Coetzee, J. Ellis, M. du Plessis. **Scorer:** Pen: D. Snyman

Lions: JPR Williams, W. Steele, I. McGeechan, R. Milliken, J.J. Williams, P. Bennett, G. Edwards, I. McLauchlan, R. Windsor, F. Cotton, G. Brown, W. McBride (capt),R. Uttley, F. Slattery, M. Davies **Scorers:** Pens: P. Bennett 3; DG: G. Edwards

Referee: Max Baise (South Africa)

Second Test

22 June, Pretoria
South Africa 9 The Lions 28
HT: 3-10 Att: 63,500

South Africa: I.McCallum (D. Snyman, L. Vogel) C. Pope, P. Whipp , J. Snyman, G. Germishuys, G. Bosch, P. Bayvel, N. Bezuidenhout, D. Fredrickson, H. Marais (capt), K. de Klerk, J. Williams, M. du Plessis J. Ellis, D. McDonald. **Scorer:** Pens: G. Bosch 2, DG: G. Bosch

Lions: JPR Williams, W. Steele, I. McGeechan, R. Milliken, J.J. Williams, P. Bennett, G. Edwards, I. McLauchlan, R. Windsor, F. Cotton, G. Brown, W. McBride (capt),R. Uttley, F. Slattery, M. Davies **Scorers:** Tries: J.J Williams 2, P. Bennett, G. Brown, R. Milliken; Con: P. Bennett; Pen: P. Bennett; DG: I. McGeechan

Referee: Cas de Bruyn (South Africa)

Third Test

13 July, Port Elizabeth
South Africa 9 The Lions 26
HT: 3–7 Att: 55,000

South Africa: A. Roux, C. Pope, P. Cronje, J. Schebusch, G. Muller, J. Snyman, G. Sonnekus, N. Bezuidenhout, P. van Wyk, H. Marais (capt), M. van Heerden (K.de Klerk), J. de Bruyn, P. Fourie, J. Ellis, J. Kritzinger **Scorer:** Pens: J. Snyman 3

Lions: JPR Williams, A. Irvine, I. McGeechan, R. Milliken, J.J. Williams, P. Bennett, G. Edwards, I. McLauchlan, R. Windsor, F. Cotton, G. Brown, W. McBride (capt),R. Uttley, F. Slattery, M. Davies **Scorers:** Tries: J.J Williams 2, G. Brown; Con: A. Irvine; Pens: A. Irvine 2; DG: P. Bennett 2

Referee: Cas de Bruyn (South Africa)

Fourth Test

27 July, Johannesburg
South Africa 13 The Lions 13
HT: 6–10 Att: 75,000

South Africa: A. Roux, C. Pope, P. Cronje, J. Schebusch, G. Muller, J. Snyman, P. Bayvel, N. Bezuidenhout (R. Stander), P. van Wyk, H. Marais (capt), J. Williams, M. van Heerden, J. Kritzinger, J. Ellis, K. Grobler **Scorers:** Try: P. Cronje; Pens: J. Snyman 3

Lions: JPR Williams, A. Irvine, I. McGeechan, R. Milliken, J.J. Williams, P. Bennett, G. Edwards, I. McLauchlan, R. Windsor, F. Cotton, C. Ralston, W. McBride (capt),R. Uttley, F. Slattery, M. Davies **Scorers:** Tries: A. Irvine, R. Uttley; Con: P. Bennett; Pen: A. Irvine

Referee: Max Baise (South Africa)

1977 New Zealand

Captain: Phil Bennett (Llanelli and Wales)
Manager: George Burrell (Scotland)
Coach: John Dawes (Wales)

Squad

Fullbacks

B.H. Hay	Boroughmuir	Scotland
A.R. Irvine	Heriot's FP	Scotland

Three-Quarters

D.H. Burcher	Newport	Wales

G.L. Evans	Newport	Wales
S.P Fenwick	Bridgend	Wales
C.M.H. Gibson	North of Ireland	Ireland
I.R. McGeechan	Headingley	Scotland
H.E.Rees	Neath	
P.J. Squires	Harrogate	England
J.J. Williams	LlanellI	Wales

Half-backs

R.P. Bennett (capt)	Llanelli	Wales
J.D. Bevan	Aberavon	Wales
A.D. Lewis*	Cambridge University and London Welsh	
D.W. Morgan	Stewart's Melville FP	Scotland
D.B. Williams	Cardiff	

Forwards

W.B. Beaumont*	Fylde	England
G.L. Brown	West of Scotland	Scotland
T.J. Cobner	Pontypool	Wales
F.E. Cotton	Sale	England
W.P Duggan	Blackrock College	Ireland
T.P. Evans	Swansea	Wales
A.G. Faulkner*	Pontypool	Wales
N.E Horton	Moseley	England
M.I Keane	Lansdowne	Ireland
A.J. Martin	Aberavon	Wales
A. Neary	Broughton Park	England
P.A. Orr	Old Wesley	Ireland
G.Price	Pontypool	Wales
D.L Quinnell	Llanelli	Wales
J. Squire	Newport	Wales
P.J.Wheeler	Leicester	England
C. Williams	Aberavon	Wales
R.W. Windsor	Pontypool	Wales

*Replacements

Tour Record:	P 26	W 21	D 0	L 5	F 607	A 320
Test Series:	P 4	W 1	D 0	L 3		

18 May	Wairarapa-Bush	Masterton	W	41-13
21 May	Hawke's Bay	Napier	W	13-11
25 May	Poverty Bay-East Coast	Gisborne	W	25-6
8 May	Taranaki	New Plymouth	W	21-13

1 June	King Country-Wanganui	Taumarunui	W	60–9
4 June	Manawatu-Horowhenua	Palmerston North	W	18–12
8 June	Otago	Dunedin	W	12–7
11 June	Southland	Invercargill	W	20–12
14 June	New Zealand Universities	Christchurch	L	9–21
18 June	**NEW ZEALAND**	**Wellington**	**L**	**12–16**
22 June	Hanan Shield Districts	Timaru	W	45–6
25 June	Canterbury	Christchurch	W	14–13
29 June	West Coast-Buller	Westport	W	45–0
2 July	Wellington	Wellington	W	13–6
5 July	Marlborough-Nelson	Blenheim	W	40–23
9 July	**NEW ZEALAND**	**Christchurch**	**W**	**13–9**
13 July	New Zealand Maori	Auckland	W	22–19
16 July	Waikato	Hamilton	W	18–13
20 July	New Zealand Juniors	Wellington	W	19–9
23 July	Auckland	Auckland	W	34–15
30 July	**NEW ZEALAND**	**Dunedin**	**L**	**7–19**
3 August	Counties-Thames Valley	Pukekohe	W	35–10
6 August	North Auckland	Whangarei	W	18–7
9 August	Bay of Plenty	Rotorua	W	23–16
13 August	**NEW ZEALAND**	**Auckland**	**L**	**9–10**
16 August	Fiji	Suva	L	21–25

First Test

18 June, Wellington
New Zealand 16 The Lions 12
HT: 16–12 Att: 43,000

New Zealand: C. Farrell, B. Williams, B. Robertson, W. Osborne, G. Batty, D. Robertson, S. Going, B. Johnstone, T. Norton (capt), K. Lambert, F. Oliver, A. Haden, K. Everleigh, I. Kirkpatrick, L. Knight **Scorers:** Tries: S. Going, G. Batty, B. Johnstone; Cons: B. Williams 2

The Lions: A. Irvine, P. Squires, I. McGeechan, S. Fenwick, J.J. Williams, P. Bennett (capt), B. Williams, P. Orr, R. Windsor, G. Price, A. Martin, M. Keane, T. Cobner, T. Evans, W. Duggan **Scorers:** Pens: P. Bennett 3, A. Irvine

Referee: Peter McDavitt (New Zealand)

Second Test

9 July, Christchurch
New Zealand 9 The Lions 13
HT: 6–13 Att: 50,000

New Zealand: C. Farrell, B. Williams, W. Osborne, L. Jaffray, M. Taylor, D. Bruce, S. Going, B. Johnstone, T. Norton (capt), W. Bush, F. Oliver, A. Haden, K. Everleigh, I. Kirkpatrick, L. Knight **Scorers:** Pens: B. Williams 2

The Lions: A. Irvine, J.J. Williams, I. McGeechan, S. Fenwick, G. Evans, P. Bennett (capt), B. Williams, F. Cotton, P. Wheeler, G. Price, W. Beaumont, G. Brown, T. Cobner, D. Quinnell, W. Duggan **Scorers:** Try: J.J. Williams; Pens: P. Bennett 3

Referee: Brian Duffy (New Zealand)

Third Test

30 July, Dunedin
New Zealand 19 The Lions 7
HT: 10-4 Att: 43,000

New Zealand: B. Wilson, B. Ford, B. Robertson, W. Osborne, B. Williams, D. Bruce, L. Davis, J.McEldowney, T. Norton (capt), W. Bush, A. Haden, F. Oliver, G. Mourie, I. Kirkpatrick, L. Knight **Scorers:** Tries: I. Kirkpatrick, A. Haden; Con: B. Wilson Pens: B. Williams 2; DG: B. Robertson

The Lions: A. Irvine, J.J. Williams (I. McGeechan), D. Burcher, S. Fenwick, G. Evans, P. Bennett (capt), B. Williams (D. Morgan), F. Cotton, P. Wheeler, G. Price, G. Brown, W. Beaumont, T. Cobner, W. Duggan **Scorers:** Try: W. Duggan Pen: A. Irvine

Referee: Dave Millar (New Zealand)

1980 South Africa

Captain: Bill Beaumont (Flyde and England)
Manager: Syd Millar (Ireland)
Coach: Noel Murphy (Ireland)

Tour Record:	P 18	W 15	D 0	L 3	F 401 A 244
Test Series:	P 4	W 1	D 0	L 3	

1983 New Zealand

Captain: Ciaran Fitzgerald (St Mary's College and Ireland)
Manager: Willie John McBride (Ireland)
Coach: Jim Telfer (Scotland)

Tour Record:	P 18	W 12	D 0	L 6	F 478 A 276
Test Series:	P 4	W 0	D 0	L 4	

1989 Australia

Captain: Finlay Calder (Stewart's Melville FP and Scotland)
Manager: Clive Rowlands (Wales)
Coach: Ian McGeechan (Scotland)

Squad

Fullbacks

P.W. Dods	Gala	Scotland
A.G. Hastings	London Scottish	Scotland

Three-Quarters

J.A. Devereux	Bridgend	Wales
I.C. Evans	Llanelli	Wales
J.C. Guscott	Bath	England
M.R. Hall	Bridgend	Wales
S.R. Hastings	Watsonians	Scotland
B.J. Mullin	London Irish	Ireland
C. Oti	Wasps	England
R. Underwood	Leicester and RAF	England

Half-backs

C.R. Andrew*	Wasps	England
G. Armstrong	Jedforest	Scotland
C.M Chalmers	Melrose	Scotland
A.Clement*	Swansea	Wales
P.M.Dean	St Mary's College	Ireland
R.N. Jones	Swansea	Wales

Forwards

P.J Ackford	Harlequins	England
F. Calder (capt)	Stewart's Melville FP	Scotland
G.J. Chilcott	Bath	England
W.A. Dooley	Preston Grasshoppers	England)
M.Griffiths	Bridgend	Wales
J. Jeffrey	Kelso	Scotland
D.G. Lenihan	Cork Constitution	Ireland
B.C. Moore	Nottingham	England
R.L. Norster	Cardiff	Wales
D. Richards	Leicester	England
R.A. Robinson	Bath	England
S.J. Smith	Ballymena	Ireland
D.M.B Sole	Edinburgh Academicals	Scotland
M.C. Teague	Gloucester	England

D.B. White   London Scottish   Scotland
D.Young   Cardiff   Wales

*Replacements

Tour Record:	P 12	W 11	D 0	L 1	F 360	A 192
Test Series:	P 3	W 2	D 0	L 1		

10 June	Western Australia	Location	W	44-0
14 June	Australia B	Location	W	23-18
17 June	Queensland	Location	W	19-15
21 June	Queensland B	Location	W	30-6
24 June	New South Wales	Location	W	23-21
27 June	New South Wales B	Location	W	39-19
1 July	**AUSTRALIA**	**Sydney**	**L**	**12-30**
4 July	ACT	Location	W	41-25
8 July	**AUSTRALIA**	**Brisbane**	**W**	**19-12**
15 July	**AUSTRALIA**	**Sydney**	**W**	**19-18**
19 July	NSW Country	Location	W	72-13
23 July	ANZAC XV	Location	W	19-15

First Test

1 July, Sydney
Australia 30 The Lions 12
HT: 15-6 Att: 39,433

Australia: G. Martin, A. Niuqila, L, Walker, D. Maguire, D. Campese, M. Lynagh, N. Farr-Jones (capt), C. Lillicrap (M. Hartill), T. Lawton (M. McBain), D. Crowley, W. Campbell, S. Cutler, S. Tuynman, J. Miller, S. Gourley **Scorers**: Tries: G. Martin, L. Walker, D. Maguire, S. Gourley ; Cons: M. Lynagh 4; Pen: M. Lynagh; DG: M. Lynagh

The Lions: G. Hastings, I. Evans, M. Hall, B. Mullin, R. Underwood, C. Chalmers, R. Jones, D. Sole, B. Moore, D. Young, P. Ackford, R. Norster, D. White, F. Calder (capt), D. Richards **Scorers**: Pens: G. Hastings 2, C. Chalmers; DG: C Chalmers

Second Test

8 July, Brisbane
Australia 12 The Lions 19
HT: 12-6 Att: 20, 525

Australia: G. Martin, I. Williams, L, Walker, D. Maguire, D. Campese, M. Lynagh, N. Farr-Jones (capt), M. Hartill, T. Lawton, D. Crowley, W. Campbell, S. Cutler, S. Tuynman, J. Miller, S. Gourley **Scorers**: Tries: G. Martin; Con: M. Lynagh; Pens: M. Lynagh 2

The Lions: G. Hastings, I. Evans, S. Hastings, J. Guscott, R. Underwood, R. Andrew, R. Jones, D. Sole, B. Moore, D. Young, P. Ackford, W. Dooley, M. Teague, F. Calder (capt), D. Richards **Scorers**: Tries: J. Guscott, G. Hastings; Con: R. Andrew; Pens: R. Andrew, G. Hastings; DG: R. Andrew

Referee: Rene Hourquet (France)

Third Test

15 July, Sydney
Australia 18 The Lions 19
HT: 9–9 Att: 39, 401

Australia: G. Martin, I. Williams, L, Walker, D. Maguire, D. Campese, M. Lynagh, N. Farr-Jones (capt), M. Hartill, T. Lawton, D. Crowley, W. Campbell, S. Cutler, S. Tuynman, J. Miller, S. Gourley **Scorers**: Try: I. Williams; Con: M. Lynagh; Pens: M. Lynagh 4

The Lions: G. Hastings, I. Evans, S. Hastings, J. Guscott, R. Underwood, R. Andrew, R. Jones, D. Sole, B. Moore, D. Young, P. Ackford, W. Dooley, M. Teague, F. Calder (capt), D. Richards **Scorers**: Try: I. Evans;; Pens: G. Hastings 5

Referee: Rene Hourquet (France)

1993 New Zealand

Captain: Gavin Hastings (Watsonians and Scotland)
Manager: Geoff Cooke (England)
Coach: Ian McGeechan (Scotland)

Squad

Fullbacks

A. Clement	Swansea	Wales
A.G Hastings (capt)	Watsonians	Scotland

Three-Quarters

W.D. C Carling	Harlequins	England
V.J.G Cunningham*	St Mary's College	Ireland
I.C. Evans	Llanelli	Wales
I.S.Gibbs	Swansea	Wales
J.C. Guscott	Bath	England
S. Hastings	Watsonians	Scotland
I. Hunter	Northampton	England
R. Underwood	Leicester and RAF	England
T. Underwood	Leicester	England
R.M Wallace*	Garryowen	Ireland

Half-backs

C.R. Andrew	Wasps	England
S. Barnes	Bath	England
R.N. Jones	Swansea	Wales
C.D. Morris	Orrell	England
A.D. Nicol*	Dundee HS FP	Scotland

Forwards

M.C. Bayfield	Northampton	England
A.P. Burnell	London Scottish	Scotland
B.B. Clarke	Bath	England
D.F. Cronin	London Scottish	Scotland
W.A. Dooley	Preston Grasshoppers	England
M.J. Galwey	Shannon	Ireland
M.O. Johnson*	Leicester	England
J. Leonard	Harlequins	England
K.S. Milne	Heriot's FP	Scotland
B.C. Moore	Harlequins	England
N.J. Popplewell	Greystone	Ireland
A.I. Reed	Bath	Scotland
D. Richards	Leicester	England
M.C.Teague	Gloucester	England
R.E. Webster	Swansea	Wales
P.J. Winterbottom	Harlequins	England
P.H. Wright	Boroughmuir	Scotland

*Replacements

Tour Record:	P 13	W 7	D 0	L 6	F 314	A 285	
Test Series:	P 3	W 1	D 0	L 2			

22 May	North Auckland	Whangarei	W	30–17
26 May	North Harbour	Auckland	W	29–13
29 May	New Zealand M ori	Wellington	W	24–20
2 June	Canterbury	Christchurch	W	28–10
5 June	Otago	Dunedin	L	24–37
8 June	Southland	Invercargill	W	34–16
12 June	**NEW ZEALAND**	**Christchurch**	**L**	**18–20**
16 June	Taranaki	New Plymouth	W	49–25
19 June	Auckland	Auckland	L	18–23
22 June	Hawke's Bay	Napier	L	17–29
26 June	**NEW ZEALAND**	**Wellington**	**W**	**20–7**
29 June	Waikato	Hamilton	L	10–38
3 July	**NEW ZEALAND**	**Auckland**	**L**	**13–30**

BRITISH AND IRISH LIONS STATISTICS

First Test

12 June, Christchurch
New Zealand 20 The Lions 18
HT: 11–9 Att: 38,000

New Zealand: J. Timu, E. Clarke, F. Bunce, W. Little (M. Cooper), I. Tuigamala, G. Fox, A. Strachan, C. Dowd, S. Fitzpatrick (capt), O. Brown, R. Brooke, I. Jones, J. Joseph, M. Jones, Z. Brooke **Scorers**: Try: F. Bunce; Pens: G. Fox 5

The Lions: G. Hastings (capt), I. Evans, J. Guscott, W. Carling, R. Underwood, R. Andrew, D. Morris, N. Popplewell, K. Milne, P. Burnell, A. Reed, M. Bayfield, B. Clarke, P. Winterbottom, D. Richards **Scorers:** Pens: G. Hastings 6

Referee: Brian Kinsey (Australia)

Second Test

26 June, Wellington
New Zealand 7 The Lions 20
HT: 7–9 Att: 39,000

New Zealand: J. Timu, J. Kirwan, F. Bunce, E. Clarke, I. Tuigamala, G. Fox, J. Preston, C. Dowd, S. Fitzpatrick (capt), O. Brown, R. Brooke, M. Cooksley (I. Jones), J. Joseph, M. Jones, Z. Brooke **Scorers**: Try: E. Clarke; Con: G. Fox

The Lions: G. Hastings (capt), I. Evans, J. Guscott, S. Gibbs, R. Underwood, R. Andrew, D. Morris, N. Popplewell, B. Moore, J. Leonard, M. Johnson, M. Bayfield, B. Clarke, P. Winterbottom (M. Teague), D. Richards **Scorers:** Try: R. Underwood; Pens: G. Hastings 4; DG: R. Andrew

Referee: Patrick Robin (France)

Third Test

3 July, Auckland
New Zealand 30 The Lions 13
HT: 14–10 Att: 47,000

New Zealand: J. Timu (M.Cooper), J. Kirwan, F. Bunce, L. Stensness, I. Tuigamala, G. Fox, J. Preston, C. Dowd, S. Fitzpatrick (capt), O. Brown, R. Brooke, I. Jones (M. Cooksley), J. Joseph, M. Jones (Z. Brooke), A. Pene **Scorers**: Tries: J. Preston, S. Fitzpatrick, F. Bunce; Cons: G. Fox 3; Pens G. Fox 3

The Lions: G. Hastings (capt), I. Evans, J. Guscott, S. Gibbs, R. Underwood, R. Andrew, D. Morris, N. Popplewell, B. Moore, J. Leonard, M. Johnson, M. Bayfield, B. Clarke, P. Winterbottom, D. Richards **Scorers:** Try: S. Gibbs; Con: G. Hastings; Pens: G. Hastings 2

Referee: Patrick Robin (France)

1997 South Africa

Captain: Martin Johnson (Leicester and England)
Manager: Fran Cotton (England)
Coach: Ian McGeechan (Scotland)

Squad

Full backs

N.R. Jenkins	Pontypridd	Wales
T.R.G Stimpson	Newcastle	England

Three-Quarters

A.G, Bateman	Richmond	Wales
N.D. Beal	Northampton	England
J. Bentley	Newcastle	England
I.C. Evans	Llanelli	Wales
I.S. Gibbs	Swansea	Wales
W.J.H. Greenwood	Leicester	
J.C. Guscott	Bath	England
A.G. Stanger*	Hawick	Scotland
A.V. Tait	Newcastle	Scotland
T. Underwood	Newcastle	England

Half-Backs

K.P. Bracken*	Saracens	England
M.J. Catt*	Bath	England
M.J.S Dawson	Northampton	England
P.J. Grayson	Northampton	England
A.S. Healey	Leicester	England
R. Howley	Cardiff	Wales
G.P.J Townsend	Northampton	Scotland

Forwards

N.A. Back	Leicester	England
L.B.N. Dallaglio	Wasps	England
J. Davidson	London Irish	Ireland
A.J. Diprose	Saracens	England
R.A. Hill	Saracens	England
M.O. Johnson (capt)	Leicester	England
J. Leonard	Harlequins	England
E.R.P. Miller	Leicester	Ireland
L.S. Quinnell	Richmond	Wales
N. Redman*	Bath	England
M. Regan	Bristol	England
T.A.K Rodber	Northampton	England

G.C.Rowntree	Leicester	England
S.D. Shaw	Bristol	England
T.J.Smith	Watsonians	Scotland
R.I. Wainwright	Watsonians	Scotland
P.S, Wallace	Saracens	Ireland
G.W. Weir	Newcastle	Scotland
B.H. Williams	Neath	Wales
K.G.M. Wood	Harlequins	Ireland
D. Young	Cardiff	Wales

*Replacements

Tour Record:	P 13	W 11	D 0	L 2	F 480	A 278
Test Series:	P 3	W 2	D 0	L 1		

24 May	Eastern Province XV	Port Elizabeth	W	39–11
28 May	Border Basil	East London	W	18–14
31 May	Western Province	Cape Town	W	38–21
4 June	Mpumalanga	Witbank	W	64–14
7 June	Northern Transvaal	Pretoria	L	30–35
11 June	Gauteng Lions	Johannesburg	W	20–14
14 June	Natal	Durban	W	42–12
17 June	Emerging Springboks	Wellington	W	51–22
21 June	**SOUTH AFRICA**	**Cape Town**	**W**	**25–16**
24 June	Free State	Bloemfontein	W	52–30
28 June	**SOUTH AFRICA**	**Durban**	**W**	**18–15**
1 July	Northern Free State	Welkom	W	67–39
5 July	**SOUTH AFRICA**	**Johannesburg**	**L**	**16–35**

First Test

21 June, Cape Town
South Africa 16 The Lions 25
HT: 8–9 Att: 46,100

South Africa: A. Joubert, J. Small, J. Mukder, E. Luebbe (R. Bennett) A. Snyman, H Honiball, J. van der Westhuizen, O. du Randt, N. Drotske, A. Garvey, H. Strydom, M. Andrews, R. Kruger, A. Venter, G. Teichmann (capt)
Scorers: Tries: O. du Randt, R. Bennett; Pens: H. Honiball, E. Luebbe

The Lions: N. Jenkins, I. Evans, S. Gibbs, J. Guscott, A. Tait, G. Townsend, M. Dawson, T. Smith (J. Leonard), K. Wood, P. Wallace, M. Johnson (capt) J. Davidson, L. Dallaglio, R. Hill, T. Rodber **Scorers:** Tries: M. Dawson, A Tait; Pens: N. Jenkins 5

Referee: Colin Hawke (New Zealand)

Second Test

28 June, Durban
South Africa 15 The Lions 18
HT: 5-6 Att:52,400

South Africa: A. Joubert, A. Snyman, P. Montgomery, D. van Schalkwyk, P. Rossouw, H Honiball, J. van der Westhuizen, O. du Randt, N. Drotske, A. Garvey (D. Theron), H. Strydom, M. Andrews, R. Kruger (F. van Heerden), A. Venter, G. Teichmann (capt) **Scorers:** Tries: P. Montgomery, A. Joubert, J. van der Westhuizen

The Lions: N. Jenkins, J. Bentley, S. Gibbs, J. Guscott, A. Tait (A. Healey), G. Townsend, M. Dawson, T. Smith, K. Wood, P. Wallace, M. Johnson (capt) J. Davidson, L. Dallaglio, R. Hill (N. Back) T. Rodber (E. Miller) **Scorers:** Pens: N. Jenkins 5; DG: J Guscott

Referee: Didier Mene (France)

Third Test

5 July, Johannesburg
South Africa 35 The Lions 16
HT: 13-9 Att:52,400

South Africa: R. Bennett, A. Snyman, P. Montgomery (H. Honiball), D. van Schalkwyk, P. Rossouw, J. de Beer (J. Swart), J. van der Westhuizen (W. Swanepoel), O. du Randt (A. Garvey), J. Dalton (N. Drotske), D. Theron, H. Strydom, K. Otto, A. Venter, R. Erasmus, G. Teichmann (capt) (F. van Heerden) **Scorers:** Tries: P. Montgomery, A. Snyman, J. van der Westhuizen, P. Rossouw; Cons: J. de Beer 2, H. Honiball; Pens: J. de Beer 3

The Lions: N. Jenkins, J. Bentley, J. Guscott (A. Bateman), S. Gibbs, T. Underwood (T. Stimpson), M. Catt, M. Dawson (A. Healey), T. Smith, M. Regan, P. Wallace, M. Johnson (capt) J. Davidson, R. Wainwright, N. Back, L. Dallaglio **Scorers:** Try: M. Dawson, Con: N. Jenkins; Pens: N. Jenkins 3

Referee: Wayne Erickson (Australia)

2001 Australia

Captain: Martin Johnson (Leicester Tigers and England)
Manager: Donal Kenihan (Ireland)
Coach: Graham Henry (Wales)

Tour Record:	P 10	W 7	D 0	L 3	F 449	A 184
Test Series:	P 3	W 1	D 0	L 2		

2005 New Zealand

Captain: Brian O'Driscoll (Leinster and Ireland)
Manager: Bill Beaumont (England)
Coach: Clive Woodward (England)

Squad

Full-Backs

I.R. Balshaw	Leeds Tykes	England
G.E.A Murphy	Leicester Tigers	Ireland
O.J Lewsey	Wasps	England
J.T Robinson	Sale Sharks	England
G. Thomas	Toulouse	Wales

Three-Quarters

M.J. Cueto*	Sale Sharks	England
G.W. D'Arcy	Leinster	Ireland
W.J.H. Greenwood	Harlequins	England
G.L. Henson	Ospreys	Wales
D.A. Hickie	Leinster	Ireland
S.P. Horgan	Leinster	Ireland
B.G. O'Driscoll (capt)	Leinster	Ireland
T.G. Shanklin	Cardiff Blues	Wales
O.J. Smith	Leicester Tigers	England
S.M. Williams	Ospreys	Wales

Half-Backs

G.J Cooper	Dragons	Wales
C.P. Cusiter	Borders	Scotland
M.J.S Dawson	London Wasps	England
C.C. Hodgson	Sale Sharks	England
S.M. Jones	Clermont Auvergne	Wales
R.J.R O'Gara	Munster	Ireland
D.J. Peel	Llanelli Scarlets	Wales
J.P. Wilkinson*	Newcastle Falcons	England

Forwards

N.A. Back	Leicester Tigers	England
G.C. Bulloch	Glasgow	Scotland
J.S. Byrne	Leinster	Ireland
B.J. Cockbain*	Ospreys	Wales
M.E. Corry	Leicester Tigers	England
L.B.N Dallaglio	London Wasps	England

S.H. Easterby*	Scarlets	Ireland
D.J. Grewcock	Bath	England
J.J. Hayes	Munster	Ireland
R.A. Hill	Saracens	England
G.D. Jenkins	Cardiff Blues	Wales
R.P. Jones*	Ospreys	Wales
B.J. Kay	Leicester Tigers	England
L.W. Moody	Leicester Tigers	England
D.F. O'Callaghan	Munster	Ireland
P.J. O'Connell	Munster	Ireland
M.E. O'Kelly	Leinster	Ireland
M.J. Owen	Dragons	Wales
G.C. Rowntree	Leicester Tigers	England
S.D. Shaw*	London Wasps	England
A.J. Sheridan	Sale Sharks	England
M.J.H Stevens	Bath	England
S.M. Taylor	Edinburgh	Scotland
S.G. Thompson	Northampton Saints	England
A.J. Titterell	Sale Sharks	England
J.P.R White*	Sale Sharks	Scotland
J.M. White	Leicester Tigers	England
M.E. Williams	Cardiff Blues	Wales

*Replacements

Tour Record:	P 12	W 7	D 1	L 4	F 353	A 245
Test (Arg):	P 1	W 0	D 1	L 0		
Test Series:	P 3	W 0	D 0	L 3		

23 May	Argentina	Cardiff	D	25–25
4 June	Bay of Plenty	Rotorua	W	34–20
8 June	Taranaki	New Plymouth	W	36–14
11 June	New Zealand MÐori	Hamilton	L	13–19
15 June	Wellington	Wellington	W	23–6
18 June	Otago	Dunedin	W	30–19
21 June	Southland	Invercargill	W	26–16
25 June	**NEW ZEALAND**	**Christchurch**	**L**	**3–21**
28 June	Manawatu	Palmerston North	W	109–6
2 July	**NEW ZEALAND**	**Wellington**	**L**	**18–48**
5 July	Auckland	Auckland	W	17–13
9 July	**NEW ZEALAND**	**Auckland**	**L**	**19–38**

First Test

25 June, Christchurch
New Zealand 21 The Lions 3
HT: 11–0 Att: 37,200

New Zealand: L. MacDonald (M. Muliaina); D. Howlett; T. Umaga (capt) (R. Gear), A. Mauger, S. Sivivatu, D. Carter, J. Marshall (B. Kelleher), T. Woodcock (G. Somerville), K. Mealamu (D. Witcombe), C. Hayman, C. Jack, A. Williams, J. Collins (S. Lauaki), R. McCaw, R. So'oialo **Scorers:** Tries: A. Williams, S. Sivivatu; Con: D. Carter; Pens: D. Carter 3

The Lions: J. Robinson (S. Horgan), J. Lewsey, B. O'Driscoll (capt) (W. Greenwood), J. Wilkinson, G. Thomas, S. Jones, D. Peel (M. Dawson), G. Jenkins, S. Byrne (S. Thompson), J. White, P. O'Connell, B. Kay (D. Grewcock), R. Hill, N. Back, M. Corry **Scorers**: Pen: J. Wilkinson

Referee: Joel Jutge (France)

Second Test

2 July, Wellington
New Zealand 48 The Lions 18
HT: 21–13 Att: 37,000

New Zealand: M. Muliaina, R. Gear, T. Umaga (capt), A. Mauger (L. MacDonald), S. Sivivatu (M. Nonu),, D. Carter, B. Kelleher (J. Marshall), T. Woodcock (C. Johnstone), K. Mealamu (D. Witcombe), G. Somerville, C. Jack (J. Gibbes), A. Williams, J. Collins (S. Lauaki), R. McCaw, R. So'oialo **Scorers:** Tries: D. Carter 2, T. Umaga, R. McCaw, S. Sivivatu; Con: D. Carter 4; Pens: D. Carter 5

The Lions: J. Lewsey, J. Robinson, G. Thomas (capt), G. Henson (S. Horgan), S. Williams, J. Wilkinson (S. Jones), D. Peel, G. Jenkins (G. Rowntree), S. Thompson (S. Byrne), J. White, D. O'Callaghan (M. Corry), P. O'Connell, S. Easterby, L. Moody, R. Jones **Scorers**: Tries: G. Thomas, S. Easterby Con: J. Wilkinson; Pens: J. Wilkinson 2

Referee: Andrew Cole (Australia)

Third Test

9 July, Auckland
New Zealand 38 The Lions 19
HT: 24–12 Att: 47,500

New Zealand: M. Muliaina, R. Gear, C. Smith, T. Umaga (capt), S. Sivivatu L. McCalister, B. Kelleher (J. Marshall), T. Woodcock (C. Johnstone), K. Mealamu, G. Somerville, C. Jack (J. Ryan), A. Williams, J. Collins, R. So'oialo, S. Lauaki

(M. Holah) **Scorers:** Tries: T. Umaga 2, A. Williams, R. Gear, C. Smith; Cons: L.McAlister 5; Pen: L. McAlister

The Lions: G. Murphy (R. O'Gara), M. Cueto, W. Greenwood, G. Thomas (capt) (S. Horgan), J. Lewsey, S. Jones, D. Peel (M. Dawson), G. Jenkins (G. Rowntree), S. Byrne (G. Bulloch), J. White, D. O'Callaghan, P. O'Connell, S. Easterby, L. Moody (M. Williams), R. Jones (M. Corry) **Scorers**: Try: L. Moody; Con: S. Jones; Pens: S. Jones4

Referee: Jonathan Kaplan (South Africa)

2009 South Africa

Captain: Paul O'Connell (Munster and Ireland)
Manager: Gerald Davies (England)
Coach: Ian McGeechan (Scotland)

Squad

Full-backs/Three-quarters

T.J. Bowe	Ospreys	Ireland
L.M. Byrne	Ospreys	Wales
G.W. D'Arcy*	Leinster	Ireland
K.G. Earls	Munster	Ireland
L.M. Fitzgerald	Leinster	Ireland
R.J. Flutey	London Wasps	England
S.L.Halfpenny	Cardiff Blues	Wales
R. Kearney	Leinster	Ireland
U.C. Mone	Harlequins	England
B.G. O'Driscoll	Leinster	Ireland
J.H. Roberts	Cardiff Blues	Wales
S.M. Williams	Ospreys	Wales

Half-Backs

M.R.L Blair	Edinburgh	Scotland
H.A. Ellis	Leicester	England
J.W. Hook	Ospreys	Wales
S.M. Jones	Scarlets	Wales
R.J.R O'Gara	Munster	Ireland
W.M. Phillips	Ospreys	Wales

Forwards

T.R. Croft	Leicester	England
S. Ferris	Ulster	Ireland
R.W. Ford	Edinburgh	Scotland

J.J. Hayes*	Munster	Ireland
J.P.R. Heaslip	Leinster	Ireland
N.J. Hines	Perpignan	Scotland
G.D. Jenkins	Cardiff Blues	Wales
A.R. Jones	Ospreys	Wales
A.W. Jones	Ospreys	Wales
L.A. Mears	Bath	England
E.A. Murray	Northampton Saints	Scotland
D.F. O'Callaghan	Munster	Ireland
P.J. O'Connell (capt)	Munster	Ireland
T.A.N. Payne*	London Wasps	England
A.T. Powell	Cardiff Blues	Wales
M. Rees	Scarlets	Wales
S.D. Shaw	London Wasps	England
A.J. Sheridan	Sale Sharks	England
P.J. Vickery	London Wasps	England
D.P. Wallace	Munster	Ireland
M.E. Williams	Cardiff Blues	Wales
J.P.R Worsley	London Wasps	England

*Replacements

Tour Record:	P 10	W 7	D 1	L 2	F 309	A 169
Test Series:	P 3	W 1	D 0	L 2		

30 May	Royal XV	Rustenburg	W	37–25
3 June	Golden Lions	Johannesburg	W	74–10
6 June	Free State Cheetahs	Blomfontein	W	26–24
10 June	Sharks	Durban	W	39–3
13 June	Western Province	Cape Town	W	26–23
16 June	Southern Kings	Port Elizabeth	W	20–8
20 June	**SOUTH AFRICA**	**Durban**	**L**	**21–26**
23 June	Emerging Springboks	Cape Town	D	13–13
27 June	**SOUTH AFRICA**	**Pretoria**	**L**	**25–28**
4 July	**SOUTH AFRICA**	**Johannesburg**	**W**	**28–9**

First Test

20 June, Durban
South Africa 26 The Lions 21
HT: 19–7 Att:47,813

South Africa: F. Steyn, J. Pietersen, A. Jacobs, J. de Villiers (J. Fourie), B. Habana, R. Pienaar (M. Steyn), F. du Preez (R. Januarie), T. Mtawarira (G.

Steenkamp) B. du Plessis, J. Smit (capt) (D. Carstens), B. Botha (A. Bekker), V. Matfield, H. Brussow (D. Rossouw) J. Smith, P. Spies **Scorers:** Tries: J. Smit, H. Brussow; Cons: R. Pienaar 2; Pens: R. Pienaar 3, F. Steyn

The Lions: L. Byrne (R. Kearney), T. Bowe, B. O'Driscoll, J. Roberts, U. Monye, S. Jones, M. Phillips, G. Jenkins, L. Mears (M. Rees), P. Vickery, (A. Jones), A.W. Jones (D. O'Callaghan). P. O'Connell (capt), T. Croft, D. Wallace, (M. Williams) J. Heaslip **Scorers:** Tries: T. Croft 2, M. Phillips; Cons: S. Jones 3

Referee: Bryce Lawrence (New Zealand)

Second Test

27 June, Pretoria
South Africa 28 The Lions 25
HT: 8-16 Att:52,511

South Africa: F. Steyn, J. Pietersen, A. Jacobs, J. de Villiers (J. Fourie), B. Habana, R. Pienaar (M. Steyn), F. du Preez , T. Mtawarira, B. du Plessis, J. Smit (capt), B. Botha (A. Bekker), V. Matfield, S. Burger, J. Smith (D. Rossouw, H. Brussow), P. Spies **Scorers:** Tries: J. Fourie, B. Habana, J. Pietersen; Cons: M. Steyn 3; Pens: M. Steyn 2, F. Steyn

The Lions: R. Kearney, T. Bowe, B. O'Driscoll (S. Williams), J. Roberts (R. O'Gara), L. Fitzgerald, S. Jones, M. Phillips, G. Jenkins (A Sheridan), M. Rees, A. Jones (A.W. Jones), S. Shaw, P. O'Connell (capt), T. Croft, D. Wallace, (M. Williams) J. Heaslip **Scorers:** Try: R. Kearney; Con: S. Jones

Referee: Christophe Berdos (France)

Third Test

4 July Johannesburg
South Africa 9 The Lions 28
HT: 6-15 Att:58,318

South Africa: Z. Kirchner (F. Steyn), O. Ndungane, J. Fourie (F Steyn), W. Olivier, J. Nowke (P. Spies), M. Steyn, F. du Preez (R. Pienaar) , T. Mtawarira (G. Steenkamp), C Ralepelle (B. du Plessis), J. Smit (capt) (D. Carstens), J. Muller, V Matfield, H. Brussow, J Smith, R. Kankowski **Scorer:** Pens: M. Steyn 3

The Lions: R. Kearney, U. Monye, T. Bowe, R. Flutey (H. Ellis), S. Williams, S. Jones, M. Phillips, A Sheridan, M. Rees (R. Ford),P. Vickery (J. Hayes), S. Shaw (A.W. Jones), P. O'Connell (capt), J. Worsley (T. Croft), (M. Williams) D. Wallace, J. Heaslip **Scorers:** Tries: S. Williams 2, U. Monye; Cons: S. Jones 2; Pens: S. Jones 3

Referee: Stuart Dickinson (Australia)

2013 Australia

Captain: Sam Warburton (Cardiff Blues and Wales)
Manager: Andy Irvine (Scotland)
Coach: Warren Gatland (Wales)

Tour Record: P 10   W 8   D 0   L 2   F 387   A 121
Test Series: P 3   W 2   D 0   L 1

INDEX

ACKNOWLEDGEMENTS

Many people have made this book possible for which I am extremely grateful.

Firstly, I would like to thank Steve James of *The Times* for many enjoyable hours chatting about the Lions, and all his help in the production of this book.

Thanks are also due to David Luxton of DLA, the *Daily Telegraph* for kindly allowing access to their invaluable rugby archive, and my editor Roddy Bloomfield and Fiona Rose from my publisher Hodder & Stoughton. Thanks to their expert guidance and management this book has become an enjoyable reality.

Finally, I must thank the British and Irish Lions for their valued support and assistance in this project.

PHOTO ACKNOWLEDGEMENTS

The author and publisher would like to thank the following for permission to reproduce photographs

Colorsport / Colin Elsey, Colorsport / Andrew Cowie, Bob Thomas/Getty Images, Russell Cheyne /Allsport/Getty Images, Mark Leech/Getty Images, David Rogers/Getty Images, Anton Want/Allsport/Getty Images, Steve Bardens – Offside, Colorsport / Stuart MacFarlane, Mike Egerton/EMPICS Sport/PA Images, Colorsport / Steve Bardens, Allsport UK /Getty Images, David Rogers /Allsport/Getty Images, Shaun Curry/AFP/Getty Images), Colorsport / Kieran Galvin, Stu Forster/Getty Images, Fotosport/David Gibson, Ludbrook/EPA/REX/Shutterstock, Matthew Impey/Wired Photos, Colorsport / Andrew Cowie, WILLIAM WEST/AFP/Getty Images

Every reasonable effort has been made to trace copyright holders, but if there are any errors or omissions, Hodder & Stoughton will be pleased to insert the appropriate acknowledgement in any subsequent printings or editions.